LAUREL
and
HARDY
The British Tours
Part 1 — 1926-1951
From Screen to Stage

by

"A.J" Marriot

Marriot Publishing

LAUREL and HARDY – The British Tours
Part 1 — 1926-1951
From Screen to Stage

ISBN 978-0-9521308-8-8

First Edition published November 1993
This Second Revised Edition – November 2019
Marriot Publishing
Ciudad Quesada, Alicante, Spain
Text Copyright © by "A.J" Marriot 2019
Printed via "LULU"

Written, compiled, and designed by "A.J" Marriot. Layout by "A.J" Marriot

COVER DESIGN by "A.J" Marriot

Cover artwork by Paul Wood (TT Litho, Rochester, Kent. ME1 1NN – www.ttlitho.co.uk)

FOREWORD (1993 – First Edition)

BERNARD DELFONT
Sir Bernard Delfont (knighted 1974)
Baron Delfont of Stepney
(Life Peerage 1976)

When asked to write this foreword, I was only too happy to be able to pay my respects to two comedians who have always held a special place in my affections. Watching the films of Laurel & Hardy was a staple part of my boyhood years, and one of the most enjoyable. Little did I realise that, in later years, when their film career was finished, I would be able to repay the loyalty and devotion I felt, by inviting them to play in British Theatre. What followed exceeded everyones expectations, and lifted both our careers.

Sadly, within a few years of adapting so successfully to this medium, they were forced by illness to withdraw, and the British public were denied further opportunity to see, in the flesh, the worlds two most fascinating funny men. Fate, though, had decreed that I play one more part in ensuring that they werent readily forgotten.

Whilst over in New York, on a business trip, I was approached by the producers of the American TV programme, *This is Your Life*. It was November 1954, and Laurel and Hardy were by now "resting", and living their separate lives. Ralph Edwards, the shows host, wanted the two comedians to be his next subjects, so needed an excuse to get them together without suspicion being raised. Knowing of my past relationship with the Boys, the production team hit upon the idea that I should phone Stan and Babe individually, inform them I was in town, and invite them to the Knickerbocker Hotel.

On December 1st, the plan was put into operation and the comedy duo were surprised by a camera crew, and a voice-over from Ralph Edwards announcing: "Stan Laurel and Oliver Hardy - This is Your Life."

Stan Laurel and Oliver Hardy were two lovable, gentle men, and to have been instrumental in increasing the amount of time they were able to impart laughter to their legion of adoring fans was indeed a time of great pride for me. A.J. Marriot has excellently documented these years, and in reading the book I was reminded of the many happy hours spent in the wonderful company of the two comedians.

They are sadly missed by all who had the honour and pleasure to meet them or see them working live, but within these pages is captured the spirit of those times.

(Lord Bernard Delfont – booker for all three post-war British Tours)

-----0-----

PREFACE (from 1993)

In the mid- to late-eighties, when my good friend Roy Sims – expert on Laurel and Hardy memorabilia – started to turn up ephemera which showed the two comedians to have made stage appearances in Britain, I began to ask questions which neither he nor any other Laurel and Hardy scholars could answer. Turning to the authoritative biographical works on the comedy duo, I was further frustrated by their lack of coverage on these tours.

Determined to seek out exactly when and where Laurel and Hardy had played their theatre engagements, I began to do research. The deeper I went, the bigger the mystery became. Why had Laurel and Hardy's tours not been documented by their biographers? Why didnt people want to talk about the tours? Was something being hidden? Had Laurel and Hardy wanted to forget about the tours?

Bit by bit, I began to piece together their movements here in Britain and over in Ireland, and contacted several acts who had worked with them. A handful were helpful in the extreme, but the majority of enquiries were disappointing: a few didnt wish to help; some were able to remember nothing; and others related only nonsense.

Four people who could have solved the great untold mysteries of the British tours – Stan and Ida Laurel, and Oliver and Lucille Hardy – were sadly departed from this world, long before my research began. It was then that newspapers became a great source of information — providing reliable dates, along with interesting comments and reviews from the time. Like "Chinese whispers," personal accounts often become distorted and/or embellished over the years, whereas the contemporary viewpoints in newspapers remain unaltered – hence the prominence of quotations from this medium, within this book.

In most cases, those articles thought to contain inaccuracies or fabrication have been commented upon and corrected, where possible. Many others were treated as garbage, and dumped.

This book, as a story, is not complete, and never could be – not even if the original manuscript, which was twice as long as this book, had been published. It is meant only to supply details of the theatres at which Laurel and Hardy played; the hotels at which they stayed; the acts with whom they worked; some of the people they met; the functions they attended; their modes of transport; and the impact they made on the British public, both off-stage and on, during the British tours. Plus, of course, I aim to present you with the best picture possible of the real men behind the screen and stage characters.

After hearing many myths and rumours, and very little else about Laurel and Hardys British tours, readers will, I trust, find the information they are looking for within these pages.

I hope you get as much fun out of reading it, as I got out of researching it.

"A.J" Marriot

1993

o-o-0-o-o

As the above was written for the 1993 book, I have done a second Preface for this edition.

PREFACE (2019)

In 1987, when I first began research for the first edition of this book, technology was somewhat limited. The computer I worked on was an Amstrad PCW 8256; which was basically a typewriter – with a screen. I often chuckle at the specification: "now with 250kb of memory" – which is about one saved page of text. I am not, however, knocking the Amstrad. It made the chore of re-editing and re-typing twelve drafts oh so much easier.

What was missing in those days, which we now take for granted, was the Internet. Much of my source material came from around THREE HUNDRED people, with whom I had to correspond by letters – that's mail sent by post, and NOT email. Take into consideration that the minimum number of letters to any one person or company was usually four or five, with some up to twenty, and you can see that the total number of letters I mailed was over two thousand.

Photographs of Laurel and Hardy in Britain were particularly hard to obtain. These days you can go on the Internet, do a Google search for "Laurel and Hardy," and thousands of images will instantaneously appear. Back during my research years though (1987-1993) you had to contact the agencies which held the original photographs, borrow them, send them off to a processing laboratory, and have prints made, which was all very laborious and expensive. The alternative was to copy photos using a photocopying machine, the results for which, in those early days, were comparable to charcoal sketches.

To find information on Laurel and Hardy's tours was also very laborious. The second way, after collating the accounts of people who were there at the time, was to search out contemporary write-ups from the newspapers printed in the towns and cities where Stan and Ollie did their shows. However, at that time, no-one knew where and when they had appeared, and it was a full two years of researching before I had the complete schedule for the 1932, 1947, 1952, and 1953-54 tours.

These contemporary newspapers were a valuable source of dates, venues, and reviews of the stage shows Laurel and Hardy did, not only in Britain, but also in Europe, and the USA; plus Chaplin's pre-film stage years. The major problem, then, was that I had to go through actual "hard" copies of the newspapers in the hope of finding the required information. In total, I spent over one hundred and fifty days in the British Newspaper Library (which was then in London) — skimming through newspapers from early morning, until they kicked me out at closing time.

I also did my own "British Tours" when visiting other libraries — namely ones in North Shields, Blackpool, Liverpool, Birmingham, and Northampton. Plus, I visited many towns and cities to interview people who were a part of the story, and also do reconnaissance on the locations of hotels, theatres, houses, and venues Laurel and Hardy had visited. These included: Ulverston (3 times), Glasgow (twice), Rutherglen, Edinburgh (twice), North Shields (twice), Tynemouth (twice), Newcastle (twice), Blyth (twice), York, Leeds, Bradford (twice), Todmorden (twice), Bolton, Morecambe (twice), Blackpool (3 times), Southport, Liverpool, Rhyl, Hanley (twice), Stoke, Barkston, Bottesford, Butlins Skegness (twice), Peterborough (twice), Coventry, Birmingham (twice), Northampton, Cardiff, Bristol, London (165 times), Willesden, Ealing, Brixton, Lewisham, Finsbury Park, Camberwell (3 times), Lambeth, Southend (3 times), Margate (twice), Romney Hythe & Dymchurch Railway (3 times), Brighton, and Southsea. What a busy day that was.

The rest of the newspaper cuttings were obtained by a constant stream of begging letters to the actual newspaper companies, and libraries. [See Acknowledgements!]

Take all that into account and then consider that, these thirty-plus years later, most people think that "doing research" is going on-line and doing a Google search. I actually had one Laurel and Hardy fan who wrote on a Facebook site: "We don't need authorities or books on Laurel and Hardy, as all the information is on the Internet," which is comparable to saying: "We don't need archaeologists digging up sites of historic interest, as all the artefacts are to be found in museums. I hold nothing but disbelief for such a misguided mentality.

In the first edition of this book the early chapters detailed Stan Laurel's life: from birth — right through to his teaming with Hardy in 1927. In this edition, however, the early years have been omitted, and we come in at the point of the story where both Hardy and Laurel arc working at the Hal Roach Studios, in California. However, fear not, for you can read the definitive account of Laurel's stage appearances, pre-Hardy, in my book: "*LAUREL – Stage by Stage*," which takes in ALL known stage appearances Stan made, on both sides of the Atlantic, before going full-time into films. [You can also read a similar treatment I did on Charlie Chaplin, by purchasing the book "*CHAPLIN – Stage by Stage.*"]

Leaving out Laurel's solo stage career has not, however, led to a smaller page count, as several stories and events which have come to light since publication of the first edition have been added. Plus, there is a vastly increased number of illustrations — mainly contemporary photographs which were not available, or even known about, first time around. The text is also expanded by the inclusion of extracts from scores of letters written by Stan Laurel for which my thanks go to Bernie Hogya for an exchange arrangement.

Obviously, I sought to correct any mistakes and omissions I made in the first edition but, as usual, will accept bouquets and brickbats for this one. However, if all you have to offer is one spelling mistake, or even one mising hypen, please keep it to yourself. This is no time for levity.

"A.J" Marriot

-----0-----

B.S. I deliberately misspelt "missing hyphen" just to test your reaction.

o-o-0-o-o

KEY

Laurel **&** Hardy = on-screen – Laurel **and** Hardy = off-screen

(*ibid.*) = previously mentioned

(*circa*) = around this time

(*sic*) = copied correctly from original

[Square brackets] = author's comments.

[FILM] = refer to Film Footage and TV Broadcasts. (P167-170)

All grammatical errors and mis-spellings in the "Laurel Letters" have been left in.

Stan used the abbreviation 'bus' for different meanings. 1) for "show business" 2) when referring to the number of theatregoers. eg. "bus' was bad." 3) meaning the visual comedy in their act, which is too lengthy to write out a description for. eg. "bus' with swapping hats."

Any other mistakes are attributable to the author.

-----0-----

CONTENT

THE END

o-o-0-o-o

DEDICATION

This book is dedicated to two men, without whom the British stage tours would never have happened: (Lord) Bernard Delfont, and his agency partner for many years – Billy Marsh.

BERNARD DELFONT

I, the author, was living in Blackpool in Blackpool in 1989, and was privileged to interview Lord Delfont in the Presidential Suite of the Savoy Hotel, when he was on a visit there.

When the interview was over, I told Lord Delfont I was hosting the Stan Laurel Centenary Convention in Blackpool, over the weekend covering 16 June 1990, and asked if he would like to attend. Without skipping a beat, he said: "Yes."

Seven months later, he duly came all the way from London to attend the Banquet, in the Baronial Hall of the Winter Gardens complex — the very room where Laurel and Hardy had been guests at a Banquet in 1932 (see page 37).

When I asked Lord Delfont why he had so readily agreed to come he told me that Laurel and Hardy had done him such a big favour in the early days when he was trying to get established, that he wanted to give something back.

-----0-----

BILLY MARSH

When Billy Marsh responded to an appeal I put in the *Stage* newspaper, for information on the British tours, I had no inkling that his help would go far beyond any limits I could have wished for. Firstly came an invite to his London office, for an interview. Next was an exchange of around 15 to 20 letters and several phonecalls in which he gave additional information, or corrections, to what I had written. Later he invited me to his house near Regents Park, where I handed over one of the drafts of the book — the feedback for which ran like this:

Billy: That's a great story, but where's the dirt?

AJM: I'm not putting any dirt in it.

Billy: Well it won't sell.

AJM: OK! if that's the case, it won't sell.

I gave Billy a list of every artiste who had appeared in the Laurel and Hardy shows, and he returned it with a short description of their act. An amazing memory, and such a nice gentleman to boot. He also knew all there was to know about every theatre in the country.

Billy, too, came to our Blackpool Centenary Weekend event. In fact, he stayed for the whole weekend. On the first night I did an hour-long interview with him, in front of all the Conventioneers. He was such a modest man, that when I pushed him to tell us about his managing Morecambe and Wise, Tony Hancock, Bruce Forsyth, Keith Harris, and other big names, he skipped any praise he was due by asking me to move on.

Billy and Lord Delfont hadn't communicated with each other for three years, and so my approach to him was a bit tentative when I had to broach the subject that they would be sharing the top table. I was thrilled therefore when, just before leaving Blackpool, Billy said to me: "Thanks for getting us back together, 'A.J'. We came up in the car together.

How ironic that Lord & Marshy had got Laurel & Hardy back together, and the Laurel & Hardy event had got these two back together.

And so all three of us have now paid back what we owe to Messrs. Stan Laurel and Oliver Hardy. I trust you will enjoy the results.

o-o-0-o-o

THE PROLOGUE

On 3 June 1954 two ageing comedians went unnoticed as they waved goodbye to England from the stern of a ship bound for America. The skinny red-haired one had first made a similar journey over forty years earlier; and, watching the shoreline fast disappearing, could not help but reflect on the intervening years – years that had seen him rise from a struggling music-hall artiste, to one of the world's best-loved film comedians. This accolade was shared by the huge man standing at his side – his inseparable business partner for the last twenty-eight years.

In 1932, almost at the peak of their film career, the two had popped over to England for a supposed holiday; but, between leaving home and getting back, were under continuous siege from massive crowds of delirious fans. Fifteen years later came a return to Britain, to work in the variety theatre – the medium in which the skinny one had learned the basics of his trade. This visit too had people turning out in their thousands just to see them 'in person.'

In the early 1950s, two more British tours had followed, but the public's urge to fight and jostle to see them was sorely diminished, and the numbers paying to see them in the theatres was severely reduced.

To understand why these two screen legendary comedians – both now in their sixties, and of ailing health – had gone from making films in America to working in British theatres, we must first go back to the Hal Roach Studios, in California, USA, in the mid-nineteen-twenties:

o-o-0-o-o

CHAPTER 1

A LOT OF FUN

Oliver Norvell Hardy commenced work at the Hal Roach Studios, in Culver City, in January 1925, three months before Stan Laurel. Roach had brought in Hardy to play supporting roles to other comedians in the "Roach All-Star Comedies." These included Charley Chase, Frank Butler, Clyde Cook, Max Davidson, James Finlayson, Glenn Tryon, Mabel Normand, Theda Bara, and the 'Our Gang' kids. Such was the genial atmosphere and the enjoyable working conditions at the Roach Studios that it quickly earned the nickname – 'The Lot of Fun.'

Laurel, meanwhile, wasn't even in front of the camera. Despite his having made over fifty solo films, from as far back as 1917 (most in his own series of comedies), Laurel had been taken on by Roach purely as a writer and gag-man – a position he was happy to be in as, at the time, he didn't rate himself as a film comedian.

Laurel's interest soon spread to all aspects of film production, for which he was rewarded by being trained as a director. One year on and Stan had co-directed a handful of films, including three with Oliver Hardy – who was by then under contract with Roach.

One day in June 1926 Hardy was unable to turn up for filming, having badly scalded his arm at home, while basting a leg of lamb he had taken from the oven. Hal Roach, unable to find an immediate stand-in, pitched Laurel into the role. Liking Stan's contribution to the finished film, *Get 'Em Young*, Roach gave him the go-ahead to write himself a part in the next picture.

Both Laurel AND Hardy *were* in Hal Roach films.

The problem was … they weren't in *the same* films.

Not yet … anyway.

Hardy had by then recovered sufficiently to return, whereupon the two of them inadvertently appeared in the same film. For Stan Laurel and Oliver Hardy, the wheels had been set in motion. It was now only a matter of time!

Further films ensued in which the two of them appeared, until, by a process of almost "natural selection," the potential of playing them as a team was spotted and exploited.

Early portrait, wherein the Derby hats are not yet established as their trademark attire. Nor have they yet taken to Laurel always being positioned on the left.

Come July 1927 the screen partnership of 'Laurel & Hardy' was considered bankable enough for them to be launched as a major comic force. Before the plan could be put into action, however, the Hal Roach Studios broke for their annual summer holidays. "Babe" Hardy (a nickname he had acquired when he first went into films – circa 1914) and his wife Myrtle went on a long sea voyage, sailing from Los Angeles to Havana, Cuba.

Stan chose to go to England, which he hadn't visited since leaving in October 1912 with the Fred Karno Company of Comedians.

[Read my book: "LAUREL – Stage by Stage" for details of Stan's stage years.]

On 2 July 1927 Laurel sailed from New York on the White Star liner the *Homeric*. After disembarking at Southampton seven days later, he travelled to London to spend a few days with his father, who was then living in Ealing, West London. Next he journeyed north to Grantham, Lincolnshire, to see his sister, Beatrice Olga. Although staying at the George Hotel, in High Street, Stan arranged to have tea with Olga, a little further down High Street, at the Palace Café. However, the power of film soon caught up with him, in the form of the many filmgoers who recognised him, and stayed around to gawp. Soon a crowd had gathered and so, being unable to deal with the increasing demands for handshakes and autographs, the English-stage-comedian-turned-Hollywood-film-actor decided it would be safer to retire to the hotel.

It's a wonder that Laurel was so recognisable; as, just before leaving for England, both he and Hardy had had the heads shaved, for a cameo role in the Roach film *Call of the Cuckoo*.

With Stan on the trip was his wife Lois, whom he had married as recently as 23 August 1926. Pressure of his film work had prevented the newly-married couple from taking a proper honeymoon, so they took this opportunity to have one now; and, on 14 July flew from Croydon Airport to Paris, where they spent the next thirteen days.

They may well have flown in this Imperial Airways HP42 Air Liner, which looks like it has been knocked up by a boffin, in his back yard, using only wood and canvas.

Honeymoon over, it was time to head home, and so on 27 July, Stan and Lois boarded the White Star liner *Majestic*, at the French port of Cherbourg.

7245 S.S. "Majestic" 56,621 tons gross. Length 915'; breadth 100'.   White Star Line.

Barring the removal of funnels, ship design has barely changed in the last one hundred-plus years, which is hardly something you can say about passenger aircraft.

Although this was, for Laurel, an obvious "holiday/come family reunion/come honeymoon," he had very cleverly sold the idea to Hal Roach of it being a scouting mission to find new ideas for comedy films, for which Roach subsequently paid his expenses. One of the earliest Laurel & Hardy films, *Duck Soup*, was actually adapted from a stage sketch, *Home From the Honeymoon*, written by Stan's father in 1906. Using this as a lever, Stan had somehow convinced Roach that it was well worth his paying a visit to Mr. Jefferson Snr. to see if he had any more suitable scripts which could be adapted. How Laurel got this past Roach, when it was so obvious he was going to see his father anyway, brings Roach's usually shrewd business qualities into question – especially when one considers, using hindsight, that not one more line of script was forthcoming from Arthur Jefferson. And how Stan got Roach to pay for his honeymoon to Paris, makes Roach seem even more gullible – even if Laurel managed to manufacture a tie-in with *Home From the Honeymoon* to the Laurels coming "home from their honeymoon."

In all, Laurel was away for almost six weeks – 29 June till 7 August – and thus missed the first week of the Roach Studio restart. During that week, Hardy had appeared in the film *Love Em and Feed Em* , along with Roach comedian Max Davidson. There is a fair possibility that Davidson was brought in to play the role which had originally been allocated to Laurel; so now we can only imagine how much better the film would have been if he had been available.

The good news for Laurel was that, during the period he had been enjoying an all-expenses-paid holiday, Hal Roach had signed a distribution deal with the film company Metro-Goldwyn-Mayer. This was a great move on so many levels. Roach's previous distributor's task was to get picture-house managers to take his films. MGM, however, had their own vast, magnificent and numerous venues, and would be more than willing to give extra finance to Roach to produce quality films to be shown in them. The deal was to commence on 1 September 1927, which meant that *Hats Off*, the first Laurel & Hardy short to be shot after Laurel's return, benefitted greatly from the might of MGM's publicity machine. This Roach-MGM combination launch was comparable to that given for a major feature-film, in which every device – from billboards; advertising balloons; trucks with posters pasted on their sides, posters in stores; and even a parade outside the cinema – was employed; and seemed to be making a statement to the film world that: "Laurel & Hardy are here – and here to stay."

Hats Off – the film in which 'the Boys' (the nickname Laurel gave to the screen characters of 'Stan and Ollie') are salesmen, trying to sell a washing machine to a potential buyer who lives at the top of a long, steep flight of steps – was a great vehicle with which to promote them as a newly-formed team. Almost everything which makes up the characters of the Boys can be found in this film, but there is one major problem – THE FILM can't be found! Amazingly, although it probably had more prints made than any other L&H film to date, there is no known copy in existence.

What is thought to be the closing gag-shot, following a huge brawl, in *Hats Off*.

The new screen double-act pushed on through 1928 – releasing such silent classics as *Putting Pants On Philip, Leave 'Em Laughing, The Finishing Touch, From Soup to Nuts, Their Purple Moment, Two Tars, Liberty, Wrong Again*, and *That's My Wife* – to the third week in December 1928, where we find them making their finest silent film, *Big Business*.

In November 1928 the first "talkie" had hit the screens (Al Jolson's *The Jazz Singer*). Not wanting to miss out on this new craze, Roach had sound equipment installed at the Hal Roach Studios over the Christmas break of 1928-29.

The Laurels, had had sound in their home almost a year earlier, but this was the sound of a baby daughter — born 10 December 1927.

When Laurel and Hardy went back to work in January 1929, the sound equipment was still not fully up and running, so they continued making silents – *Double Whoopee, Bacon Grabbers*, and *Angora Love*. It was the last week in March before the first Laurel & Hardy talkie was made — *Unaccustomed As We Are*. Next came two more talkies: *Berth Marks*, and *Men O' War* — with time taken out to film a cameo role in the MGM extravaganza *Hollywood Revue of 1929*.

On Friday 28 June 1929, and by now having achieved celebrity status, Stan and Babe were included among a list of Hollywood A-listers who were invited to the opening of the newly-built Fox Theatre, San Francisco – the major stars being Marion Davies, Janet Gaynor, Wallace Beery, Joan Crawford and Douglas Fairbanks, Jr.; Will Rogers, Loretta Young, Buster Keaton, Lupe Velez, Harry Langdon, and Charley Chase.

The *San Francisco Chronicle* described part of the opening night as follows:

Then came Will Rogers to introduce the stars. Waves of laughter swept the mighty throng as he brought each dainty beauty across the big stage, or escorted each broad-shouldered man star to take his bow. His comments on each, and their smiling replies, raised chuckles to guffaws, and thunders of applause swept the theatre as the audience paid tribute to their favourites.

The line-up was followed by Fanchon and Marco's California Capers, which had a company of two hundred artistes. Then at 9.30 the audience watched the world premiere of the film *Behind That Curtain*. The whole presentation was enhanced by the sounds of a forty-piece orchestra, and a fifty-voice choir.

So why am I including this, when you are feverishly trying to get to the beginning of "The British Tours"? Well that is because of the significance of the show at the Fox Theatre. Just five months after the opening, Laurel and Hardy chose to chance their arm there, and partake in a programme in which they were to be featured not just as the characters on the screen, but also 'live on stage.'

This was an extremely risky gamble. First question that had to be asked was: "Could Laurel and Hardy cut it as live performers?" Being the main attraction, they would have to justify the admission fee which the several thousand patrons would be paying to see them over the six-day, four-shows-daily appearances (Fri-Thu 22-28 November 1929). If Laurel and Hardy failed, the two years of hard work they had put into building their reputation as the funniest screen double-act could be destroyed overnight. The contemporary reviews inform us how they fared:

The crowds yesterday at the Fox Theater were very probably attracted by the promise of seeing those deliciously droll fellows, Stan Laurel and Oliver Hardy, but they had much else to be thankful for.

There is a good "crook and detective" picture The Girl From Havana, *plus a Laurel and Hardy screen comedy,* They Go Boom, *which will make you laugh even if you have the toothache.*

But it was, really it was, Laurel and Hardy in the flesh that everybody waited for, and howled over. They are funny fellows, and they do a lot of rough-housing, so much that, when they finish, Rube Wolf is in his union suit, their director James Parrott, is minus coat, shirt, porus-plaster and waistcoat: a man in the audience is stripped of his clothes in the aisle and thrown into the orchestra pit, and both Stan and Ollie have barely enough clothing to keep within the law.

Their act is a riot of laughs. Perhaps they are just a bit funnier, this pair of rowdy comedians, in the picture than they are on the stage.

Maybe it was a mistake to play them against themselves. They Go Boom *is tremendously funny.*

(*San Francisco Chronicle* – Saturday 23 November 1929)

Broadcasting 'live' on radio, on the forecourt of Grauman's.
[Note the handprints and autographs in the cement paving slabs.]

[For full details of all of Stan and Babe's stage shows and public appearances in America, read my book: "LAUREL and HARDY – The U.S. Tours."]

The risk of doing the live show had probably been taken to make a quick buck, after both Stan and Babe had lost huge amounts of money in investments in the recent Wall Street Crash ("Black Tuesday" – 29 October 1929). It would be several years before the stage experience would be put to use doing further live shows, but that was a second medium they could do without for now, as there were still many more classic comedy films to be made.

Fast forward to 21 July 1932, and Laurel and Hardy's film credits to date numbered around thirty-three silents, thirty shorts (if one includes cameos in other films), and two features – *Pardon Us*, and *Pack Up Your Troubles*. It was time to take a well-earned break.

It had been five years since Stan had last seen his dad, and so for him to use the summer break at the Roach Studios to visit England, was an obvious choice. What was far from obvious was that Babe Hardy, who could have taken his holidays anywhere in the world, chose to go with Laurel. This speaks volumes for the high regard the two partners had for one another. After all, they had worked side-by-side for those five years, plus had attended show business events outside the studio, so one could be forgiven for thinking that the last thing they would want to do would be to go on holiday together. But, as Hardy was proud of the fact that he was of both English and Scottish ancestry, his desire to go there was increased. That Britain boasted many fine golf courses also had more than a little bearing on the matter for keen golfer, Hardy.

Babe decided to have his wife Myrtle accompany him, in the hope of saving their eleven year marriage. He had been having an affair with an attractive divorcee by the name of Viola Morse, so thought the vacation might help to patch things up. Stan, though, left his wife Lois at home, insisting: "She doesn't like crowds and travelling, and is not over strong, so preferred not to make the trip." The truth was that Laurel's marriage was also on the rocks, and Lois could not face the ordeal of making the trip in order to keep up appearances.

o-o-0-o-o

CHAPTER 2

A FEW WEEKS' GOLFING AND FISHING

As Stan and Babe understood it, the trip was purely a social call to the "Old Country," where they could take in a few weeks of golfing and fishing. The film company MGM had different ideas, though. Having, themselves, drawn up the travel plan for their ever-rising comedy stars, MGM organised around it a massive publicity campaign, in both Britain and America. Consequently, when Laurel and Hardy came to change trains at Chicago, on their near-four-day train journey from California to New York City, thousands of fans and photographers confronted them. The comedy duo's first thought was that there was someone in an adjacent compartment whom the crowd were waiting to see; but, when the mob continued to clamour more and more for their attention, it soon become frighteningly obvious that this was not the case.

Wanting to get away from the situation as quickly as possible, Stan and Babe fought their way through the swarm to catch their connection for New York City. Once on the train they had much cause to speculate as to the reason for the recent scene and, in the end, may well have dismissed it as a publicity stunt manufactured by MGM to raise interest in the release of their latest film. The reason Laurel and Hardy couldn't believe all the adulation was for them was that, as far as they were concerned, all they had done for the last five years was make short, supporting films for the main cinema features. In the Hollywood star system this meant they didn't shine very brightly. The public, though, had other views.

Convinced that the nightmare reception was over, Stan and Babe settled back with thoughts only of enjoying the peacefulness of the British countryside, and the hospitality of its people. Little did they know that their nightmare had just begun, and the likes of the reception at Chicago was to be repeated at every stop. Mob number two, on New York Broadway, was even bigger.

Stepping out of the train at New York. Luckily, they had that mobile panic-room behind them.

The press were out in force, and the presence of the two stars, plus the newsreel cameras, whipped the crowd to a point of hysteria, and it was only with a great deal of assistance from members of the New York Police Force that Laurel and Hardy were able to board the Cunard liner *Aquitania*, and set sail for England.

Boarding ship did not afford them instant relief, as they still had to contend with the attentions of the two-thousand-plus passengers and crew – as did fellow travellers Douglas Fairbanks Jr. and his wife, Joan Crawford. After the first few days at sea, and following repeated appeals from the captain for the celebrities to be left alone, Babe came out of enforced isolation, and joined in with the entertainment. Amongst other invites, he accepted one to view the ship's engines, and another to referee a boxing match. Stan however declined the two, and seldom came out of his cabin.

In one incident Babe almost regretted, for life, popping out of his cabin – well, popping his head out, at least. He related:

> Near Cherbourg I heard a noise above my cabin. I put my head out of a porthole to see what was amiss, and a heavy weight came down about three inches from my head. If it had caught me, I don't know what would have happened. At first I thought it was one of Stan's tricks, but the incident was too serious to be funny. It turned out that it was a depth-weight being lowered. It frightened me very much at the time.

On 23 July 1932, the *Aquitania* arrived at Southampton, England, to be greeted by the unbelievable and totally unexpected sight and sound of thousands of waving, cheering fans – whistling Laurel & Hardy's signature tune – *The Cuckoo Song*.

[Many Americans call it *The KuKu Song* – thus interpreting the actual bird call as one note, repeated; when it is so obviously two different notes. There is also an arrangement called *The Dance of the Cuckoos*, but the most favoured is *The Cuckoo Song*. Stan himself said in the magazine *Ideas and Town Talk*: "We call it *The Cuckoo Song*. I don't think it boasts a name really."]

Whilst the crowd were showing their delight, and confetti was falling like snow, Laurel was running up and down the passenger deck shouting, "Where's mi dad?" Hardy, meanwhile, was regaling some of the dozens of pressmen who had swarmed aboard with stories of their exploits on board the *Aquitania*. These began: "I'll be glad when I can get Stan off this boat. I have had a terrible time with him, you know ..."

Shortly, Laurel returned to his partner's side, dragging with him an elderly, nattily-dressed gentleman. "Babe, meet Dad," said Stan. A.J. introduced the party to Venetia – his second wife, and Stan's stepmother. Also in the party were Dr. & Ethel Falconar, friends of Laurel's wife Lois, who were to remain with them throughout most of the holiday.

Whilst the comedians were still on board, the *Sunday Post* recorded the following quotes:

"After our holiday," said Hardy, "we go back to Hollywood to complete our contract, which still has about two years to run." Then contradicting a statement he had made only a minute earlier, Hardy continued:

"Stan has behaved perfectly on the voyage. He is a thorough little gentleman and the finest fellow in the world. Since 1927 [*sic*] when we first started to work together, we have never had a cross word."

Although the part of this statement concerning Stan's behaviour was said very tongue-in-cheek, the latter part, extolling Stan's human qualities, was straight from the heart, and Babe meant every word of it. Stan returned the compliment in an equally sincere manner: "*Ollie is the kindest man I know. He wouldn't hurt a fly. It's a pleasure to work with him*".

On the dock, the comedy stars received an invitation, on behalf of the Mayor of Tynemouth, to be guests at a civic lunch, during their forthcoming visit to Tyneside. Laurel sent the reply:

I shall be happy to accept it, I am looking forward tremendously to renewing acquaintance with Tyneside. I have almost forgotten what it looks like, but not quite. I expect that when I go there I shall remember people and places where I spent happy times in years gone by. I shall be delighted to be in North Shields again.

Laurel also sent a message via the *Sunday Sun*, to all his friends in the North East.

By the time you are reading this I shall be home! Only those who have been away from England for years realise how the Old Country tugs at the heart-strings. No matter how happy, how successful, you may be in new surroundings, your thoughts go back longingly to the friends you left behind. You want to see the old places and old faces again. I have kept in touch with several of my old friends in the North Country, and I am looking forward keenly to seeing the changes and developments that have taken place in the long years I have been absent. With me, of course, comes my great friend and great comedian Oliver Hardy.

Whilst the VIPs were in customs, word came through that the Minister of Labour had forbidden Hardy to undertake "any form of employment – paid or unpaid," during his stay in England. The decision was quickly over-ridden, after the intervention of Sam Eckman, Managing Director of MGM London Pictures, who was on hand to take care of such formalities. Had he not been, Babe could not have made any personal appearances. Had Hardy known how events would turn out over the next forty-eight hours, he would have prayed that permission be denied.

Having satisfied the pressmen, and the customs officials, Laurel and Hardy now had to fight their way through the ever-demanding crowd to board the train for London. Amidst further cheering, flag-waving and confetti-throwing, the train finally managed to pull out of Southampton Docks, one hour late.

Arriving at Waterloo station, they were met by a similar scene to the one at Southampton, with over a thousand pairs of lips whistling *The Cuckoo Song*.

The Boys meet their Waterloo [fans].

Laurel and Hardy on their arrival in London.

With forty photographers moving, and the crowd getting pushier and pushier, Stan exclaimed:

What a reception. I never imagined anything like this. If my old friends in the North Country are only half as enthusiastic, I shall be thoroughly happy.

Four hundred porters had volunteered for duty that day at Waterloo Station but, even so, the pressure of the crowd was so great that the two comedians became separated. Hardy couldn't figure out how it happened. He said he just climbed into a taxi and arrived at the Savoy Hotel, where only the hall porter was on hand to greet him. By the time Laurel arrived, and the confusion was resolved, there was no time for them to rest and freshen up before giving the press reception – arranged by MGM.

Pictured is Sam Eckman, from MGM London Pictures, who stayed with the two Hollywood stars through-out the London part of this publicity tour. Here he is briefing the Boys for the press reception at the Savoy Hotel.

Eckman can also be seen in the above, sandwiching comedian and newspaper columnist Bobby Howes between himself and Hardy.

Special interest was held by those newsmen in attendance from the places Laurel and Hardy were expected to visit: Tynemouth, Newcastle, Edinburgh, Glasgow, Birmingham, Blackpool, Leeds, Sheffield, Liverpool, Hull, and Manchester. Asked if they had any business commitments in England, Laurel said: "No, but we do intend to study audiences with a view to catering for them in future films." (There goes Laurel's attempt to get some research payments out of Hal Roach for this, his second visit to England.)

With the reporters gone, Laurel and Hardy were able to get to their hotel rooms, to change. After dinner in the Savoy restaurant, they retired to their rooms – Babe to rest, and Stan to talk with his dad and his sister Olga and her husband Bill, who had now joined the party.

The following day, Sunday 24 July 1947, a *Daily Herald* reporter found the Jeffersons in Stan's room at the Savoy, still reminiscing:

> 'Come in and join the family party,' said Stan greeting him with a broad smile. 'I've been waiting for this reunion for five years, saving up all I had to say, and we haven't got past the old times yet. Ollie the great old scout has shuffled off and left us to it. He went to see the 'Changing of the Guard' this morning. They must have heard he was coming and were afraid he might get up to something, 'cos they didn't have it,' he announced, and his peel of laughter bounced off the ceiling. 'So he's gone to the Cheshire Cheese to have a few cheeses. Reckon he's full of - er - cheese by now.'

Rather than enter Fleet Street via the Strand, Hardy takes a diversion along the Victoria Embankment.

[AJM: The Cheshire Cheese is a public house in Fleet Street, frequented by journalists]

As the Jeffersons' afternoon tea-party continued, the reporter was replaced by one from the *Daily Sketch*, who recorded the conversation as follows:

> 'As for the boy, well ... ,' said Mr Jefferson, then after a while, 'A good boy. A very good boy. Success hasn't spoiled him. It's something to say that.'
>
> 'He's still the same kid,' said his sister. The boy hung his head modestly.
>
> 'Seems to me,' said Jefferson, 'that comedians are born, not made.'
>
> 'You said a lot, dad,' said the boy.
>
> 'I always go to see him in the pictures,' Mr. Jefferson added. 'In our home in Shields in the old days I could see he had something in him. Always being funny, he was. So I made him a little theatre in the attic. Spent the day there, he and his sister Olga. Well what I say is, "what's bred in the bone" ... '

Here, the account ends. The amusing observation about this conversation is the way Stan's dad refers to him as "the boy" — he was forty-two at the time.

Tea at the Savoy with Stan's dad and step-mother, Venetia.

Later that evening, Stan and Babe went to a performance of Noel Coward's play, *Cavalcade*, at the Drury Lane Theatre. In a letter written later to a fan some years, Stan revealed:

```
... saw Noel Coward's stage production of 'Cavalcade', that
too is a wonderful memory - sitting in the actual Royal Box
with the powdered wig dept. in attendance.
```

But, at the end of the performance of *Cavalcade*, it wasn't the actors on the stage who were given a standing ovation by the packed house, but the two comedians sitting in the Royal Box. The cast didn't seem to bear a grudge as, after the show, Stan and Babe were guests at a private party given for them backstage. Also in attendance were their fellow passengers from the Atlantic crossing, Doug & Joan (Crawford) Fairbanks [pictured].

An advert in Monday's *Evening Standard* read: "*Leicester Square Empire. Tonight, personal appearance of LAUREL & HARDY at 9 p.m.*" As a consequence, an estimated two thousand people turned up, giving Leicester Square the appearance of Trafalgar Square on a New Year's Eve.

Once again the media had instigated the formation of a huge crowd, into which the precipitation of Laurel and Hardy served as the catalyst for a reaction of hysteria.

In the melee which followed, with the crowd frantic to get a look inside the comedians' car, one of the doors was torn from its hinges. Inside, Stan and Babe were terrified they were about to be crushed, for the car appeared to be giving them as much protection as a paper bag. They managed to gain entrance to the theatre only with some strong-arm support from a squad of policemen. On route, Laurel glanced upwards to see his name in lights above the theatre entrance and remarked to the *Daily Herald* reporter shadowing him:

Looks great, but kind of wasteful. But you should see the lighthouse in the graveyard at Ulverston in Lancashire where I was born. They put it up when I was a kid, a tombstone with a light on top. It was the Eighth Wonder of the World to me. Ever since then it's been my ambition to have a tombstone like that.

[AJM: Any rich, Americans paying attention?]

Once inside the cinema, after the showing of the Laurel & Hardy film *Any Old Port*, the house-lights went up and the Boys walked on stage. The audience clapped and cheered for several minutes. Once the noise had abated, Hardy expressed their genuine gratitude for the great welcome they had received, whilst Stan interjected some cause for slapstick retribution. Asked, afterwards, how he felt about the welcome, Hardy told a *Daily Sketch* reporter:

'I did feel like crying. You see I often get that way. I'm not ashamed of crying, you know,' he added, 'I love to go and see sob-stuff films. I just sit there and cry and cry.'

[AJM: Perhaps THAT'S the reason he's called 'Babe.'].

On Tuesday 26 July the newspaper *Radio Programme* page announced:

LAUREL & HARDY TO BROADCAST TO-NIGHT.

Laurel & Hardy, the British [*sic*] film comedians will broadcast for the first time to-night. They are due to appear at the microphone at 10.35, and their performance will last only five minutes. What they talk about will be kept secret until then.

The 'On Air' appearance, broadcast nationwide from the BBC studios in London, was causing great excitement as, that week, a huge exhibition of radios was on at the London Olympia. "Radio" (to misuse a line from one of Laurel and Hardy's films) was "still in its infancy," so personalities of the status of Stan Laurel and Oliver Hardy, being introduced *live* into people's homes, could only help to boost its popularity. The *Manchester Evening News* said prophetically:

"This will be one of the occasions when Televisors would be really appreciated."

Bert Tracey's view of Laurel and Hardy during their BBC radio broadcast, in London.

Television, then, was even more so in its infancy, but in the public's mind enough for Stan's father also to prophesy, when commenting on the decline of the theatre: "*Whatever next ... ? Pictures televised direct to our firesides?*"

Although no recording of Laurel and Hardy's radio broadcast exists, it is known that Hardy sent greetings to a Mr. Bert Tracey. This would seem rather a strange thing to do as, at the time, Bert Tracey was watching Oliver Hardy through a plate glass window in the studios. Bert's mother, however, received the greetings at her home in Victoria Park, Manchester, where Hardy said he was looking forward to meeting her the following Tuesday. Tracey was spending the evening with Laurel and Hardy, prior to travelling to the North of England with them.

[AJM. Bert Tracey's connection with Oliver Hardy went back to 1916, when they were in films together with Vim Comedies, in Florida.]

In a later article in the *Manchester Chronicle*, Tracey described the broadcast as follows:

The BBC's magnificent new studios astonished Oliver. In spite of the self-possession an actor is supposed to have, the two stars looked like a couple of criminals about to be electrocuted as they seated themselves at the little table before the microphone.

Some stuff was written for them to broadcast, but they just slung it away and carried on with one of their little quarrels.

Immediately after the broadcast, Stan and Babe hurried round to the Strand Theatre, where Ivor Novello's play *Party* was playing. Backstage they were introduced to members of the cast by Leslie Henson, and again met up with Doug and Joan Fairbanks, plus Ivor Novello himself.

Through such late nights the Boys were now extremely tired, so spent the morning of Wednesday 27 July resting. In the evening, they went to the Coliseum Theatre, in St. Martin's Lane, WC2, to watch the play *Casanova*.

Top left: Jack Barty — Right column: Jack Barty, Douglas Wakefield, Billy Nelson.

Backstage, they met three of the principal actors: Jack Barty, Duggie Wakefield, and Billy Nelson. Within the year, all three comedy actors would find themselves employed at the Hal Roach Studios– which suggests that Stan had influenced their being employed by Roach.

[AJM: Wakefield and Nelson starred in their own films, but Barty did cross over into one film with Stan and Ollie – *The Laurel-Hardy Murder Case*, in which he played the part of 'Jitters' the butler.]

Barty, Wakefield, Nelson – in the 1933 Roach comedy *Twin Screws*.

Upon leaving the Coliseum, our subjects officiated at the opening of the new Screen Artistes Federation Club, in Archer Street, after which they were wined and dined by their hosts. [**FILM**]

Leaving early, they joined up with the rest of their party at the train station, and caught the overnight 'sleeper' to Newcastle. I hope they *were* able to sleep, for, from now on in, sleep was going to be a precious commodity.

o-o-0-o-o

CHAPTER 3

TYNE AND WEAR – TIRED AND WORN

Upon pulling in at Newcastle Central at the unsavoury hour of 5:49am, a car took them to the Grand Hotel, Tynemouth, where few people other than a keen posse of reporters and a couple of policemen were around. Hardy made no secret of his tiredness, and promptly cancelled the round of golf arranged for later in the day, adding, with an unusual tinge of bitterness:

> "I'm just sleepy. Everybody wants me here and there. I'm just like a mannequin on a string."

As one of Hardy's main intentions in coming to Britain was to sample her golf courses, he must have indeed been feeling fatigued. Laurel, too, was feeling the pace:

> 'This is supposed to be a holiday, but our tour of England has been extended so that we have to cut out Madrid and Berlin. It's good to be back in Tynemouth,' he yawned, 'but I feel I must have a rest. I'm going to bed.'

By then it was 8am, but at 10:30 both comedians appeared for breakfast, where Stan's niece Eileen Jefferson (daughter of his older brother Gordon) had travelled from Newcastle to meet her famous Uncle. News of Laurel and Hardy's arrival had spread, and a large throng began to gather outside. At a breakfast table in the hotel, a *Shields Gazette* reporter asked Laurel how he was enjoying his return visit to North Shields:

> I've just arrived, but I'm pleased to see the place again. Hardy and I came over for a holiday, but we have not had a moment to spare. All the time I was in London I hadn't time to go for a walk. I would like to have had the chance of a walk round the town to see some of the places I remember as a boy, but it cannot be done. We are just rushing about saying 'Hello' and then we are gone again. I am looking forward to the luncheon and seeing the councillors. I want to see if I can recognise any of them.

Breakfast over, the Mayor and Mayoress of Tynemouth – Alderman and Mrs. J.G. Telford – arrived to escort them to North Shields Town Hall. Upon its arrival, the mayoral car was surrounded by a crowd of several hundred people determined to get a good look at the local hero. A police cordon some fifty yards long, which had been holding the crowd at bay, snapped like a cheap necklace. Once again, as was now becoming all too regular, Laurel and Hardy were buffeted around in their car like a toy boat in an angry sea. As soon as the police cordon regrouped and ringed the car, Stan and Babe emerged to the sound of tremendous cheers. Making their way through hundreds of outstretched hands they reached the sanctuary of the Town Hall where, stepping out from his vantage point between the palms and potted plants which bedecked the corridors, a *Sunderland Echo* reporter asked Laurel:

> 'What do you think of Mr Hardy?'

> 'He's worth his weight in diamonds,' replied Stan.

> Then to Hardy, 'What do you think of Laurel?'

> Hardy's 18 stone frame quivered with mirth: 'Coming through that crush just now I was mighty glad to be Hardy, but if ever I wish I were anyone else – it's Laurel.'

These were not empty words, spoken to appease a reporter's curiosity, but were a genuine indication of the high regard in which the two partners held each other.

The reception in the Mayor's Parlour included amongst the guests: the chairman from each of the council committees; local theatre and cinema managers; two representatives from MGM; and members of the press; plus many of the people whom Stan had known as a boy, when he had lived in the neighbouring town and fishing port of North Shields (1897-1905).

Arrival at the Town Hall in the mayoral car. The guy in the light trilby, left, is thought to be John Hutchinson – MGM rep' on this leg of the tour.

After cocktails, the honoured guests were taken across the road to the Albion Assembly Rooms. On the way over, despite a strong presence of police, the pressure of the mob split them up.

This could be the first-ever version of a picture in which you are asked: "Where's Ollie?" But it's actually showing how far Stan and Ollie became separated, during their short walk across the Town Hall Square to the Albion Assembly Rooms.

During luncheon Stan and Babe were constantly having to swap their knives for pens, in order to sign the almost continuous stream of papers which were thrust at them, but both men took it in good spirits.

In proposing a toast, the Mayor recalled when Stan's father was himself a councillor (elected 1 November 1900). In reply to the toast, it was Stan who spoke first. In quiet tones he began:

> Mr. Mayor, Aldermen, Councillors, and old pals, I do not know what to say for the marvellous reception. I was not born in North Shields, but I feel that I just belong here. I am proud to be amongst you all. I owe a lot to Mr Hardy for making it possible for me to be in this position to come here and enjoy your wonderful reception. I feel I want to thank everybody personally. God Bless you all.

Then it was Hardy's turn:

> Mrs. Hardy and I want to stay here for ever. You have accepted us and made us feel at home. From the bottom of my heart I wish to thank you. I have never in all my life met with such hearty people, such kindly people, such courteous people, or such considerate people.

Considering that Oliver Hardy had no roots whatsoever in Tynemouth, and had been afforded its hospitality for only a couple of hours, this tribute would seem to be a bit over the top. It would, however, not be the last time Babe "laid it on."

Earlier, Hardy had confided to a reporter: "*Mr. Laurel wants them to give him 'the Freedom of the City' but, if the Mayor of Tynemouth is wise, he will do nothing of the kind.*" The Mayor must have taken Hardy's advice, for the luncheon ended with no such ceremony.

Stan's boyhood pals Alfred Chambers, John Armstrong, John Bell, and two others get a private meeting, in the seclusion of the backyard of the Assembly Rooms.

Feeling nonplussed, Stan sneaked out and went round to 8 Dockwray Square with the intent of surveying, in solitude, the home which had meant so much to him as a boy. He was denied the opportunity however, due to the vast volume of people who had anticipated his move and were awaiting his arrival. The crowd allowed him to mount the steps to his former home, but he was unable to get inside and look around due to the change in occupancy of the dwelling.

When the Jeffersons lived there (1897-1902) they had had sole occupancy of the house; but now, in 1932, it was subdivided and lived in by several families. Laurel was to say of his lost moment: *"It is a place for sentiment with me. I belong to Dockwray Square."*

After being extricated from the crowd by a police snatch-squad, Stan was driven to a second former home, Ayton House, where the Jeffersons had lived from 1902 till 1905. Here he was met by a much smaller gathering. [Note John Hutchinson again, above.]

The photo at left has been identified many times as Stan with his mother outside 8 Dockwray Square, which is wrong on both counts. The property is Ayton House, Ayres Terrace, Preston Village – on the outskirts of North Shields. The Dockwray Square house is shown at right.

The lady seeing off Stan to school is most-likely Mary Taylor, one of two live-in domestics.

For Laurel, it was then back to the Grand Hotel, where he was reunited with his comedy partner. First on the agenda was a group photo with staff and locals at the back of the hotel; and then a publicity shot, with the reception committee and the hotel manager, on the hotel steps.

Most of the photos taken on the day were shot by Roland Park – one of Stan's boyhood pals. The lady centre (dark coat, cloche hat) is his wife; and the girl in all-white and the boy on her left are their children. Behind the boy is the hotel manager.

Between Stan and Babe is hotel manager, J.G. Ratcliffe, who commissioned the shooting of footage on these steps, and of the imminent proceedings, and managed to appear on film in both locations, at the same time – a master of camera-hogging.

On schedule at 3pm, Laurel and Hardy were driven the short journey from the hotel to the Plaza Cinema. As soon as Stan got out of the car, everyone wanted to touch, kiss, or shake hands with him. The Tynesiders' show of affection was unbounded, for they were meeting not just any film star, but one whom they regarded as one of their own. The party of dignitaries next led their guests to the rear of the cinema, where the huge open-air terrace, adjacent to the beach, had been laid out with seats, on a specially-built wooden platform.

Above left is the view of the Plaza from the Grand Hotel, and right is the reverse view.

Between Babe and Stan is the Mayor of Tynemouth, Alderman J.G. Telford, accompanied by Mrs. Teleford, and other civic dignitaries

Of the two comedians Ollie was up first and, following a rather dramatic speech in which he paced up and down the rows of seated on-lookers. He then finished by addressing the people on the beach, with the words: "*I will be down amongst you all soon.*" [FILM]

With the masses now baying for Stan, he rose and, in trying to give back the love they were radiating, allowed himself to be pushed, pulled, kissed, hugged, patted on the back, and shook hands till it hurt. He signed autographs, and posed for photographs with whomsoever commanded his presence. When the number of people approaching him didn't seem to be decreasing, he addressed them thus: "I love you all. I would like to shake hands with you all and say 'Thank You.' It is the greatest day of my life." He continued, "I shall always remember this visit to Tynemouth." Then, obviously choked with emotion, he regained his seat and proceeded to wipe away real tears of sentiment, whilst his partner could do nothing to console him.

The number of attendees was swelled by six hundred children who came under the charity banner of the 'Sunshine Fund.' In a gesture which only two people with the warm, human spirit which Laurel and Hardy possessed would care to volunteer, they presented gifts (donated to the charity by J.G Ratcliffe) to all six hundred children.

Stan, Babe, and Mr. Ratcliffe discussing how to go about handing out the 600 presents.

Laughing and joking throughout, Stan and Babe managed this mammoth task with unfailing grace and humour, and brought more pleasure to the children than if Saint Nicholas himself had been present. [Fortunately, silent film footage taken of the events outside the Plaza, for showing in local cinemas, is still in existence. **[FILM]**

As the party started to leave the esplanade, the two stars were again mobbed. When Stan and Babe finally got away, they flopped straight into their beds back at the Grand Hotel.

At 9 o'clock the two comedians were driven the nine miles to Newcastle-upon-Tyne, where they made a walk-on appearance at the Queen's Hall, in Northumberland Street; followed by a similar one at the Stoll Picture House, in Westgate Road. Outside both venues their car was again besieged, and they had to go through the now customary ritual of being manhandled.

Sometime during the earlier visit to North Shields, Laurel had managed to meet up with Horace Lee – former manager of the Theatre Royal, in North Shields. [Laurel's father Arthur Jefferson had been Manager and Lessee of the Theatre Royal between 1895 and 1905 so Stan would have known Horace when he was working for his father at the theatre. Horace then took over the role of manager, himself. Laurel said of Lee, in a letter written in 1955:

```
I used to call him Uncle Horace - a sweet guy. I had the
pleasure of seeing him again in '32. it was an emotional
meeting, both cried like kids.
```

Another side of Stan was shown to us by the reporter from the *Shields Hustler*:

What struck us all was Stan's sweet naturalness. Success hasn't spoilt him, as it does so many people. He has not developed a swelled head, and his old friends in North Shields were glad of that. There is something sad to witness men who have succeeded in forgetting themselves, and putting on airs – airs that invariably do not become them. Stan is 'being himself' and we like him all the better for it.

Friday, after breakfast, whilst waiting on Newcastle Central Station, the Boys were kept busy signing autographs, and talking to the press. Laurel left the following message for the people of Tyneside:

God bless everybody. I love them all. Tyneside people do not alter – they are as good as ever.

Hardy joined in:

You're all just fine. I feel that America could not have made me feel more welcome.

Arthur Jefferson was on the platform, but remained behind to continue his own reunion with the people of Tyneside. His wife Venetia, however, left with Stan's party. Stan hugged and kissed his dad and said goodbye.

As the train pulled away, the pair leant through an open window and Stan waved his cloth cap whilst Ollie waved his straw boater. The people of Tynemouth responded by giving them a final rousing cheer. In Scotland, others had yet to stake a claim on the returning hero.

o-o-0-o-o

CHAPTER 4

SCOTLAND FOR THE BRAVE

Rather than being an uncontrollable mob, the one-thousand-strong crowd at Edinburgh's Waverley Station could be described only as "boisterous." For their restraint, they were treated to a series of antics from Stan and Ollie which resulted in the reception being the jolliest of the whole trip. But allowing the public freedom of access to the celebrities soon proved too much; so the police force dislodged them from the crowd, and escorted them to the North British Station Hotel. Inside, both heaved a sigh of relief – pleased to have escaped a bruising for once.

Laurel pointing out the escape route over the rooftop of the North British Station Hotel, to avoid the mob below.

In the afternoon, following a well-earned rest, the Boys took an escorted walk around Edinburgh Castle, and went unmolested. The event was recorded on film, but a letter written by Laurel to a fan in November 1957 revealed something the camera had missed:

EDINBURGH CASTLE, CHANGING THE GUARD.

Yes, I visited Edinburgh Castle in '32. Oliver was with me, his first trip to Scotland, we did'nt get a chance to enjoy looking around on account of the crowds who followed us there, to get autographs & snap shots, handshaking, etc. also requests to kiss babies & many more Gals.

I can see poor Babe now, pretending to be very pleased, but giving on the side his famous 'Burned up' expression, then quickly changing to a jovial side again.

I often wished I had been able to slot that situation into a film, it would have been a riot.

Frame Grabs of footage of Laurel and Hardy arriving at Waverley Station, then entering and exiting the North British Station Hotel; later followed by a tour of Edinburgh Castle.

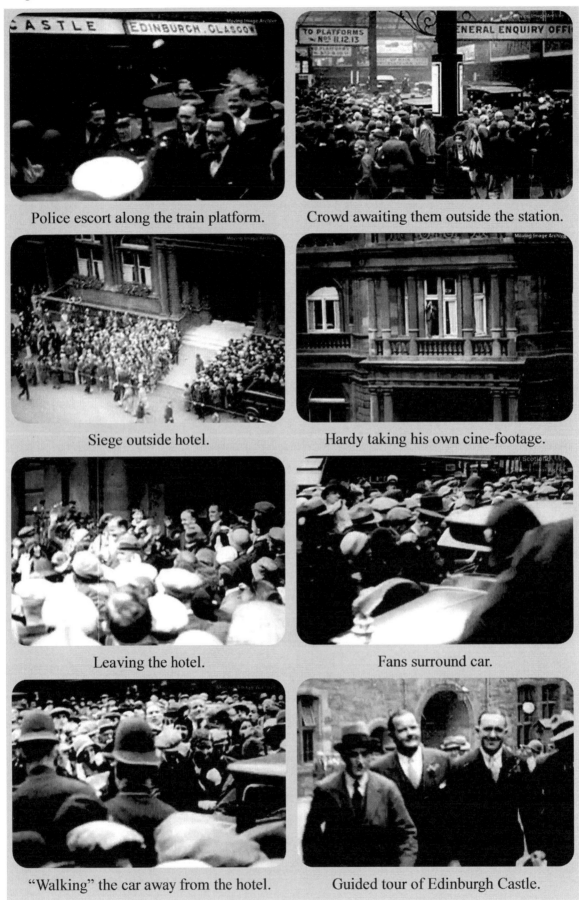

Police escort along the train platform.

Crowd awaiting them outside the station.

Siege outside hotel.

Hardy taking his own cine-footage.

Leaving the hotel.

Fans surround car.

"Walking" the car away from the hotel.

Guided tour of Edinburgh Castle.

[**FILM**] Film held in the National Library of Scotland

Although the daytime events had gone off well, the evening was to hold a very different atmosphere. With only one public appearance having been arranged in Edinburgh, it was not surprising that crowds had gathered hours before the comedians' arrival. The scenes which followed were admirably caught on film by local cinematographer Alan J. Harper. At 7:30pm, as Laurel and Hardy's car pulled up at the Playhouse Theatre, pandemonium broke loose. People brushed past the police, and ringed the car – jostling, cheering and waving – prompting the VIPs to dash for the safety of the foyer. Meanwhile, the audience of three thousand inside the Playhouse was being kept happy watching the Laurel & Hardy film *Laughing Gravy*. **[FILM]**

When the house-manager, Mr. Ellis, introduced Laurel and Hardy on stage there was several minutes of deafening applause. Filling in with comic interplay, the comedy duo waited for the ovation to subside and, when the vast audience became hushed, Hardy started his customary address. In his speech he told the people of Edinburgh how thankful they were for the wonderful reception they had been given that night, and also for the kindness they had been shown since their arrival in Britain. He went on to say, modestly, that they had been more than adequately rewarded for the little efforts he and his partner made to amuse and entertain, by that reception, and continued:

> When I come here again I'm coming in a big limousine, and I am going to 'do' this country properly, even though it may take about three months. I have so many "Scotch" friends in Hollywood, and I want to see the country from which they came. This visit is all too short, but even so it has meant that we shall have to cut out going to part of the Continent, for which we sail on the 24th of next month.

Laurel then broke into the conversation with his plea to be heard, after which their 'business' ended with Ollie booting Stan off the stage. All things being finished inside the Playhouse, Laurel and Hardy had next to work out an escape plan. Looking outside, the pair could see that the crowd had in no way diminished, so police reinforcements were called for. When Stan, Babe, and Myrtle dashed for the car, the fans on the opposite pavement, being denied a view of the comedy duo, surged across the road en bloc. But before the scene could turn ugly, four mounted police horses intercepted and, employing their hulk and pounding hooves, scattered the mob in seconds. Just to make sure the crowd didn't re-form and follow the stars to their hotel, the mounted police then accompanied the car down Leith Walk, back to the hotel. **[FILM]**

By 9:30pm the party was packed-and-ready on the railway platform, this time at the Caledonian Station, where fans demanded Stan and Babe's constant attention right up to the last second of the train pulling away. Little did the Boys know that, whilst enjoying the journey west to Glasgow, this was the lull before the storm and, in less than ninety minutes, their lives and those of many fans would be in peril.

o-o-0-o-o

On 30 July 1932 thousands of people were crowded into the Los Angeles stadium, USA, to witness the opening parade of the two thousand athletes in the Olympic Games. Countless flags were being waved, and a choir of one thousand sang the National Anthem. The "President's Dinner" was attended by scores of film stars. On the eve of all this, eight thousand people were crowded into Glasgow Central railway station, to witness the attraction of just TWO celebrities. Countless flags were being waved, and a massed choir of eight thousand whistled the anthem – not the National Anthem, but Laurel and Hardy's anthem – *The Cuckoo Song*. This reception was to grab bigger headlines, nationwide, than the Olympics, and the scene to greet Laurel and Hardy was one not seen in Glasgow before, or since:

The Central Station was jammed solid with people long before the train was due and, even at that early stage, extra police had been drafted in, for it was obvious there were going to be problems. The train drew in at 10:47pm and the comedy duo could be seen standing in the doorway of a Pullman car. Upon descending from the train, there was time for a little fun, as only the reception committee had been allowed onto the platform.

Hardy using the bagpipes as a way of warding off the attacking horde awaiting them as soon as they leave the safety of the station platform.

The trouble came when, upon exiting the platform, the celebrities were confronted by a solid mass of eight thousand spectators, packing every available square-inch of the concourse. The efforts of the police could not prevent those at the front of the crowd from being squashed against the platform barriers, so action had to be taken quickly. A posse of seven policemen ringed the celebrities and tried to lead them out through the station entrance. Such was the pressure of the crowd, though, that an involuntary diversion was made to a subway, which led to a side exit. So tightly packed was it that voluntary movement was almost impossible, and men and women in the crowd struggled desperately to escape being crushed.

When people started getting hurt, panic set in, and the air became filled with the sounds of shouting and screaming. Many people collapsed in a faint, and had to be borne over the heads of the crowd to a place of safety, where they could receive treatment. Only the prompt action of the police in holding back part of the crowd helped to relieve the situation.

As the two comedians emerged into Hope Street, a rush was made towards them by the crowd in front of the Central Hotel. It was then that, owing to the pressure of numbers, a section of the stone balustrade skirting the wall of the hotel collapsed onto the pavement. The falling masonry bowled over several on-lookers, but then formed

MANY INJURED IN
RUSH TO SEE
LAUREL AND HARDY.
VICTIMS PRECIPITATED INTO MANHOLE.

BALUSTRADE KNOCKED DOWN

NINE persons were taken to hospital and dozens more had to be attended to in the street in Glasgow last night when the most extraordinary crowd scenes which have ever been witnessed in and around the Central Station attended the arrival from Edinburgh of the famous screen comedians, Laurel and Hardy.

WOMEN TRAMPLED ON.

MAN FALLS UNDER TRAMCAR.	THE INJURED.
	NINE people were taken to the Royal Infirmary. They were:—

in a heap which, by chance, prevented others from falling into the basement below.

By a miracle only the two people trapped under the debris were injured, but the incident created a wild stampede for safety, during which a number of people were hurt.

Fifteen minutes after Laurel and Hardy's arrival, the scene was one of devastation. People were limping around looking for shoes, hats, or coats which had been lost in the mad crush. Others were being treated for minor injuries. Ambulance wagons and police reinforcements had been rushed to the area, and eight men suffering from leg injuries were taken to the Royal Infirmary.

Meanwhile Laurel and Hardy had staggered into the hotel, exhausted and badly ruffled. Stan was deathly pale, and looked as if he were about to pass out at any moment. Babe was first to recover, and was soon up and wise-cracking. Stan, however, remained badly shaken, and made his feelings of panic known. Outside, so many people were still hanging around that the Boys decided it was best to show themselves. Stepping outside would have been suicidal, so they ascended to a first-floor window balcony, and spent a few minutes "mugging" to the lustily cheering crowd below. Then Babe, with a slight gesture of his hand, signalled for silence and, as his call of *"We'll be seein' ya!"* carried over the heads of the throng, he and his partner gave a final wave and slipped back inside the hotel.

Many pickpockets had taken advantage of the earlier situation, and five had been arrested. Even the stars themselves had suffered personal losses, when souvenir hunters had committed the effrontery of removing articles from Stan and Babe's pockets. Laurel was most dismayed to find his fifty-guinea wristwatch missing. Fortunately, Mr. Hutchinson (the MGM tour rep') had had the foresight to hold the Boys' wallets, which contained huge sums of money. The losses, though, were minor compared with the reality of the implications of their continuing "welcomes," which was that Stan Laurel and Oliver Hardy were now two very frightened men. Describing his ordeal, Stan said:

> I was so tightly wedged in the crowd, I thought my last hour had come. I couldn't breathe, my clothes were torn, and I almost lost a shoe.

The first "reception committee" they had encountered, in Chicago, which they thought was a one-off, had now become a recurring nightmare, getting progressively scarier. At breakfast, Stan was to say:

> I've never seen anything like it, have you, Babe? The scenes at Southampton and London were just Sunday School picnics compared with that rodeo at the station. Nothing that has happened in the States or elsewhere can compare with our experiences last night.

The tragic irony of the situation is that the organisers were worried only a handful of people would bother to turn up at that late hour. Station officials, who were totally unprepared for the vast numbers, and had erected no barriers to keep them at bay, were held to blame. The feelings of those making up that seething, swaying, pushing, panicking, hysterical mass must not be dismissed too lightly. Although Laurel and Hardy had escaped unhurt, the event could not be treated as high prank. Even though the crowd's motives were for the pursuit of innocent curiosity, there was a definite risk of people being killed. Laurel himself was to state: *"Honestly, we escaped with our lives only by a miracle."*

Stan and Babe were the first to admit that accolades like this they could do without and, in the early hours of the morning, in a desperate attempt to obtain a bit of sanity from their fans, they sneaked over to the offices of the *Evening News* and had the following plea inserted in Saturday's paper:

> Many, many thanks for your very kind welcome. We appreciate your overwhelming reception, but we would like to remind you that we are here on a joy trip for the good of our health. To those who were injured at the station last night, we offer our sincere regrets, and we hope they are now none the worse for their experience. We never expected anything like Glasgow's welcome, and our visit here will be all the happier now, if we are allowed to go around just like a couple of rubber-necks [tourists] on vacation.

Babe looking frustrated as Stan uses one-finger to type the appeal going in the *Glasgow Evening News*.

After a limited amount of sleep the Boys managed to make it for breakfast, where they were joined by A.B. King J.P. (booker for the Scala Cinema), accompanied by 'Projector' (the nom-de-plume of the cinema columnist for the *Evening News*). A large crowd had gathered outside the hotel hoping to catch a glimpse of the two comedians; but, as Hardy had left for Western Gailes Golf Course and Laurel had gone straight back to bed, they were left disappointed. Later Stan entertained an old friend, William Walker of Tollcross, Glasgow, and together they talked of their school days in the Glasgow suburb of Rutherglen, and of the joint shows they had put on. Willy recollected that when Stan began to earn good money from films, he had written: "*Come out here. It's money for jam.*"

On his return to the hotel, Babe, who had won the grand sum of half-a-crown at his game of golf, found Stan answering fan mail. One letter was from a schoolboy requesting a signed photo, and had three-halfpence enclosed for return of post. The plea was cleverly tagged with words which would be a challenge to anyone's conscience: "*My Mum told me it's a waste of time writing, as you are sure to ignore my request.*" Little did his Mum know that Stan's devotion in such matters was unrivalled, and that during his show business years he was to write letters, and sign photographs, totalling in the thousands. Thus it was that this one request amongst many was fulfilled, and a signed photo, plus the original three-halfpence, was sent by return.

The presence of the Glasgow City Police Force for that afternoon's visit to the Scala Cinema could hardly have been described as "subtle." Determined to stop similar scenes to those witnessed at the Central Station, the police escort had swollen to fifty, backed up by six mounted policemen. The foot patrol was employed to link arms along the length of Sauchiehall Street, and to stop the crowd of over three thousand from breaking through.

The entrance was designated a no-go area by the ominous presence of two large police horses which, to further assert their authority, were actively prancing up and down on the spot. The stamping hooves must have conveyed the message to the crowd not to enter into the reception area, as nothing so much as a toe came near. Laurel and Hardy also benefitted from the presence of four of these magnificent creatures flanking their Daimler car when, on their arrival at 4pm, twenty or thirty of the more foolhardy members of the gathering slipped through the police cordon and rushed the car. Determined to stand no such nonsense, the police brusquely swept the offending people back into the ranks. Other members of the crowd were now left in no doubt as to the treatment they could expect if they tried a similar manoeuvre.

With only a brief wave, Stan and Ollie stepped from the car, and quickly disappeared inside. Conducting the welcoming ceremony in the foyer of the Scala might well have led to some outsiders forcing their way in, and others in the auditorium vacating their seats and coming to see what they were missing; and so the whole party — Stan, Babe, Myrtle, and their travelling companions — were escorted to the rooftop for a press-shoot. There, Mrs. Falconer and Myrtle were presented with bouquets by the cinema manager's daughters.

The *Glasgow Sunday Mail* further informed us of the gifts that Laurel and Hardy were given:

So many souvenirs have been collected by Laurel and Hardy during their few days in Glasgow, that they are compelled to buy four more steamer trunks. They were delighted when, at La Scala, they were presented with "Old Keg" and "White Hart" whisky bottles almost the size of themselves, by Mr. James McVey, who also made them other liquid gifts of more normal dimensions.

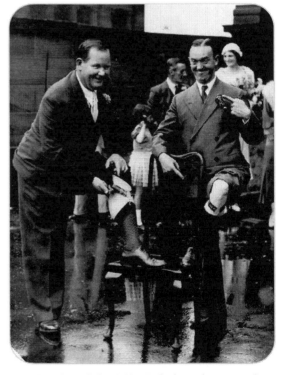

La Scala Directors are to be congratulated on the special effort they made during Laurel and Hardy's visit. The theatre has gained a tremendous amount of prestige through the directors' enterprise in bringing them to Glasgow.

Both Stan and Babe were whisky lovers — they would even go on to write a stage sketch about the effects of drinking it (*Birds of a Feather* – 1953) – so it must have been worth it to them to have travelled to its place of origin to sample it. The big downside is that, at the bottom of the label it reads: "Sole and Direct Importers: CALIFORNIA WINE & LIQUOR CORP." Had they known that, they could have saved themselves twelve thousand miles of travel in coming to pick up a bottle. As one famous Scotsman might well have said: "Dohhh!"

I hope, for Hardy's sake, that Laurel's bottle is a prop.

With all the formalities having been conducted on the rooftop, an attempt was then made to sneak the party through the auditorium, where the audience were being treated to a Laurel & Hardy film, and into the board room. The ploy failing, and the comedians being recognised, resulted in some comedy by-play: Ollie, of the screen character, berated Stan for allowing them to be spotted, and Stan duly responded by pretending to burst into tears. The tears soon became real though, when the film ended, and the comedy couple addressed the packed auditorium:

'We have never experienced a reception like this, and we are feeling ... ,' said Hardy. Stan interjected, 'Let me speak too,' he said. 'We want to thank you for this wonderful reception. I only wish my dad were here to see.'

Laurel then told the audience, in an emotionally choked voice, of the wonderful feelings he had on being back in Glasgow. He went on to relate his early experiences in entertainment in Glasgow, and his association with the Metropole Theatre. Choking on his sobs, he just managed to utter "*Thank You,*" before having to turn away. The audience, though, had noticed the tears, and there was an audible gulp in response. Rallying to his partner's aid, Hardy declared, "*I'll cheer him up,*" and the spell was broken by a fit of laughter from both sides. But then Laurel broke down again, when the vast audience, accompanied by the cinema organ, sang the traditional Scottish song, "*Will Ye No' Come Back Again.*" This is considered a huge compliment in Scotland and, when Stan eventually came off stage, it was quite a while before he recovered.

That evening, the Laurel and Hardy party went on a mystery tour with some of their friends. Although now free from official appearances, they had decided to stay over for one more day, so that Babe could play golf on the highest-rated of the Scottish courses – Gleneagles.

The following morning, determined to honour the revised saying: "When in Scotland, do as the Scots do," Hardy duly turned up bedecked from head-to-toe in tartan golf togs. To complement the attire, he was given a tartan umbrella by Alex King (*ibid.*). But this wasn't just any old brolly – the handle was an ancient war club, and the cover was Frazier tartan. Alex King (aka: A.B. King J.P.) was the current 'Head of the Frazier Clan,' and the umbrella, which was over seventy-years old, had belonged to his predecessor.

The gift was well received as, after Babe had tempted fate by saying: "*It will probably never be opened as it seldom rains in California,*" the heavens divided, and the brolly was in use throughout the game.

Hardy was offered another gift, while still at Gleneagles, when a local golf-club-maker, George Nicholl, offered to make him a personalised set of clubs from his company's Wizard range, with Babe's features embossed on each one. These would be sent on to him, later on in the tour.

Stan, meanwhile, was still at the hotel chatting to James Reed, whom he had first got to know back in 1912, when they did some shows on the Continent, in 'The 8 Komiks' (Comiques). Stan was also one of 'The 4 Bartos' in the same show. The markings on this advert were done by him.

Jimmy Reed was currently the manager of the Scala Cinema, where the Boys had done a walk-on the previous afternoon; but, because of all the brouhaha caused by the fans, they had been unable to spend time reminiscing. Here, at the reunion, Reed informed Stan that Ted Leo, also a former member of 'The Eight Comiques,' was now leader of the Savannah Orchestra — the resident band at the Palais-de Danse in Dennistoun, Glasgow.

[AJM: Ted and Stan *were* to meet up on this 1932 visit, but where or when is not recorded.]

Albert Pickard

Another reunion which took place on the roof of the Scala was between Stan and Albert Pickard, former manager of the Britannia Theatre. Upon meeting him Stan's eyes filled with tears, and he recounted to the press:

My dad didn't suspect I had a hankering after the stage. He allowed me to go on occasionally as a newsboy or other small character, at the Metropole, but I used to slip along to the Britannia when those try-out nights were on. Mr Pickard was the man who really gave me my chance on the stage, and I'll never forget him for it.

[AJM: Sorry to say, but my own research leads me to believe that the Talent Show was not held on the stage of the Britannia Theatre, at all. In the photo you can just see a building on the left, in the process of construction. When completed, around the turn of the century, it was accessible via a doorway off the staircase leading to the balcony of the theatre, and it was here that I believe the Talent Show took place. The Britannia had a full music-hall show running nightly, and so it is unlikely that, on a Friday night, those who had just put in a good week's work would suffer the efforts of a batch of awful amateur acts. Friday was also heavy drinking and zero tolerance night, when even professional acts weren't always well-received; so to put amateurs in front of them, would be like throwing the Christians to the lions. I surmise that the Talent Show was used to channel in the overflow of patrons when the theatre was full. That's my theory, and I'm stuck with it.

Another doubt I have is the oft-quoted date of June 1906 for Stan's appearance, as mid-summer 1907 fits his timeline much better.]

The Britannia Music Hall – housed on the first floor, in the Panopticon building (circa 1898). Lessee A. E. Pickard 1906-1920

Monday 1st August found Laurel and Hardy on Glasgow Central Station, awaiting the 10:05am train which would take them to Preston, on the first leg of their journey to Blackpool. Concerning the crowds which were bound to be awaiting them, a tearful Laurel confessed, "*I'm scared to death.*" Hardy was less pessimistic and, smiling confidently, said: "*We've had plenty of practice with crowds here. We'll just have to wait and see.*" The scene that morning gave them no cause for concern. In contrast to Friday night's madness, the cold light of day revealed the crowds to be politely reserved and, as Stan and Babe walked across the platform, there were only polite comments such as, "*There's Laurel and Hardy.*"

In fact, the cause of most of the gathering wasn't Laurel and Hardy at all, but was the usual huge number of travellers prevalent on a Bank Holiday, plus the addition of a throng of train-spotters attracted by the *Royal Scot* on the opposite line. There were however some ardent fans around Laurel and Hardy's reserved compartment, for whom Stan and Babe spent fifteen minutes signing autographs. Happily, Stan had got his watch back, after a girl had found it on the platform on Friday night and handed it in to the police.

As soon as the guard's whistle blew, there was a rush of people to the comedians' open window to say farewells. With a station policeman running alongside the train to stop any further contact, one young wag shouted: "*Hey, Mr Laurel, where's your buzzing tooth?*" (A reference to a line in the recently released Laurel & Hardy film *Pardon Us*.) "*I guess I had that taken out long ago,*" was the last thing anyone heard as the train pulled away.

Again Laurel and Hardy's fate was about to be placed in the lap of the gods, and soon they would find themselves once more in the lions' den.

o-o-0-o-o

CHAPTER 5

LANCASHIRE HOTCHPOTCH

Monday – 1ˢᵗ August 1932

From Glasgow, Stan and Babe had to change trains at Preston. Upon their arrival at 2:20pm they were greeted by officials of the Blackpool Tower Company, and a Mr. Hutchinson (*ibid.*). Stan's father and Dr. & Mrs. Falconer were also noted to be back with the touring party.

The two comedians told the pressmen they were having a great time, but hadn't seen much. Laurel was recorded as wearing: "A pepper and salt suit, and a light cap," while Hardy was dressed in "a brown suit and cap." This 'lost' newspaper photo gives us some idea of the scene.

Laurel and Hardy, the film comedians, being welcomed at Preston Station this afternoon by Mr. C. N. Wilkinson, the Liverpool representative of the Metro-Goldwyn-Mayer Co.   Photo: "The Lancashire Daily Post,"

Miss Nora Barrie, daughter of a Preston cinema-manager, then presented the Boys with a huge cheese. This was an in-joke, taken from the 1930 film *The Rogue Song*, in which Stan swallows a fly when taking a bite of cheese, thus emitting a buzzing sound every time he opens his mouth.

To avoid stepping into the crushing jaws of a giant crowd at Blackpool North Station, it had been decided to drive the remaining sixteen miles. So, looking nervy as a crowd began to gather, Stan made for the car, and soon the motorcade of four limousines set off for Blackpool, via Lytham St. Annes.

En route, they pulled over to savour a slice of the peaceful-ness of the Fylde countryside and, unhampered by any crowd, posed on this five-barred gate, under Hardy's tartan umbrella. It was as well they did, for it would turn out to be the only peaceful moment they were to have whilst in Blackpool.

After passing virtually unnoticed along the South Promenade, the car then hit trouble: for the crowds awaiting its passengers extended from Central Beach right up to, and past, the North Pier.

The Metropole is the huge building to the right, with a car park running around the left-hand side. This whole area would have been packed with expectant fans.

TALBOT SQUARE, CENOTAPH, AND HOTEL METROPOLE, BLACKPOOL 18

So many onlookers were gathered at the front of the Metropole Hotel that the manager requested police reinforcements. Some of these mounted the car running-boards but, even so, the drivers could not get into the hotel car park, so drove past and dropped off their charges at a side entrance – leading into the Metropole Suite and Ballroom. However, Laurel and Hardy weren't completely in the clear as, once inside, they were mobbed by hotel guests from the Regency Lounge. They managed to escape via the lift and went straight to their rooms, after which it was made clear to all guests that the two celebrities were to be allowed to rest.

The fans outside though had other ideas and, making their presence known, forced Stan and Babe into showing themselves on the front balcony, overlooking the car park and promenade. The huge cheers which followed attracted the attention of those on the nearby beach, who also got a wave when the two Hollywood comedians showed themselves on a side balcony (pictured). "See you tonight," Hardy informed the crowd. Stan nodded in agreement, and the two returned inside for a belated sleep. Police remained on guard around the hotel, to ensure their peace wasn't broken further.

Metropole Hotel – overlooking the beach

Of their thoughts on Blackpool, Hardy later informed an *Evening Gazette* reporter:

> This is my first visit to England, and believe me, I've had such a wonderful reception, I wouldn't mind living here always.

"Amazing," said Stan.

"I had no idea Blackpool was such a wonderful place," said Hardy.

Stan added:

> I have never been to Blackpool before, though I have always wanted to. We came here on vacation, but it's turned out to be the hardest work we've ever had in our lives. We've been in such a rush that we have not been able to call on all many of the friends we came especially to see. But we don't mind that. We are so overwhelmed by our reception that we'd do anything to show our gratitude to film-goers over here.

Hardy added:

> We never expected all this enthusiasm. It's a thousand per cent more than we ever dreamed of.

In a rare interview, Myrtle Hardy said of her partner:

> My husband is just a big, shy boy. He would like to spend his holiday taking quiet rides into the country. I am afraid we shall all get back home again needing another holiday to get over the effects of this one. But we won't get it. They start work again the minute they get back.

Laurel, feeling he had in some way cheated the fans by not allowing them personal contact, explained to a *Lancashire Daily Post* reporter:

> We appreciate the honour of their welcome, but we simply could not face it. In Glasgow, it was terrible. We were mobbed by thousands of people, and honestly, we only escaped with our lives by a miracle. We could not face any more. When we saw the crowd this afternoon, it made us nervous.

Little did Laurel know that the size of the crowds that evening was to increase many-fold, and considerably more subterfuge would be called for to gain the two celebrities safe passage.

First port of call was the Winter Gardens complex. From the Metropole this would normally be only a two-minute car ride; but between the point of departure and the point of arrival were an estimated ten thousand people – all determined to see their heroes. The crowds were so dense that the journey lasted twenty minutes, and the resultant traffic chaos throughout Blackpool took some thirty minutes to clear.

After fighting their way inside the Winter Gardens, the two comedians were able to sit down to a belated dinner, laid on for them by Ald. Tom Bickerstaffe JP (chairman of the Tower and Winter Gardens' board) in the mediaeval-style Baronial Hall. The meal was preceded by the Mayor – Councillor L. Newsome JP – welcoming the Hollywood stars to Blackpool; and ended with Tom Bickerstaffe proposing the loyal toast.

With the private dinner over, it was time for the VIP guests to go and meet the fans awaiting them in the adjacent Empress Ballroom. If the numbers in the street had seemed unbelievable, the scene in the ballroom was staggering. Here, nine thousand people had crammed into what was supposedly a three-thousand-capacity room. Laurel and Hardy walked on stage to a deafening roar and, awaiting a lull, Hardy asked, "*Can you hear me?*" to which nine thousand voices bellowed out a deafening "*Yes!*" Stan, who appeared fit to burst into tears, teased "*I can't hear you.*" The crowd bellowed again, at which the comedy couple went into a knockabout routine.

THE TOWER AND WINTER GARDENS COMPANIES

WELCOME

LAUREL

AND

HARDY

TO-DAY

FOR

BLACKPOOL'S BANK HOLIDAY

See Them To-Night

AT THE

Tower and Winter Gardens

WHERE THEY WILL DEFINITELY APPEAR IN PERSON

Here, the Empress Ballroom is well-under its capacity of 3,000. So imagine, if you will, 9,000 people in there.

Having appeased the crowd, the Boys went backstage and were led out of the Winter Gardens complex through a back exit.

[AJM: They may have been taken out through a tunnel which led from under the Tower Circus to the Palace Building on the seafront. The Alhambra Theatre was on the site before the Palace, and the tunnel was built specifically so that acts performing in both the Tower Building and the Alhambra Theatre on the same evening, could get to and from each venue with the minimum of hindrance. However, it did cater for the dual purpose of famous acts wanting to get out of either building, without having to run the gauntlet of their fans waiting outside.]

Over at the Palace building, on the seafront, the combined audiences in the Palace Variety Theatre and the adjacent Picture Palace totalled three thousand.

Those in the cinema side were having a foretaste of what was to come, with the showing of the Laurel & Hardy film *Helpmates*. Again, the reception when the Boys walked on stage was tumultuous.

Blackpool Tower Ballroom

Having satisfied both houses with the same formula of interchange, the duo popped next door (maybe back through the tunnel) into the world-famous Tower Ballroom, to repeat the performance for the six thousand fans awaiting them there.

By staying on to shake hands and sign autographs afterwards, Laurel and Hardy thought the crowds outside would have dissolved; but once again the tenacity of the people in just wanting to cast their eyes on the two of them had been grossly misjudged, for the route back to the hotel was filled with almost as many people as when they had first ventured out. It was gone midnight before the crowd finally relinquished their hold, and the two battle-weary stars were able to get back to their hotel rooms.

To appreciate what is going on here, you really need to step back, and take in the reality of seeing Laurel and Hardy 'live' on stage. Blackpool has always attracted the cream of British show business — actors, singers, comedians, recording stars, speciality acts and, of course, in later years, the biggest British TV stars,

But this was something far above that. Firstly, Laurel and Hardy weren't an act who spent three seasons of the year touring all the clubs and theatres around Britain, and then spending the summer season at a holiday resort. They were HOLLYWOOD STARS. The audiences had spent the last five years crying with laughter at the Laurel & Hardy screen characters, in over sixty of their films. Never in a million years did they expect to ever see those two characters in real life, for films aren't real life — they are a whole different, fantasy world, and that fantasy doesn't extend into the real world. And yet, that is exactly what was happening here.

Imagine if you will, that you were in the Blackpool Palace Cinema in 1932, watching a Laurel & Hardy film and then, as it ended and the lights went up, the two men behind those characters walked out on stage. What a mixed feeling of incredulity, disbelief, euphoria, and amazement the audience must have felt. The presence of most big stars will promote similar feelings, but add in that people were being brought up on film after film starring these two characters, and that here they were, over five thousand miles from their place of origin, waving and speaking to the audience members. What an incredible and emotional event that must have been, for all who were privileged to be there.

[American stars such as Marlene Dietrich, Bob Hope, Judy Garland, Frankie Laine, Nat King Cole, and Frank Sinatra *did* visit Blackpool, but L&H were the fore-runners – by years, and by status.]

Here in 1932, having been seen by just about everybody in Blackpool, but having savoured none of the sea-side atmosphere, Laurel took a very chancy gamble and, around 1:30am, slipped out past the police escort, accompanied only by the MGM rep' John Hutchison. Stan must have felt he had been transported to the moon, for the seafront was almost deserted, and he was able to walk the full length of the promenade to the Pleasure Beach, and back again, without once being challenged. With two sticks of Blackpool rock to show for his adventure, and without being ungrateful for the earlier welcome, the Lancashire lad was to regard this as the highlight of his Blackpool stay.

[AJM: Just why a stall-holder was selling toffee rock at that time of morning, I can't explain; unless eating rock was the equivalent of today's late-night drinkers needing to gorge themselves on burgers or kebabs].

Tuesday – 2nd August 1932

Blackpool North Station

The Tuesday morning departure time had been kept secret but, even so, thousands of people were awaiting Stan and Ollie as they emerged from the hotel and scrambled into their car. With fans climbing onto the running boards, and autograph books being thrust through the windows, the car made slow progress out of the forecourt through the narrow gap made by the police. The fans waving and cheering at the departing car thought it was going to go along the seafront and on to Preston, but it made a diversionary turn and headed for the North Station, where it dropped off its famous fares. Here, with only minutes to go before the train arrived, a sizeable crowd had no time to gather, but this did not stop those who were already on the platform from burying the Boys under a deluge of autograph and hand-shaking requests.

Viewing his right hand, still sore from the hand-shaking the day before, Stan remarked to a *Daily Post* reporter:

If this goes on much longer I shall have to use my left hand. I must have shaken hands 10,000 times since I arrived in England, and my partner has an even greater record. But Blackpool has been wonderful. The crowds were twice as big as those at Glasgow, but they gave us a chance to breathe.

Now we are looking forward to going back to work, for a rest. Honestly, we came here for a holiday, but up to now we have not been able to pay a single visit to our friends.

Hardy added:

Before leaving America, I had never even heard of Blackpool, but after seeing it, I am surprised that more isn't done to make it known to the Americans.

The last word on the Blackpool visit must, however, go to the writer of this article in the *Blackpool Gazette* which, place name apart, serves as a fitting epilogue to the whole British tour.

At Blackpool we get many notable visitors, and if this week more people have been interested in the two film comedians, Laurel & Hardy, than in the eminent divine, the Archbishop of York, it is merely a reflection of the times. If the leading statesmen of the world, headed by President Hoover and Mr. Ramsay McDonald, had walked in procession through Blackpool they would not have excited more interest than these two comedians. Intellectuals may come and go almost unnoticed. Laurel & Hardy are mobbed with friendliness and cheers where'er they show their familiar faces.

Can you wonder that in these hard and serious times we welcome people who make us laugh? Laurel & Hardy's humour is broad, but it is clean. Therefore, they are public benefactors, and this is why Blackpool's visitors this week cheered them with a heartiness which surprised these two modest and simple fellows. Yes, quite simple and modest fellows who, if they were not victims of a whirlwind publicity campaign organised by the film company which employs them, would be contentedly touring the British countryside, unnoticed.

Laurel & Hardy clown with zest for the money it brings. They are under no delusions as to their importance in the world, or to what awaits them. They know that their day as film favourites is a short one [AJM: Slight misjudgement, there!]. So they are frankly opportunists, glad to take the public's smiles and dollars, and ready for the next phase when it comes – supersession by new idols bringing new ideas.

If only the visit had been a few days earlier, or a few days later, the Boys would have been able to savour more of the solitude they so desired for, by an extreme case of bad luck on their behalf, they had arrived in Blackpool on its busiest Bank Holiday to date.

350,000 BESIDE THE SEASIDE

Amazing Rush by Road and Rail

SUNSHINE REVELS

Blackpool has to-day smashed all known records
"Biggest ever" say the railway and transport experts.
350,000 visitors
116 special trains
3,000 motor coaches and buses
20 trains arrived before 7 am.

Whatever followed could only be an anti-climax.

On the journey to Manchester, Stan and Babe received no peace whatsoever. Every time the train stopped at a station, there was a mad scramble of autograph hunters pawing at their window. One elderly gentleman deserves a mention for his enterprise in obtaining the individual autographs of both Stan Laurel *and* Oliver Hardy. He procured Laurel's signature at Blackpool's North Station, but was unable to get Hardy's. Undaunted, he boarded the train and awaited the next stop, at Preston. Here, he jumped from his third-class carriage, and ran the length of the train to Hardy's first-class compartment. His efforts were blocked by a horde of people who had been waiting on the platform with a similar aim. Realising the train would be pulling out before his turn came, he sprinted back to his carriage. At Chorley, and then Bolton, he repeated this procedure, only to be stymied at each attempt. Finally his tenacity paid off at Salford, and he departed, happily clutching his hard-earned reward.

These scenes were only a minor inconvenience compared with the terrible sense of foreboding that Stan and Babe had for yet another "close encounter of the herd kind" – at Manchester. Their fears weren't totally unfounded but, because most people had returned to work that day, only around four hundred were at Victoria Station to greet them.

WHERE'S OLLIE?

Although this crowd was much smaller than the ones in Blackpool, 400 people can still cause one heck of a scrum.

Normally, to find Stan and Ollie you need to look for a ring of policemen, and they ought to be in the middle. But even the police-ring has been broken apart, and Ollie is nowhere to be seen.

Hardy, stepping out from the shelter of the station, gained a laugh from the crowd when he opened his famed tartan umbrella and remarked to Stan: "*They say it rains in this locality, Stanley,*" and glanced heaven-ward as if expecting an instant response.

After the customary mobbing, cheering, and autograph signing, albeit on a much smaller scale, the party was driven away to the Midland Hotel, in the city centre.

A small press reception had been set up, at which the duo were anxious to impress that they were "dead tired." Stan reiterated the remark that they had come to see England but, so far, had managed to see only: "*people, hotels, more people, theatres, and yet more people.*" He demonstrated by opening one of his travelling

Left is Frank Lisbon, who Stan had worked with in the Fred Karno sketch *Skating* (1910) and had taught the cast how to roller skate.

trunks that, even when they left England, he would still have to spend many an hour in dealing with the demands of their English admirers, for he had amassed hundreds of fan letters.

> 'There are thousands more in London,' he added, 'plus the ones I've already sent on to Hollywood. I should hate to disappoint anybody if we did not answer those letters. The writers would think we were high hat, and that's not so. All these letters will be answered, but goodness knows when. I shall take them all back to Hollywood and answer them as best I can.'

James Blakeley (left) – proprietor of cinemas (Northern Exhibitors); and his son, John E. Blakeley – film producer.

Thankfully, not all fans made demands on the Boys' good nature. Some derived pleasure from giving. One such man was James Blakeley, a local film producer, who presented the comedy duo with a two-hundred-foot clip from *Hats Off*, a Laurel & Hardy film which had been shown in England some five years ago. How sadly ironic that *Hats Off* and *The Rogue Song* (the film which prompted the presentation at Preston) are the only two of the one-hundred-plus Laurel & Hardy films, of which there are no known prints.

At the start of the press meeting in the Midland Hotel, Hardy had retired to a corner, away from the line of questioning. When approached he would murmur only that he was tired and hungry and, after a while, succumbed to his hunger pangs and drifted off in search of food. Stan was in total sympathy with Babe's condition, and felt genuine guilt that he had brought him to England with the promise of sightseeing and playing golf. He explained to an *Evening News* reporter:

> 'Poor old Hardy, he's even more tired than I am. Everybody recognises him – he just can't escape.' He continued, "There's Hardy", they all shout, and make a dash for him. But me – well I'm not so conspicuous. I just look an ordinary sort of fellow. Poor Hardy's big and bulky and you can't miss him. When we're together there's no escaping the crowd. England is a wonderful place and the crowds are marvellous but they won't give us a rest. We have wandered through London, Newcastle, Glasgow, and Blackpool, and now we are in Manchester and feel numb.'

> He added, 'I want this afternoon to myself to gather my thoughts. When working for films, we keep regular hours – going to bed at 9-30 p.m. and getting up at 6-30 a.m. – but the crowds here won't let us rest.'

With that, everyone got the message and left. At 6:30pm the two comedians made their scheduled arrival at the New Oxford Picture Theatre, where the police were having difficulty in restraining a large crowd. The roadway was clear of cars as, even in those early days, parking was banned. It was decided to work this in their favour. Instead of riding in one of the limousines normally made available to them, the Boys took a taxi. As taxis picking up and dropping off fares is a common sight, Laurel and Hardy's was ignored, and the pair were able to sprint from the cab to the entrance before the crowd had time to act. They still had problems inside the theatre though, when many members of the capacity audience tried to waylay them.

Meanwhile, feeling cheated, the crowd outside hung on. An awaiting car signalled that Stan and Ollie were about to emerge and, as they did so, the two were precipitated into the grasping hands of what had now become a mob. Following a struggle lasting some minutes, the car pulled away and proceeded to Bert Tracey's home in Victoria Park. After the promised cup of tea with Tracey's mother (*ibid.*), the party left for the Manchester Opera House, where they were sneaked in and ensconced in a private box.

After catching only the last act of the production *The Night of the Garter*, the Boys were led backstage and introduced to Leslie Henson, the producer, at whose invite they were in attendance. For those experiencing *déjà vu*, Leslie Henson had proffered the same hospitality the previous Wednesday, on their visit to the Strand Theatre, in London.

The courtesy call having been honoured, Stan and Babe retired to the Midland Hotel to prepare for the following day's battle.

Leslie Henson

Having fought off the Lancastrians, they were now going to have to take on the Yorkists.

o-o-0-o-o

Chapter 6

THE TOUR LEEDS TO LONDON

Wednesday – 3rd August

The Leeds newspapers had been advertising Laurel and Hardy's visit for over a week, prompting two thousand people to turn up for their 1:07pm arrival at New Station. Stepping from the train, the celebrities were met by a wall of pressmen – sandwiched in between which were Stan's Uncle John, Aunty Nant, and their daughter Mary. Introducing the threesome, Stan said jokingly to a reporter: "They come from the Heavy Woollen District – Crackenedge" (a reference to the family's latest address in Crackenedge Lane, Dewsbury). Barriers kept the crowds away from the platform, so the Boys were able to walk freely to the station exit. Consequently, for the first time on the tour, it was the comedians themselves who made the headlines, and not the crowd. Standing in the back of an open-topped car, moving at a snail's pace, Stan and Ollie waved and bowed to the cheering masses on the extremely short journey to the adjacent Queens Hotel. Hardy later commented: "We've just got to smile – it's all so darned wonderful."

Queens Hotel – press conference

Safely inside the hotel, the comedy duo stuck to the formula which had served them best over the past few visits, namely — hold a press conference; shake hands with civic dignitaries; get rid of everyone except friends; have a chat; go and rest.

Upon retiring, the party stepped into the lift to go to their rooms, with Hardy last to enter. As the lift doors closed and the attendant pressed the button, the lift gave a resounding shudder and, at half its usual pace, struggled gainfully upwards. During the laboured ascent, Babe stood with that look of pained determination normally given by the "screen" Ollie when things just won't go right. Hardy wasn't at his lifetime heaviest, but eighteen-stone is still a lot for man or machine to contend with.

At 7:30pm Stan and Ollie were driven the few yards across the road from the Queens Hotel to the Majestic Cinema, where thousands awaited them, inside and out. Thanks to the efficiency of the police escort, they gained access to the cinema without too much of a struggle. Their appearance on stage was greeted with rapturous applause, and it took several attempts to break the laughing mood before they were able to get into their "serious" speech. Having thanked the people for the magnificent welcome, the pair closed with the sincere words: *"Thank you all, and God Bless you."*

Stepping outside onto the cinema's rooftop balcony, overlooking the City Square, the Boys found it "black" with people. Waving to the fans below, and then their party at a window in the Queen's Hotel, to their right, they ad-libbed some business wherein Laurel, in pretending to lose his balance and almost fall off the balcony, is rescued by Hardy. After the speech, which Hardy opened with: *"I would like to ask you all round for a cup of tea,"* the two returned inside.

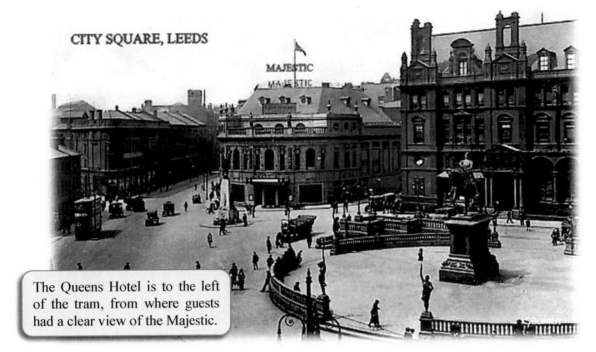

CITY SQUARE, LEEDS

The Queens Hotel is to the left of the tram, from where guests had a clear view of the Majestic.

The day after Laurel and Hardy's appearance, the *Leeds Mercury* printed an article which tried to analyse why some people gained so much joy from turning out to see the two film stars, and why others frowned on such behaviour. Those against questioned the mentality of people who had nothing better to do than, quote: "gape at a couple of clowns going from a train to their hotel." One critic declared it was "all vamped-up publicity," whilst another stated: "the papers ought to have more sense than to encourage a fuss like this." One veteran posed the question: "Don't you think this shows how neurotic people are becoming, getting into a fever over nothing?" Mentioning two former stars of the legitimate theatre, the veteran went on to say:

> When they appeared, people didn't crush each other's toes to get near them. They didn't have to be rescued by the police from their own admirers. There was more sense in those days. We were level headed then.

The article defended the fans by saying:

> Laurel & Hardy are two very likeable artistes, and it would be very surprising indeed if filmgoers did not want to see them in the flesh. For this sad old world always wants laughter. It wants it more than ever just now, and these two gentlemen cause more laughter than any other laughter-makers in the world. 'What are they really like?' is a natural question.

And went on:

> Chaplin is still the master genius of films, but already his early films seem historical, and whilst we wait for his infrequent pictures, Laurel & Hardy are making new friends every week. In Leeds there is probably not a day goes by without half a dozen cinemas showing their comedies.

> The star-building policy in the film world means that when a company gets hold of a really attractive player, his or her [or their] fame is magnified and megaphoned to the ends of the earth. The comedians are sure to come off best. Their mimicry speaks a language understood from Iceland to the Fiji Islands, and the reputations of Laurel & Hardy leap lightly across all frontiers.

The article finished:

> Indignant non-filmgoers may grumble at Leeds for giving such a princely reception to a couple of laughter-makers, but that is nothing to what we shall see in time. Whether we like it or not, we have got to get used to all this in our brave new world. For the first time in history, the clown will have an audience of millions, representing every race and language.

The protests did not noticeably put anyone off, for the following morning (Thursday 4th August) there was a large contingent of fans awaiting the two stars as they left the Queen's Hotel. The crowd were however very restrained, and their idols were able to walk across the station yard, located right behind the hotel, and mount the platform unchallenged. For this, the on-lookers were rewarded with the spectacle of the two comedians switching into their screen characters, and going through a whole string of familiar gestures – some of which were captured on cine-film by an enterprising amateur film-maker.

Boarding the 11am train, Laurel and Hardy disappeared into a carriage, only for their heads to reappear immediately through the open window. In so doing, the resulting pretend clash of heads gained further laughter from the gleeful on-lookers. Hardy then played his *piéce de résistance* and convulsed the crowd by producing his own cine-camera and putting the filmmaker through the same intrusion he had earlier been made to suffer. With that, the train pulled out and the view of one straw boater and one cap were the last signs that the bright presence of Stan Laurel and Oliver Hardy had withdrawn from the drab Leeds morning.

One hour later the intrepid travellers were thirty-three miles further south, in the Yorkshire city of Sheffield. Following a tumultuous welcome, they rested at the Grand Hotel. After lunch, both Stan and Babe slipped out to purchase some of Sheffield's famous silverware, then later in the afternoon entertained friends in the hotel lounge. There, Hardy was delighted to receive the personalised golf clubs which had been promised him by George Nichol when he had played at the Gleneagles Golf Course.

Pictured is the 2-iron, showing the cartoon image of Hardy, which had been stamped into every club. Babe is thought to have used these on occasion, but gave them away to friends in the early fifties, when his golfing days had ended. Recipient of the 5-iron was Bing Crosby, a club that was later rescued from the "Lost and Found" bin in a municipal golf course, for the price of one dollar.

In the evening the duo made appearances in front of the 6:30 and 9:00 houses at the Cinema House, Fargate, and entertained the audiences with their usual party pieces.

Friday 5th August. Around noon, ten thousand people were awaiting Laurel and Hardy's imminent arrival at Birmingham. However, the New Street Station premises were guarded by railway officials and police, and entry was permitted to bona-fide travellers only. At 1:26pm the train carrying the two stars duly delivered them at the platform, where they were met by the customary welcoming committee and a throng of pressmen. Accompanied by great rousing cheers as the awaiting fans outside the station caught sight of them, the party jumped into a taxi, and took off. Although their hotel, the Queen's, was very near, it was impossible to take a direct route as the mass of people extended along its length. The taxi therefore took the long way round and, as soon as it stopped at its destination, Stan and Babe dashed inside. The crowd was still outside baying for attention, so the two stars made an appearance from the safety of an upper floor balcony, before retiring inside to rest.

Their rest didn't last long, as the reception committee rounded them up and shepherded them over to the ambiguously named "Council House" – a civic centre of vast proportion. Inside, they were officially welcomed to Birmingham by the Mayor – Alderman W.W. Saunders, whilst, outside, three hundred fans cheered them on.

Their evening appearance was at the Gaumont Cinema, where the comedy duo performed their usual stage routine; after which they took refuge in the manager's office until the huge crowd outside had dispersed, before sneaking back to the hotel for a good night's rest. A second visit, to the West End Dance Hall, had been planned but it is thought this was cancelled.

BIRMINGHAM

LOST PHOTOS – from various Birmingham newspapers.

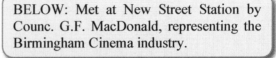

BELOW: Met at New Street Station by Counc. G.F. MacDonald, representing the Birmingham Cinema industry.

ABOVE: Fresh off the train, at Birmingham New Street Station.

BELOW: The crowd awaiting them at the Birmingham Council House.

BELOW: Received by Deputy Mayor – Alderman. W.W. Saunders – at the Council House.

Waving from the balcony of the Council House.

BELOW: With Gaumont Company officials, at the Gaumont Palace.

Saturday 6th August: The two travel-dizzy film stars boarded the 8:40am train to London where, upon arrival, they re-booked into the Savoy Hotel. Having now fulfilled all the enforced MGM press engagements, Laurel and Hardy were effectively able to disappear for a while from the eye of the national press, and it was then that Stan got to spend some quality time with his father:

Arthur Jefferson (aka: "A.J") was an extraordinary showman. His first job of note was as an actor, commencing in the eighteen eighties. He soon turned his hand to concurrently managing theatres – his first being in Ulverston, Lancashire. A long spell as actor and theatre manager in Bishop Auckland followed, and then came a move to North Shields, where Stan was finally able to live a family-life with his parents, older brother Gordon, and younger sister Olga Beatrice.

Between 1895 and 1905 Arthur Jefferson built himself a bit of a show business empire, with the lesseeship of the Borough of Tynemouth Hippodrome, and the Theatre Royals in Blyth, Wallsend, Hebburn, and North Shields. In 1901 he took on the Metropole Theatre, in Glasgow, but left it in the hands of an acting-manager, and continued to run his businesses from North Shields. Then, in 1905, the Jeffersons took up residency in Glasgow to manage the Metropole full-time, and it was the turn of the North East theatres to be handed over to acting-managers.

By 1910, A.J. had severed all ties with his North East theatres, and then, in 1912, left Glasgow and moved to London where he set himself up as a show business agent. It was also the year he got married to his second wife – Venetia. His first wife, Madge (Stan's mother) had passed away in 1908. In 1917 Arthur and Venetia moved into "Drayton House," 49 Colebrook Avenue, Drayton Green, Ealing, West London, from where he continued to run his Agency. It was to this address that son Stan came to visit him on or around 8th August.

A surprising story about Drayton House is that it gets a mention in the Laurel & Hardy film *Pack Up Your Troubles* – for which filming had been completed as recently as June. In the scene immediately after

49 Colebrook Avenue – 2012   49 Colebrook Avenue – 1932

their violent eviction from the wedding ceremony – where Ollie is trying to dowse the flames issuing from the seat of his trousers (after being shot with a 12-bore shotgun), Stan refers to the directory from which they have methodically been going through all the listings for "Smith," and then announces: *"The next address is 49, Colebrook Avenue. It's just around ..."* The film was only to be released in the States in September, and even later in Britain, so Jefferson Snr. would have to wait a little while longer before he could fully appreciate this personal in-joke.

Accompanying Stan on the visit to see his father were Babe and Myrtle, where their party enjoyed hospitality both inside the house, and in the garden. It was while they were all outside that some amateur footage was shot. There is a panning shot showing the façade of Drayton House, and the ladies in the garden, but then the main focus is on Stan standing with his father and step-mother Venetia in the doorway.

It would seem as though Arthur Jefferson was accustomed to the old style of having a photograph taken, wherein the subject has to stay stock-still for a few minutes, as Jefferson Jnr. has to point out that it is a movie-camera — meaning that one can MOVE. Laughing at his own naivety "A.J" unfreezes his face, and beings to play to the camera. [**FILM**]

"You can move, dad.
It's a movie-camera."

"Oh yeh! I'm so used to
keeping still for ten minutes."

[Frame stills from the 1932 footage shot at Colebrook Avenue]

Following an enjoyable afternoon, and then tea with the Jeffersons, the whole party left for an 8pm appearance at the Walpole Cinema, in Ealing. This was A.J's "local" where, the previous November, he had given himself the pleasure of mounting the stage, prior to a screening of *Jailbirds* (the English release of the Laurel & Hardy film *Pardon Us*) to inform the patrons that the thin one in the film was his son. To demonstrate the power this relationship afforded him he had added that, if ever Laurel and Hardy visited England, he would endeavour to make it possible for them to be received on this very stage. Nine months later the wish had become a reality. By request, there had been no publicity, but word-of-mouth had ensured a good turn-out.

LOST PHOTO – Taken outside the Walpole Cinema, with the manager Mr. H. Usher.

The atmosphere was very homely, and Laurel was touched by the sentimentality afforded him by the audience, and by his father.

Hardy, after expressing appreciation at being received like this, "*a stranger in a strange country*," was quoted by the *West Middlesex Gazette* as saying of his partner:

> I have never had a more marvellous friendship or feeling for anybody in my life. He has been a great pal. I had never met his father until I came over, but I knew I should meet just such a man, one of the finest men I have had the pleasure of meeting.

In his reply Stan said:

> You can never realise what a wonderful feeling it is to be received in the way in which we have been received all over the country. When we go back to America we will carry back memories which will live with us during the rest of our lives.

Hardy having left the stage, A.J stood alone with Stan and said:

> So alive to do honour where honour is due, the British public have lavished their kindness and their affection on my dear boy and his partner. Realise your own feelings under these circumstances and my own poorness of speech in trying adequately to thank you.

With that, a renewed burst of cheering broke out and the guests left to go next door to the Walpole Hall, and be entertained in private. The audience meanwhile were able to compare real-life with screen image, when the Laurel & Hardy film *Chickens Come Home* was shown.

Two days later (10 August) A.J., Venetia, and Stan's sister Olga waved the two comedians off at Victoria Station, on the first leg of their train journey to Paris. Hardy, assuring those present that he was going to rest when they left England, expounded: "*We shall stay in Paris for ten days, and hide from everyone.*" It was not to be.

Rare gag-shot of Laurel and Hardy and their entourage at Victoria Station, awaiting the arrival of the *Golden Arrow*, which would take the comedy couple on to Paris.

Far left is cigar-smoking Sam Eckman (*ibid*), and far right (half in shot) is Venetia.

After disembarking from the *Golden Arrow* at the Gare du Nord, Paris, the party was ushered into the Customs Office. This ought to have been a refuge from the assembled crowd, but led to the debacle of fans climbing over obstacles to get near to the two stars.

Upon exiting they were picked up by a car, which had been sent by no less a person than the President of France – Albert François Lebrun – and were chauffeur-driven through Paris like national heroes, waving to the crowds, and into the Champs Élysées. [**FILM**]

Wanting to gain some publicity, Claridges released the information that Laurel and Hardy were staying as their honoured guests, free of charge. But Stan and Babe had wanted to stay low-key while they were in Paris.

Now that everyone knew where to find

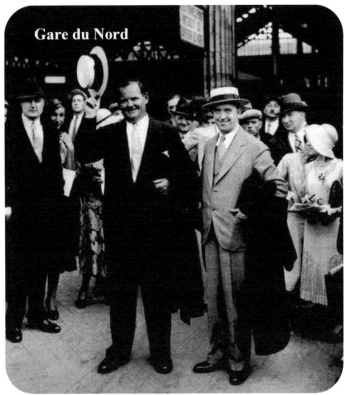

Gare du Nord

them, they could find no peace. Reluctantly, after only five days, they gave up, and – also cancelling their planned sightseeing tour of Deauville, Berlin, Antwerp, Brussels, and Madrid – returned to London (Monday 15th August).

Laurel pointing out who blabbed their location to the press.

At least they had learned where the Lido de Paris and the George V Hotel were, which would stand them in good stead in the later years.

o-o-0-o-o

Chapter 7

THE FAB TWO

Now free from pre-planned events on their itinerary, Stan and Babe were able to select which London attractions to attend – within reason, of course; as they were still able to magically conjure up a crowd in an instance.

One evening, the two of them put on their best bib-and-tucker to go and watch the musical *The Cat and the Fiddle*; at the Palace Theatre, Shaftesbury Avenue, after which they went backstage to pay their compliments to one of the stars of the show – French singer-actress Alice Delysia.

One addition to their work schedule they *would have*

Alice Delysia

welcomed was the premiere for their latest feature film. On the sea crossing from New York, Stan had written:

July 14th. '32

My Dear Friend Jimmy [Reed]:-
We have just finished another feature picture entitled:-
"PACK UP YOUR TROUBLES." I am looking forward to it doing
enormous business. it's a good picture Jimmy & everybody
that has seen it, thinks that it is the best thing that we
have made. We are expecting to have a trade showing of it
in LONDON, so you will probably get all the dope on it from
that source.

And a month later, Stan was still hoping the screening would happen:

Aug.14th. '32.

Dear Henry [Ginsberg]:-
Am anxiously hoping the Feature will get here before we
leave - know we can give it a great send off & do a lot of
good for all concerned.
Returning to London tomorrow to discuss Phonograph Record.

Well at least the latter did take place. The 18th of August was the hottest day in England for two years, but Stan and Babe took no advantage of this, and ended up in the Columbia Gramophone Recording Studios, in St. John's Wood, where they made a commercial disc-recording entitled, *Laurel & Hardy in London*. [see page 170]

Taken during the actual recording of *Laurel & Hardy in London*.

In October 1964, when sending a tape recording to a fan, Stan wrote:

```
The record you refer to on "Voice of the Stars" was made in
London by the Columbia Recording Co. & titled "Dance of the
Cuckoos". First side was expressing our thanks to the
British public for the kind & generous reception they had
accorded us during our short visit - the 2nd. side was a
Columbia Orchestra arrangement of our theme music. I
understand this was released under the Metro-Goldwyn-Mayer
label in 1932.
```

Listening to the recording, at the studios.

```
During World War 2nd. The
Columbia bldg. was Blitzed
& all the 'Master' record
prints were destroyed, I
assume ours was among them.
This recording was the only
one we ever made - I know
of no others - if any, I
imagine must be a copy of
"Dance of the Cuckoos".
```

[AJM: Laurel has got hold of some wrong information here. He must have read somewhere (post-WWII) that the Columbia Studios had been bombed, but I am thinking that these would have been the ones Columbia had in "Petty [Petite] France" – Westminster SW1, before moving to the new premises in St John's Wood, in 1931. The latter definitely didn't suffer any bomb damage, and has been in continual use since then. The actual name of these studios is "ABBEY ROAD" and, at the time Stan wrote the letter, four lads called "John, Paul, George, and Ringo" (aka: 'The Beatles') had been recording there for the last two years.]

Another barely-known visit Stan made, was to see top London comedian Max Miller. Author John M. East reveals this account Laurel gave him, in his biography of "The Cheeky Chappie."

> I saw Max Miller's act three times. The first time was in the early 1930s when I went back to 'Old Blighty' for a holiday. Just by chance I booked a seat at the Holborn Empire. Max was on the bill; I guess he'd just hit the big time.
>
> No doubt about it, he was a great comic. I'd never seen any artist involve the audience so much. They'd do anything he wanted them to do - like lambs to the slaughter.

Marta Eggerth

And on a daytime visit, Laurel paid a visit to Elstree Studios where, it is believed, he discussed the possibility of Laurel & Hardy films being made there. Currently all was fine at the Roach Studios, but the time wasn't too far away when Laurel would be looking for pastures new. While there, he mixed business with pleasure by flirting with German actress Marta Eggerth, on the set of *Happy Go Lucky* (Released as: *Where is the Lady*) and said "Hello" to Stanley Lupino – who was also making a film there (perhaps *Sleepless Nights*).

In a letter to a fan, Stan said of Lupino:

```
Stanley Lupino is the father of Ida
Lupino. He was a popular Stage Star,
but never saw him work. I knew several
of the Lupino family but never met Ida.
```

Over the next six days a few people managed to get their pictures in the paper, posing with Stan and/or Ollie, among whom was Scottish international footballer, Alec Jackson.

Alec Jackson, rated by many as the finest footballer of his era, deserves a book written about him in his own right – the story of a man who hit the highest peak, then retired from the game while still there. (Date and location not known.)

Somewhere on this tour Stan also bumped into Jack Buchanan, of whom he said: "*He was a charming personality and, of course, a great artiste in his particular line.*"

Come 24 August, and having enjoyed a few days free from unwanted attention, Laurel and Hardy bid their farewells to Stan's father, step-mother, and sister, Olga Beatrice, at Paddington Station, and travelled by train to Plymouth, to board the *SS Paris* and sail for New York. It was as close as they could make it to following in the wake of the Pilgrim Fathers.

A.J, Venetia, and Olga playing a last game of "rock, paper scissors" before the Boys set off for their return to California.

During the six-to-seven-day crossing, Stan and Babe had time to reflect on the staggering reception they had received in Britain, and in France. In a later letter Laurel wrote:

U.S.A. Oct 4th. 1932

Dear Mr. & Mrs. Wray

Pardon delay in answer to your Kind letter. Our mail was so large — Just couldn't handle it — sent it back here unopened — so have just read yours. Sorry I didn't have the opportunity of meeting you during my visit to Shields — especially you knowing the Family as well as you did — But am sure you realise how impossible it was — It was a grand home coming for me — I'll never forget it — Bless them all, it was so genuine — it hurt me — There was nothing I could say or do to show my sincere gratitude.

It was very sweet of you to mention re my little Brothers grave — I thought of it while I was there , but was unable to go where I wanted to go — even my Mothers grave in Glasgow — I didn't have a chance To visit. My whole time was taken up with Public — Press - & Photographers.

I went over for a rest — but came back a nervous wreck. However, If I died from it all — it would be a humble way of showing my appreciation. Again many thanks for your Kind   Thoughts.

        My Sincerest Good wishes always!

                Stan Laurel

Let us not forget that, before visiting Britain, Stan and Babe had made only two feature films, the latest of which, *Pack Up Your Troubles*, had not (as we already know) even been released there. Having been kept in the cocoon of Hollywood, the comedy couple had had no idea how widespread their previous films were being distributed, and how popular their short-films were with cinema audiences – both inside and outside America.

They had of course appeared before huge crowds in and around Hollywood, but those appearances had had the full Hollywood glitz and glamour behind them. The events had also been attended by a whole host of film stars; whereas, on this overseas tour, Laurel and Hardy were the sole attraction. No wonder they had been totally surprised and overwhelmed by it all.

And the journey wasn't over yet. First off, they had to face what New Yorkers had to throw at them when the *SS Paris* docked in New York Harbor on 30 August. Immediately, a flash-mob of pressmen swarmed board — for whom Stan and Babe gave some quick quotes, and put on a range of comic poses.

Too late for shuffleboard – they're about to shuffle off-board.
RIGHT: Observe that Stan is tearful, owing to Ollie standing on his hand.
(Makes a change from standing on his foot). In the background is Wall Street.

One journalist reported that:

Mr. Laurel said the tour was so strenuous that Hardy lost seventy pounds, while he gained twenty.

Methinks seventy pounds (five stone) is a gross over-estimate. Hardy's fighting weight in 1932 was around eighteen stone of muscle and athleticism. In later years he did shed that much weight, and more, but that was after hitting twenty-four stone, little of which was muscle.

And another report gave us:

The comedy pair brought back a script which they concocted in Paris, for their next two-reeler.

Hmm! interesting! I wonder which film script that could be. If we take it as being, literally, their next 2-reeler, then that would be *Their First Mistake*, after which came *Towed in a Hole*; but I am unable to say if either film was derived from the script written in Paris, or even if the script were ever made into a film.

SS PARIS

Life on board is serene until, that is, the press invade – then it's action stations.

Bottom right: It is believed that the dogs in this photo of the Boys at NY Harbor were added later, for a gag.

While in Paris, Stan had written ahead, to the Roach Studios manager, with an appeal for help with re-entry into the United States and other bureaucracy he and Babe were about to face.

Aug.14th.'32.

```
Dear Henry [Ginsberg]:-
Quimby cabled me re playing Capital on our way back - Just
had to turn it down - (dog tired). We are leaving for home
Aug. 24th from Plymouth instead of Havre (S.S. Paris)
arrive N.Y. Aug. 30th (Warwick Hotel.) Would greatly
appreciate it, if you could arrange to have some one from
the N.Y. office meet us & help us through the Customs, it
would save us a lot of time.
```

[AJM: Laurel is referring to the Capitol theatre (built in 1919), which since 1924 had become Loew's flagship movie palace for MGM Films. As such, it hosted world premieres of MGM films. The Capitol also staged shows, so one would surmise that Quimby wanted to book the Boys to make a stage appearance, between film screenings, as they had done at the Fox Cinema in San Francisco, in November 1929.]

[Back in January 1927 Fred Quimby had signed a personal contract to handle the distribution of the Hal Roach films through MGM, worldwide, for the next five years. As this had now expired, he had moved on to this involvement with the Capitol.]

[MGM New York offices – 31 August. Fred Quimby, at left, and former lyricist Felix F. Feist, were both working for Loews Incorporated, the parent company of Metro-Goldwyn-Mayer. They are almost certainly the ones who answered Laurel's appeal for someone from the New York office to help them through Customs.]

B.S. If the name Fred Quimby seems familiar to you, it is because you will have seen it on the credits of MGM cartoons – most notably 'Tom & Jerry'; plus those made by Tex Avery.]

After their overnight stay at the Warwick Hotel, things turned very dark for our transients — literally. New Yorkers were able to witness a near-total solar eclipse; with the maximum eclipse (when the moon is closest to the centre of the sun) occurring at 16:33.

While using the smoke-filtered viewer to protect his eyes from the eclipse, Laurel gets them damaged from an entirely different source.

The location is thought to be behind the MGM offices, where they met Quimby.

As Stan and Babe were to get back to Los Angeles on 5 September, and the journey took three days, then it would be fair to presume they stayed an extra night in New York. If that is the case, then it is here where I would tend to place the shooting of a little sketch they did on Broadway — one which is on extant film footage. Some place this footage as having been taken on Stan and Babe's visit to New York *before* sailing for England; but, when one factors in the mob scenes and hysteria which greeted them back then, one would have to seriously question if the crowds would have given them the time, and space, to film the said scene. There *is* a crowd present, but they are fairly subdued, and allow filming to proceed without invasion.

[**FILM**] This is how the footage runs:

Laurel and Hardy are seen being driven down New York Broadway in an open-top horse-drawn taxi carriage (known as a New York 'hack'). Rather than being a mute clip of them waving to the crowds, the film takes a surprising diversion from the usual news coverage: A New York cop stops the carriage, and we are treated to a full-blown comedy sketch, wherein the cop goes through the procedure of issuing the Boys with a ticket for going through a red light.

[AJM. If I have mis-dated this footage, then you ardent film buffs will just have to scream yourselves silly. My job is to record a day by day account of several years of touring, and not to give frame-by-frame descriptions of footage examined microscopically over decades.]

[B.S. It just struck me. Could this footage be the result of what was earlier described as: "The comedy pair brought back a script which they concocted in Paris, for their next two-reeler? Possible, don't you think?]

Lois had flown to New York to welcome Stan back, but the expected hugs and kisses never materialised. During the enforced absence, Stan had given cause for Lois to lose all feelings for him, and the three-day train journey back to Los Angeles was a far from happy reunion. Unlike with the eclipse, the darkness would remain.

o-o-0-o-o

Chapter 8

THE WORM TURNS

The arrangement for Laurel and Hardy to be absent from the Roach studios had been made in an agreement dated as late as 29 June 1932 — less than two weeks before leaving for England. The terms were that their current contracts be suspended for sixty days, and the time added on to the original termination date. Why Stan and Babe hadn't made the trip to England in April, when the Roach Studio was closed, remains an unanswered question – unless it was indeed to avoid the Olympic Games.

The sixty-day absence period, ran from 10 July to 12 September. Stan and Babe had arrived back in Los Angeles on the 5 September, but it was the fourth week in September before they were back in front of the cameras. Now fully rested they were able to get back to doing what they did best — making 2-reelers.

Having made three shorts by the end of the year, their next film was not only a feature, but also their first venture into the world of comic opera – *Fra Diavolo*. This necessitated dropping the now-familiar garb of the characters of Laurel & Hardy, and dressing in period costume. Later, both comedians looked back on *Fra Diavolo* as one of their favourite feature films, and dressed similarly for two others – *Bohemian Girl*, and *Babes in Toyland*.

Come the making of two more shorts in 1933, there was no doubt in anyone's mind that Laurel and Hardy were box-office stars in their own right, but it was their private lives which were grabbing the headlines. In May, Stan's wife Lois filed for divorce and, one month later, Babe filed for divorce from Myrtle. A few 2-reelers later, during which time both comedians were temporarily reconciled with their wives, they were taken out of their favourite medium and set to work on another full-length feature – *Sons of the Desert*. This was to prove one of their most popular and enduring films and, against their inner desire, ensured that more features would be forthcoming. By August 1935 they had made their last two-reeler.

Sons of the Desert had marked the end of Stan's marriage to Lois, and saw him accompanying a fresh partner, Virginia Ruth Rogers.

LOIS NEILSEN
Married 1926 – Divorced 1934

VIRGINIA RUTH ROGERS
Married 1935 – Divorced 37

Hardy's final split with Myrtle had come in May 1937. Next move in the marriage market was by Laurel when, on 1 January 1938, he took himself a new wife, Vera 'Illiana' Shuvalova, a Russian singer/dancer. He divorced her just seventeen months later.

| Stan marrying Illiana – second ceremony | Babe marries Lucille |
| 25 April 1938 | 7 March 1940 |

Moving rapidly ahead — next move in the marriage market came in March 1940, when Babe Hardy married script-girl Virginia Lucille Jones, some eight months after meeting her during the making of *The Flying Deuces.*

Also on the set of *The Flying Deuces*, the seed for a plan which was to germinate much later was planted. In his book *Laurel and Hardy – The Magic Behind the Movies*, Randy Skretvedt tells of Stan's admiration for the work of film cameraman Art Lloyd, and quotes Lloyd's wife Venice on an offer Stan made to Art:

> We were going to go to Europe for a three-year deal with Stan and Babe – they were going to make films at the Elstree studio in England; they were also going to make stage appearances there and in France.

This statement is pretty revelational as, up till that time, Laurel and Hardy had worked in the medium of live stage only that one week back in 1929 at the Fox Theatre, San Francisco. Plans for transferring their allegiances to Britain, though, had to be dramatically shelved when an event happened which was to have effects throughout the world – literally. On 3 September 1939, Britain and France declared war on Germany. Colossal as the repercussions of war were to be, however, it was a separate event, closer to home, which temporarily curtailed Laurel and Hardy's film career; for on 5 April 1940, when their contracts with Hal Roach expired, no attempt was made by either side to renew them. Roach wasn't prepared to continue with what he considered were excessive contractual demands by Laurel, whereas Laurel thought that by leaving Roach he could gain full artistic licence with another studio. Both producer and star were soon to find out to their cost that their hey-day was over.

Enjoying their newly-found freedom, the Boys accepted an invitation to attend a Red Cross benefit show at the *Golden Gate International Exposition*, on Treasure Island, in San Francisco Bay — 22 August 1940. Rather than just make a walk-on appearance, they performed a short sketch – *How to Get a Driver's License*, written by Stan – which enabled them to act in character. It is strongly believed this is the sketch which Stan had played on a short tour in January 1939. And when I say "short" – I mean "*short*." If I tell you that Stan's then wife Illiana was also in the show – singing Russian ballads – it should come as no surprise that the Laurels had a major-bust-up during these two-nights, which prompted Illiana to leave Stan and go into 'seclusion,' thus forcing cancellation of the few additional dates.

The two evenings the show with Illiana did go ahead, in Oakland, did however stand Stan in good stead, as he got to break-in *The Driver's License* sketch. His fellow stage actors were Eddie Borden and James C. Morton, both of whom had appeared in Laurel and Hardy films. One can be pretty confident that this is the sketch which Stan had in-hand ready to play live shows in England, as outlined on the set of *The Flying Deuces*. As for why Hardy wasn't on this stage 'tour,' one word was enough to keep him away — Illiana. He didn't even want to be in the same city as her, much less the same show.

Encouraged by a good response from the twenty-five-thousand-strong audience, here

With Gloria Dea, from the Aquacade show, at the *Golden Gate Exposition*.

at the *Golden Gate International Exposition*, the two comedians decided to sample the delights of more live shows. But, unable to make the trans-Atlantic crossing to England, owing to the wartime restrictions, they stayed in the USA, and played a thirteen-city tour in a variety-style show titled *The Laurel & Hardy Revue*. This began on 27 September 1940, in Omaha, Nebraska, and ended in mid-December, in Buffalo, New York.

[N.B. The noun is 'licence' – the verb is 'license.' In the US, the verb form is used for both.]

THE DRIVER'S LICENSE
With James C. Morton as 'the cop.'

Audiences were enthusiastic, and the Boys played to packed houses at every engagement. Their popularity was placed beyond doubt when, in mid-April 1941, they appeared to great acclaim at the 'Mexico City Motion Picture Industry Festival,' as guests of President Avila Camacho.

Stan and Babe probably believed that, whilst doing these shows, they were allowing time for more lucrative offers of work to pour in. But what they had failed to observe when jumping off the Roach train, was that theirs was the last wagon. All the other comedians from the same era had reached the end of the line before them. Consequently, when it came to hitching a ride with someone else, nobody was going their way. Chances of getting a lift were made even slimmer by Laurel wanting to dictate his terms to the driver, which wasn't feasible in the circumstance. Thus, when 20th Century Fox offered to take on Laurel and Hardy, it was either under their terms, or L&H would have to find another vehicle. [Thus ends this metaphor! RIP.]

The agreement, made April 1941, was to make one picture, with the option of a further nine over the next five years. The Boys would be free during this term to work for other film companies, and to make stage and radio appearances. The offer was too good to refuse, especially as both comedians had just been hit by further claims for alimony, and back-taxes. Stan had temporarily stopped one of his alimony claims when, on 11 January, he re-married Ruth; but before filming commenced he was a single man again.

GREATGUNS
Hats On

GREATGUNS
Hats Off

In character – Laurel does his trademark grin.

As himself – he shows off his new dentures.

During the making of the first film with Fox, Stan and Babe soon learned, to their extreme consternation, that they had no control whatsoever over the scripts, editing, lighting, make-up, or even the preservation of the Laurel & Hardy characters. Even worse, the production team were incapable of producing good comedy. This didn't seem to worry the studio heads, as Fox had five hundred theatres at which to show their films, regardless of the quality. Consequently the film, *Great Guns*, fired only blanks.

In November 1941, Stan and Ollie were able to get back into their stage characters, when they embarked on a tour of Caribbean army bases – again performing *The Driver's License*.

ST. CROIX

Over a period of two weeks they visited defence bases in Puerto Rico, St. Croix, Antigua, St. Lucia, Trinidad, and British Guiana – with a company calling itself *The Flying Showboat*. Other acts on the tour were Ray Bolger, John Garfield, Mitzi Mayfair, Jane Pickens, and Chico Marx.

The following month, December 1941, the Japanese bombed Pearl Harbor and provoked the Americans into joining the war. It was soon realised, however, that entertainment was still necessary to raise morale, enlighten the gloom of war, and ultimately to maintain the war effort. Thus, sport and entertainment were encouraged on a wide scale, both at home and abroad.

In January 1942, Laurel and Hardy went on a ten-city tour with another revue-style show, performing the now trusty *Driver's License* sketch – after which, they started work on their new "disaster movie" with Fox, *A-Haunting We Will Go*. Laurel firmly believed that *this time* things on set would be different – but it wasn't to be, and again they were forced to play uncharacteristic roles, and speak unfunny lines.

Post-war publicity proclaimed Laurel and Hardy to have been the first American artistes to tour Army Camps – clocking up an amazing fourteen thousand air-miles in doing so. Full story in:

LAUREL and HARDY – The U.S. Tours.

In order to forget the pain of "*Haunting*," the Boys joined the *Hollywood Victory Caravan* – the name given to a cluster of Hollywood stars, travelling by train from city-to city, and playing benefit shows in huge stadiums at each stopover, to raise money for the war effort. The debut show was in Washington DC; after which, the distinguished company set off on a tour of further cities in the East and mid-West. This took from 29 March to mid-May 1942, and ended in San Francisco.

The full complement of stars taking part was: Cary Grant, Charles Boyer, Desi Arnaz, Joan Blondell, Bob Hope, Jerry Colonna, Rise Stevens, Bing Crosby, James Cagney, Claudette Colbert, Eleanor Powell, Charlotte Greenwood, Frank McHugh, Olivia DeHavilland, Merle Oberon, Francis Gifford, Joan Bennett, Pat O'Brien, Bert Lahr and Groucho Marx (pictured) – plus eight glamorous starlets.

Groucho Marx was to relate of the tour:

I shared a dressing room with Laurel and Hardy. I've never drunk so much alcohol, but these two were pleasantly sloshed all the time I was with them. This, I thought, would be the leg-up I needed to outshine them. No way!

With the Roach Lot leased to the US Government, and having no urge to run back to 20th Century Fox, Messrs. Laurel and Hardy decided to see how green the grass was elsewhere, and signed to make two features with MGM. *Air Raid Wardens*, the first of these (shot in December 1942) also suffered from bad direction, scripting, and editing, and the suppression of the Laurel & Hardy characters. Continuing up to December 1944 Stan and Ollie made five more films, none of which came anywhere near to doing justice to their screen talents. With the MGM contract at an end, and realising that to negotiate any form of extension would be assigning themselves to further misery, Laurel and Hardy kissed a sour goodbye to the world of films.

Things were happier on the war front: 5 May 1945 witnessed the unconditional surrender of the Germans, and signalled the end of the war in Europe. The Japanese capitulated on 14 August after receiving the *very clear* and *very loud* messages which the Americans delivered to Hiroshima and Nagasaki.

With hostilities over, the Boys had nowhere to go. Filming was a closed door, and visiting Army bases was too uncomfortable, too exhausting, and not what one could term a "future." They had enjoyed their entry into stage work, but to do this on a permanent basis was not an easy prospect. By now, Vaudeville boasted only around a dozen theatres, so acts had to be prepared to work in night clubs, in cabaret, and in cinemas, to stay in full-time employment. The cinemas were enormous, seating between three and six thousand people, with the usual presentation being a forty-five-minute variety bill, sandwiched between two feature films. Somehow none of these options was the right medium for Laurel and Hardy's soft-approach humour.

With the Boys floundering, a life-line appeared from an unexpected source. Over in England a young entrepreneur, Bernard Delfont, was starting to make a name for himself, as a London-based Theatrical and Variety Agent. In just a few years Delfont had broken the monopoly of the major chain of theatrical agents, and become sole booker in seven venues. Taking advantage of the sailing de-restrictions across the Atlantic, he decided to emblazon his name on the map by placing it alongside that of "Laurel & Hardy." Delfont's first idea was to invite them over to play in pantomime; but, on being informed that they had a well-established stage act, changed his *modus operandi* and booked them on a provisional twelve-week engagement of British variety theatres, with an option for a further twelve weeks if the first term were successful.

Stan's new wife Ida – who I nicknamed "My Fur Lady," owing to her love of wearing furs.

For Stan Laurel it was the beginning of a whole new life. The war was over and, just one week after his divorce from Ruth had been finalised (30 April 1946), he had himself a new wife – Ida Kitaeva Raphael (his second *Russian* wife). Babe's wife, Lucille, was unable to join them, due to hospitalisation for a minor operation, but would be travelling across at a later date.

With the sailing of the *Queen Elizabeth* from New York, it is ironic to reflect that, thirty-five years after deserting the British stage to go and seek a new life in America, Stan Laurel was returning in the hope of mending the pieces of his broken fortunes. The worm had turned.

o-o-0-o-o

Chapter 9

SNOW JOKE!

In a sense, the war years preserved Laurel and Hardy. It was as if, in 1940's Britain, a pause button had been pressed on their careers. During the next five years the British had been too concerned about their battles with the Germans to worry about Laurel and Hardy's battles with Fox and MGM, and were unaware of the comedians' decline. Now in 1947, two years after the declaration of peace, the pause button had been released and, following all the recent devastation the British had suffered, this symbol of fun and laughter was now about to appear in their midst. To be reminded of those happy times was more excitement than the fans could contain. Thus, on 10 February 1947, as the *Queen Elizabeth* sailed into Southampton Docks, Laurel and Hardy looking down from one of the decks may well have been forgiven for saying, "Oh no! not again!" for the scene which greeted them was almost identical to the one in 1932. **[FILM]**

This French reporter greeting the Boys, with that well-known French welcome: "Be envy you!"

Because over in America their popularity had faded, the two ageing comedians were amazed at the love and loyalty which the people of England had retained for them. The press, too, never foresaw this *arrivada*, and few were on hand to record it. The biggest saviour was Pathé Newsreel, who filmed a short interview before the two Hollywood comedians disembarked. In it, Laurel and Hardy announce their intentions of making not only personal appearances, but also a film. When asked what the name of the picture is, Hardy has to ask Laurel to prompt him, at which Stan offers the name, "Robin Hood," but seemingly unsure, tags it with the line: "I think."

A US newspaper, from a week earlier, seemed to back up the claim:

> Stan Laurel and Oliver Hardy have announced that they have closed a deal with Alfred Shipman, British producer, to appear in an English musical film, "Robin Hood." Hardy will play Friar Tuck and Laurel, Little John.
>
> [AJM: 'Friar Hardy.' and 'Little John Laurel.']

But the film never grew beyond the acorn stage. You could say it was a case of: "You couldn't see the Hood for the trees."

Missing from the welcoming party at Southampton Docks were Stan's father and sister, who were both now living in Lincolnshire. Their village was snowed under, with no chance of anyone getting in or out, so Stan phoned and sent his regards.

The party then boarded the train to London where, at Waterloo Station, several thousand more fans welcomed them. The crush was so great that Laurel and Hardy were again split up. In 1932 Babe had found himself alone in a taxi. This time, desperately unnerved in the centre of the crush, he sought refuge on a bus. After showing extreme surprise as to his fare, the driver asked where Hardy wanted to go. "Anywhere, as long as it's away from here," Babe informed him, then added, "and on to the Savoy." However, his companions soon located him and, this time around, they all travelled to the hotel together, on the bus.

Hardy arriving at the bus like a little lost boy, which is soon laughed off when Stan and Ida finally find him.

The following morning Babe, Stan, and Ida went along to Caxton Hall, Westminster, to collect their ration cards, as many items were still rationed — some would remain so until the summer of 1954. Outside in the cold, the Hollywood party happily stood in line with the rest of the people in the queue. Inside, an enforced power-cut led to them registering by candlelight.

This was no isolated incident, for electricity cuts extended throughout Britain, and domestic switch-offs were twice-daily. As if post-war conditions and shortages weren't bad enough, the weather decided to add to the misery. In 1932 the Boys had arrived in July, during record-breaking temperatures. Now, here in February, the weather was particularly bad – and with the worst still to come.

At the cocktail party given that evening at the Savoy Hotel, Bernard Delfont had

CAXTON HALL

made sure to invite along the right people for, if the tour were to become successful, he would have either to persuade the management of each particular theatre to keep the show on for an extended run, or get other theatres to book it. Amongst those present were Lew Grade (Delfont's brother) from the Lew & Leslie Grade Agency; Harry Foster (Laurel and Hardy's British agent); and Val Parnell (managing director of the London Palladium); plus Hannen Swaffer and Patrick Campbell (journalists). Acting as hostess was Rosa Heppner, from the 'Association of London Theatre Press Representatives.'

"He's eating all the horse's doofers."

Within the next few days, Laurel and Hardy began rehearsals of *The Driver's Licence* sketch at one of Delfont's venues – the London Casino. Joining them was Australian comedy actor Harry Moreny, who was to play 'the cop.' Moreny had been spotted in the comedy revue show *High Time*, currently at the London Palladium, where he was playing in sketches with English comedy duo Jewel & Warriss, so his pedigree was assured.

Stan and Babe would have liked to have broken up their work schedule by going to see friends and places they had missed on their last visit, but were hampered by masses of snow from continuing cloud formations, and masses of people from continuing crowd formations — as this news snippet from 13 February will demonstrate:

Comedian Stan Laurel went out for a walk, despite the bitter weather. Within a few seconds he was protected from the wintry blasts by a milling crowd, asking for autographs.

But a couple of visits are known to have come off. One was to the Ministry of Food kitchens, in Portman Court, where the Boys were shown what a week's ration for one person looks like.

You can see Hardy thinking: "Rations for one week? That wouldn't last me one meal."

A second public appearance was a walk around Trafalgar Square, where they were again mobbed, but this time by pigeons. [How those pigeons had survived being netted and then eaten remains one of Britain's biggest war-time mysteries.]

At least one pigeon went missing that day, and now, so has the evidence.

So, after twelve days of almost non-stop rehearsing, Sunday 23 February found them on their way to Newcastle, with Stan Laurel, in the words of Hannen Swaffer: " … scared to death about the act's English debut on Tyneside."

Laurel's nervous energy was totally wasted on the reviewer from the *Evening Chronicle* who submitted only the following observations:

> Those two droles [*sic*], Laurel & Hardy, ruling an empire as wide as films can travel, hold court amid the acclamation of thousands of their delighted subjects at the Newcastle Empire this week. Here they are in the flesh, looking just as they do on the screen, with the benefit of depth as well as width. Their act, a cameo of their characteristic screen life is one of an interesting variety programme.

Whether the reviewer had bothered to go to the show, along with the "thousands of their delighted subjects," is open to speculation. Considering that a press-party had been given, plus complimentary tickets to the show, the coverage is an insult. Bernard Delfont and Billy Marsh were, however, present on the opening night, and saw nothing to cause them concern. On the contrary, the reception the packed auditorium gave the two comedians far exceeded what they, and other concerned parties, had anticipated – and that includes Laurel and Hardy themselves.

The treacherous snow-laden route the tour members had taken to get into Newcastle was worsening by the day, and there were fears that, come the end of the week, they weren't going to be able to get out. The snows had blocked most major roads, and smaller roads were totally impassable. The London to North East Railway line was also completely blocked, but steam trains with snow ploughs bolted onto the front were being put into service to clear the tracks. Coal had become a very precious commodity, as colliery workers were unable to get to work and, during the night, temperatures of −13°C were recorded.

In these arctic conditions Babe, Stan, and Ida had to while away the days in the "comfort" of the Royal Station Hotel. After their opening-night success, the Boys took Bernard Delfont and his partner Billy Marsh back there for a celebration. Babe phoned Lucille to give her the good news and, during the conversation, was informed that the temperature in California was 27°C. Going back to Stan and Ida's room, where he found the company huddled around a meagre fire, he relayed the Californian weather situation. With perfect timing, Stan picked up the last piece of coal, and throwing it on the fire declared: "Ah well, there'll always be an England." To which Hardy appended the immortal line: "Well, here's another nice mess you've gotten me into." With that, the five of them "broke up," the room shook with laughter, and the tears cascading down their cheeks warmed their faces. This was a case where the meaning of the phrase "bringing coals to Newcastle" was totally lost.

But they did manage to get out of the hotel. On Wednesday, Stan and Babe were guests of the Mayor of Tynemouth – Francis J. Mavin, who firstly had them chauffeured to Laurel's former home at 8 Dockwray Square, North Shields. At his last attempt, in 1932, Stan had been unable to enjoy the visit in solitude owing to the mass of fans but, this time, having the whole week in which to choose his moment, found the square relatively empty. Hardy was to say that Laurel was so excited as he neared his home, "He almost jumped out of the car." After a short look around, though, Stan confessed: "It's very distressing to see how the place has been knocked about during the war."

Dockwray Square as Laurel would have seen it, except that the first two houses were demolished post-war — so not by the Germans.

After also calling round to the sites of his father's former theatres, the Boro' (rebuilt in 1910) in Rudyerd Street, and the Royal, in Prudhoe Street, the party adjourned to a civic reception at the Grand Hotel, Tynemouth, followed by tea in the Mayor's parlour. As a return compliment the civic party were invited to Laurel and Hardy's show at the Newcastle Empire.

Then, on Friday, Stan and Babe were guests at a luncheon given by the Railway Electrical Engineers, at their hotel; after which they very thoughtfully made a personal house-call to local celebrity Marie Lamb to wish her a happy one-hundredth birthday. Having a telegram from the King is one honour – having Laurel and Hardy to tea is another.

Luncheon with the Railway Electrical Engineers, at the Grand Hotel, Tynemouth

Leaving the frostbitten city of Newcastle on Sunday, and travelling far inland to the city of Birmingham, might well have made the touring party think they were moving to a more temperate climate. The weathermen appeared to bear out this line of thought by forecasting a thaw within forty-eight hours; but the "thaw" turned into the heaviest snowfall of the winter, and was accompanied by gusts of wind up to forty miles per hour. Faster than man and machine were moving the snow, Mother Nature was putting it back. Olga Varona, one of the acts from the show, has vivid memories of the conditions:

> I will never forget that winter of '47 in Birmingham, with roads blocked and buses out of action all over the country. On arriving at the Birmingham Hippodrome, on the opening night, the queue of people standing in snow piled several feet high, proved how wonderful the British people were in their spirit and love of the theatre. I thought "Bless you all, you are the salt of the earth."

OLGA VARONA on vertical rope
Assisted by husband Archie Collins

Olga was an Australian gymnast, whose act consisted of aerial acrobatics on trapeze and on vertical rope, for which she was assisted by her husband, Archie Collins. Birmingham was to be her first engagement on the tour, and so having the unenviable task of closing the show added to her nervousness. On the first night, half-expecting to be playing to a rapidly emptying house, Olga got on with her act as best she knew. On finishing, she expected the polite applause of the few people who might have stayed on to watch. Imagine her amazement when she received rapturous applause from a full-house. Thoughts were now going through Olga's mind that Laurel and Hardy would not appreciate a support act receiving such acclamation. Some stars could not take this, and would have acts transferred to other shows. But, as Olga was to find out, Stan and Babe weren't like that. On future shows, when they had finished their act, they would cut short the applause, and invite the audience to save it for the next act. Then Hardy, in order to persuade the audience to stay on, would introduce Olga with the words: "she is a great artiste, and something special to watch." The subsequent months she toured with these two most unselfish of professionals turned out to be a big turnaround in Olga's career and, come November, led to her appearing on the *Royal Variety Show*. Not bad – for a complete unknown.

Of the opening night at Birmingham, the *Evening Despatch* had this to say:

> The appeal of Laurel & Hardy's act is its simplicity and good nature. Hardy bullies Laurel. Laurel takes it on the chin. And finally Laurel, having mopped up all the sympathy delivers the last blow and gets the last laugh. The triumph of the little chap – you can't beat it for a punch line.

> Thus with a little chat and a snatch of a song, is composed a charming and disarming act, worthily supported by a first-rate bill, in which chief honours go to Olga Varona for the grace and daring of her aerial acrobatics.

The *Birmingham Post* offered:

> In 1932 when Laurel & Hardy were in Birmingham last, we were trying to climb out of the depression. Today, things are not much different in point of mood. Now, as then, Laurel & Hardy make us forget that life is real and more than somewhat earnest. Their drollery, buffoonery and small-boy prankishness is achieved with consummate artistry.

The *Birmingham Mail* gave a more profound opinion:

> The great majority of their audience last night having fallen under the persistent influence of their pictorial personalities, were prepared at all costs, rapturously to acclaim, and heartily to laugh. But the few who came to scoff must have remained to laugh and even to praise. The act is perfectly rehearsed and perfectly timed. Their material is not brilliant or even outstandingly good of its kind. In script it would scarcely yield a smile, yet they cause it to become grotesquely funny, and their good natured stupidity shines through.

Basically, the last reviewer is saying that the script is very weak but, in the hands of these two masters of comedy, becomes naturally funny; and that anyone who thought Laurel and Hardy were riding on their reputations as screen comedians would, after seeing the act, have to acknowledge their tremendous stage presence.

The newspapers for the Birmingham week contained little or nothing else of the exploits of Laurel and Hardy; though, to be fair, perhaps there was nothing to tell. The *Evening Despatch* displayed a photograph of the two comedians having a cup of tea at the Midland Hotel, and managed to add a few points of interest on the structure of Laurel and Hardy's comedy, wherein Laurel declared:

> "Making comedies is the most serious business in the world." Oliver nodded in agreement and they both shook their heads rather sadly. Of their temporary lapse into music hall, Hardy said: "I love it. It's far more exciting than making films."

Laurel added:

> On the stage you get an immediate reaction and know whether the audience likes you or not. Anything we do in the comedy line has a definite reason – you can't go and fall over and make funny faces without a reason.

The *Birmingham News*, too, was affected by the inactivity of its subjects:

> What Laurel & Hardy think about Birmingham must remain a mystery, for they were too concerned with the weather to talk about impressions of anything – but the weather. Huddled over a tiny fire of cinders with two small sullen logs atop, they spoke as wistfully and with as wry a smile of sunny skies and the 28 degrees they left in Hollywood, as might any Englishman.

Having digested all this information, one can only presume that Laurel and Hardy spent the rest of the week drinking cups of tea in front of a meagre log fire. The important issue, though, is that they had had two weeks preparing their act away from the prying eyes of the London critics, and were now ready to rise up and take London by storm.

o-o-0-o-o

Chapter 10

DRIVING WITHOUT DUE CAR

The Driver's License sketch began life in 1939, without Hardy, when Stan Laurel embarked on a short stage tour of venues in America with his then wife – Illiana. With him, as fellow players in the sketch, went James C. Morton and Eddie Borden — two actors from the Roach studios.

Morton would have played 'the cop' in the sketch, a role he had had in some of the Laurel & Hardy shorts — most notably in *Tit For Tat*, and *Midnight Patrol*. Borden is noticeable in the part of the fop whom Stan and Ollie pickpocket in *Bohemian Girl*, but less noticeable in *A Chump at Oxford*, as his role required him to keep a white sheet over his head, to portray the ghost in the maze.

The Driver's License sketch was trialled again, at the 1940 San Francisco Exposition (*ibid*), which Laurel rewrote as a 2-hander — i.e. the lines the cop would normally say were spoken by Hardy.

21 Jan 1939

22 August 1940

When Laurel and Hardy took the sketch on tour, in a show with several other acts, James C. Morton was recalled to play the cop, and Hardy took over the role which Eddie Borden had deputised in.

The Laurel & Hardy Revue then ran from 27 September to 19 December 1940, and took in ten U.S. cities.

THE DRIVER'S LICENSE

DRIVER'S LICENSE 1940 — 2-hander

BABE: Oh, never mind the name. What's your address?

STAN: 254 S. uth Main Street.

BABE: 254 South Main St.......

STAN: That was before I moved.

BABE: What did you move for?

STAN: I beg your pardon?

BABE: I said - What did you move for?

STAN: Well, I couldn't get the landlord to raise the rent.

BABE: How, what on earth did you want the landlord to raise your rent for?

STAN: Well, I couldn't raise it.

BABE: Ohhhh.... Were you ever arrested for violating the traffic laws?

STAN: Once - for speeding/.

BABE: Speeding? How fast were you going?

STAN: Ten miles an hour,

BABE: Ten miles an hour? Why that's not speeding! You can go ten miles an hour anywhere.

STAN: Not on the sidewalk I couldn't.

DRIVER'S LICENCE 1947 — 3-hander

COP: What's your address?

BABE: We used to live at 254 South Main Street.

But that was before we moved.

COP: What did you move for?

BABE: Well, you see sir, we couldn't get the landlord to raise our rent.

COP: What on earth did you want the landlord to raise your rent for?

STAN: Well we couldn't raise it, could we Ollie?

COP: Listen to me very carefully. Have you ever been apprehended for contravening a traffic regulation?

BABE: I beg your pardon?

COP: Have you ever been arrested for breaking the traffic laws?

BABE: Oh yes sir, for speeding once.

COP: Speeding? How fast were you going?

BABE: Ten miles an hour.

COP: Ten miles an hour? That's not speeding, my dear boy. You can go ten miles an hour any place.

STAN: Not on the sidewalk, could you Ollie?

Hardy's original copy of the 2-hander version, plus a facsimile of the 3-hander:

After *The Laurel & Hardy Revue*, Stan and Babe reverted to the above 2-hander, when they embarked on visiting a number of Forces Bases, entertaining both Army and Air Force troops:

Entertaining soldiers at:
CAMP ROBERTS
[located on both sides of the
Salinas River in Monterey and
San Luis Obispo counties]
CALIFORNIA
8 June 1941

(3-hander)

Atkinson Field
BRITISH GUIANA
7 November 1941
with
The Flying Showboat Co.
playing troop bases in,
and around, the Caribbean.

(2-hander)

Next came the *Hollywood Victory Caravan*, a show with a host of other Hollywood stars, which played fourteen US cities during April and May 1942, raising money for the war effort by the sale of War Bonds.

So, in 1947, when Bernard Delfont asked the two screen legends to come over to England to appear in a pantomime, he was informed that they had a ready-made sketch they would prefer to perform — which is when the 3-hander version of *The Driver's Licence* was recovered from the script drawer, dusted off, and revised.

An early draft of *The Driver's Licence* is printed in its American format, in the book *The Comedy World of STAN LAUREL*, by John McCabe. In its British format it was presented in three parts – the twelve minute sketch being added to by a further eight minutes of business, front of tabs, split either side of the sketch. This is how it ran:

The Boys make their entrance to the accompaniment of *The Cuckoo Song*, then stand front of stage curtain at a microphone:

THE DRIVER'S LICENCE SKETCH

OLLIE: Good evening, ladies and gentleman ...

STAN: Can I say something?

OLLIE: (Glaring) Can't you see I'm speaking to the ladies and gentlemen? (To audience, smiling). As I was saying - good evening, ladies and gentlemen! It's a very real pleasure for Stan and me to be here with you tonight.

STAN: Say, can I say something?

OLLIE: Will you pardon me a moment, ladies and gentlemen? My friend, Mr. Laurel wishes to speak to me.

  What is it?

STAN: You're standing on my foot.

OLLIE: (Tie-twiddles to the audience.) I beg your pardon.

  And now, ladies and gentlemen, Stanley would like to say a few words to you.

STAN: What'll I say?

OLLIE: Just say, "hello everybody!" (Irritated.) But with your hat off!

STAN: Hello, everybody - but with your hat off!

OLLIE: Ooooooh!

STAN: What will I say?

OLLIE: Just make a nice, long speech.

STAN: But we haven't got time.

OLLIE: What d'ya mean, we haven't got time?

STAN: Well, we've got to get our new driver's licence. The old one perspires tomorrow.

OLLIE: You mean 'transpire.' But for once, ladies and gentlemen, Stan is right. We do have to get our new driver's licence. Come, Stanley.

  (They walk into the set in two).

  Stan and Ollie enter the police station with the "you after me" business, Ollie with a big flourish, rings the bell on the desk.)

  ENTER THE COP

Cop: Good morning, gentlemen. What can I do for you?

The cop hands Ollie an application form, and asks him to fill it in.

Ollie tells the cop that, owing to a slight accident, he can't write.

When the cop suggests that Ollie get his friend to fill it in for him, Ollie tells him that Stan can write but he can't read.

Alhambra, Brussels – December 1947

The cop then passes the application form to Stan, with the command to read it.

Stan studies the form, looks puzzled, and then reveals that he can't read that reading, because it's too close to the paper.

So the cop volunteers to fill in the form, with the words:

```
Cop:    As a rule I don't do this sort of thing, but under the
        circumstances, I'll break the rule.
```

Hearing the word 'rule,' Stan hands the cop the wooden ruler on his desk.

Ollie reacts angrily, and chastises Stan by telling him the cop didn't mean that kind of rule.

The cop next gives them a test, in the form of a hypothetical set of driving conditions.

During the cop's animated lecture, Stan delves into his lunch box. Firstly he takes out an apple which he gives to Ollie, and then a banana which he puts in his pocket.

Next he finds a cigar, which he is about to put in his mouth, when Ollie taps him on the shoulder. Stan says "Sorry," and hands the cigar to Ollie.

ABOVE: The 'Hat Swap' routine

Finally, the cop has had enough, and backs up his demand that they leave immediately by taking a gun from behind the desk. He then fires repeatedly as the Boys run out. A stage-hand immediately runs on, with the seat of his pants seemingly on fire.

Stan and Ollie re-emerge front of tabs. Hardy addresses the audience with the words: "We hoped you enjoyed our bit of nonsense," and then croons *Shine on Harvest Moon*, to which Laurel does a soft-shoe-shuffle [a routine taken from the Laurel & Hardy film *The Flying Deuces*]. Stan follows with the song *I'm a Lonely Petunia in an Onion Patch*, to which Hardy does an eccentric little dance.

The Boys close by wishing everyone 'God Bless,' and Hardy introduces the last act on the bill.

o-o-0-o-o

The above was taken at the Alhambra, Brussels, and shows the scenery on this Continental part of the tour. It appears to be the exact same backcloth they carried on their 1940 *Laurel & Hardy Revue* tour, in the US. The skyscrapers seen through the window are a bit of a giveaway.

And here is a shot from that 1940 US tour, from which one can clearly identify the same backcloth. The cop is Lew Parker, who took over the role when James C. Morton withdrew from the show, owing to illness. Having a jug of water poured down the front of his pants every night was blamed for his catching the flu.

o-o-0-o-o

Chapter 11

CAPITAL VENTURES

The London Palladium is now home to large-scale spectacular musicals but, in the thirties and forties, it played almost exclusively revue shows – with such stars as 'The Crazy Gang,' Tommy Trinder, and Jewel & Warriss. Then, when variety started to come to the fore, American acts – such as Chico Marx, Danny Kaye, Judy Garland, Jack Benny, Abbott & Costello, Bob Hope, and Bing Crosby – were invited over. Laurel and Hardy, though, were the first of the big American post-war stars to play the Palladium, and helped more than anyone to put it on the map as the must-play venue for American stars. It needed a large figurehead to do this, and none of the American imports came larger than Laurel and Hardy. So this is now the THIRD time they have led the way: firstly the 1932 British Tour, then the USO Caribbean Tour, and now this one.

Being two old screen comedians trying to establish themselves in Variety, though, may possibly have given them doubts as to whether they really had a place on this stage. Len Lowe, who was on the bill, well remembers Babe's show of nerves, and revealed:

> Hardy was in his stage costume and full make-up TWO HOURS before the start of the show. He spent the whole time pacing up and down backstage – sweating profusely.

Hardy need not have worried. *The Performer* said of their first show in front of a London audience:

> It is rarely that Variety top-liners get so uproarious a reception on their first appearance at any particular theatre as that accorded the film couple, Stan Laurel & Oliver Hardy at this house, and it was some time before the pair could even begin to get under way.

> The pair have material of no particular strength. Indeed, the script can have caused no wet towels and sleepless nights – but what they do have is the benefit of considerable film following, and in this they score heavily by exploiting to the full the various comedy mannerisms that have endeared them to so many. At the finale of this episode, the duo sang a little, Laurel danced a little, and both seemed not a little overwhelmed at the warmth of their reception.

The *Daily Express* reviewer saw the show in similar light:

> Laurel & Hardy, making their West End bow at the London Palladium last night, had the audience laughing before they appeared – as soon as the orchestra struck up their signature tune.

> They play a sketch about getting a driving licence, which ends surprisingly in a little song and dance. Their comedy is neat and amiable; all the old film tricks abound.

> The 'stage' Laurel & Hardy are somehow more like their film equivalent than one could imagine: Laurel in turns cretinous and crafty – Hardy beaming with rage, and as majestic and finicky as ever.

The *Weekly Sporting Review* revealed some hitherto unknown business which the Boys performed, in which they have a little dig at some of their Hollywood contemporaries:

Coming on to a tremendous ovation, those loveable screen comedians Stan Laurel and Oliver Hardy soon proved their worth as mirth-makers, in that they were as good and as funny as you expected them to be.

Dressed identically as you've seen them on the screen, looking and fooling about exactly as they've been doing for years in their popular pictures, Stan and "Ollie" first go through a kind of cross-talk routine, follow with a typical burlesque – "Applying for a Driving Licence," in which they are splendidly assisted by Harry Moreny – and wind up with a series of skits during which Laurel debunks Crosby and Sinatra, and Hardy does likewise to Astaire!

It's altogether a glorious chunk of tomfoolery and the comedians fully justify all the fuss made over them. If you're lucky enough to get into the Palladium, you'll love every moment Stan and "Ollie" are on the stage.

The business referred to above, wherein Messrs. Laurel & Hardy have a little dig at Messrs. Crosby, Sinatra, and Astaire, does not appear in any extant script. It must be the reviewer's description of the two songs and dances – as described in the previous chapter. The *Observer* gives mention of another bit business which does not appear in the script:

The comedians go into a trance. They play noughts-and-crosses on an invisible blackboard. Beside them a policeman glares; they consider him long enough to knock off his hat.

Many variety stars were in attendance on the first night. One man keener than most to see how well Laurel and Hardy went was comedian Tommy Trinder, as his show was to follow them in.

Outside the theatre the bad weather was still raging and, over the next few weeks, the populace were to suffer blizzards, more thaws, more floods, and a hurricane. During the height of the thaw, the Thames rose nine foot. Many homes were flooded, and the telephone lines were dead. The flooding wasn't just confined to London, but affected thirty counties in all, with roads impassable almost everywhere. The Palladium, however, stayed open and the crowds kept pouring in. As a result, Laurel and Hardy's run was extended from two weeks, to three.

On 9 March, the eve of their London debut, Stan and Babe had been guests of the 'Grand Order of Water Rats' at a 'Dinner and Cabaret Evening' at the Savoy Hotel. Part of the entertainment was an adaptation of the popular radio series *The Brains Trust*, with Tommy Trinder as question master, and Sid Field, Nat Mills, Billy Butlin, and Laurel and Hardy, as the "brains." As can be imagined, the item turned out to be a riot of laughs.

On Friday 14 March, the Laurels and Hardys visited the 'Daily Mail – Ideal Home Exhibition,' where they viewed a number of stands displaying products, new to the market. **[FILM]**

3 TONS of JOLLITY
At the 'Stack-a-Bye' stand, Hardy gives one of their steel chairs a thorough testing, with the added weight of musical entertainer Tessie O'Shea, and actress Vera Pearce. Some chair!

This delightful lady presents the two stars with a new electrical product - the 'Surran Bed-Warmer.'
[AJM: All we had to keep our feet warm, when we were kids, was a hot brick, wrapped in a rag.]

More images from the Ideal Home Exhibition

"Remember when I used to be dumb?"

The following day, Stan and Babe were out and about again; this time at the bespoke tailors 'Simpsons of Piccadilly,' where they went to cash in their clothes vouchers for new suits.

"Please sir! What can we have for these coupons?"

"How about a pair of braces each?"

Ollie not understanding the term: "Walk-in wardrobe."

And the poor manager at Simpson's had even more to contend with:

When the assistant fails to measure Ollie properly …

… Stan comes up with his own sure-fire method.

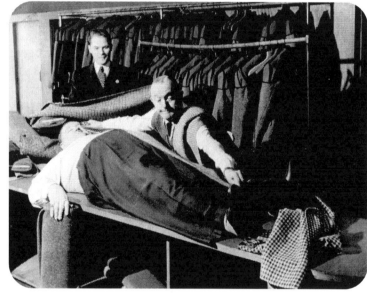

OLLIE: What do think of this one?

STAN: Fine! But isn't that the one you came in with?

In 1932, Stan's father was living in Ealing, West London; but, in 1940, fearing that a German bomb might finish him off, Arthur Jefferson had gone to live with his daughter Olga in the safety of the Lincolnshire countryside. Olga, along with her husband – William Henry Healey, ran a public house, the Plough Inn, in the small village of Barkston, near Grantham. Just after the First World War, Bill had been in the orchestra at the Theatre Royal, Grantham; and, after seeing Olga on stage, approached her at his Aunt's theatrical digs. Following a career in acting, which had started in 1912 when she was just eighteen, Olga retired from the stage, and the two had lived together a while, before marrying and taking over this tiny pub.

Back in February, when the Boys had first arrived in England, A.J and Olga had been unable to welcome Stan at Southampton Docks, as the large snowfalls had prevented them from leaving their village. So now, on 16 March 1947, with the snows cleared, and not having to move on to another venue (this being the Sunday between Stan and Babe's first and second week at the London Palladium), Laurel took the opportunity to go and visit them in Barkston. Remarkably, Oliver Hardy, who could have spent the whole day resting at the Savoy, chose to go with him. If anyone claims that these two didn't get on – they're nuts!

After disembarking at Grantham Station, the comedy duo joined the Healeys for lunch at the Red Lion Hotel, before retiring to the Plough Inn to meet up with Mr. Jefferson. A Grantham journalist was allowed access, of which he wrote in the *Grantham Journal* (21 March 1947):

> EIGHTY-SIX years-old Arthur Jefferson waited patiently at the Plough inn at Barkston on Sunday. He had put on his best blue suit, and was waiting to welcome his son – a worldwide screen personality – whom he had not seen in person for 13 years. It was a touching moment as the son, and his equally renowned and corpulent partner, walked in. Stan Laurel and Oliver Hardy had arrived!

Ida Laurel – Bill Healey – Olga Healey
Stan – Arthur Jefferson – Babe

In this country to entertain the British public, Mr. Jefferson's son, Stan Laurel, had travelled from London with his wife Ida, and his partner Oliver Hardy, and they were accompanied by Laurel's sister, Mrs. Beatrice Healey ['Olga' was her middle name], and Mr. Bill Healey, brother-in-law, landlord of the *Plough Inn*. Mr. Jefferson last saw his comedian son 13 years ago, when he spent a year with him in America.* He was overcome with joy at Sunday's reunion.

[AJM: * A.J's wife Venetia had accompanied him during their long stay in Los Angeles from August 1934 till around July 1935, but she had since died.]

"God bless you, Son" he said.

"I'll race you up the street for a pound," quipped Stan.

The article continued:

Oliver Hardy was by no means out of the picture. He enjoyed every minute of the celebration.

Earlier the screen comedians arrived quietly at the Red Lion hotel, Grantham for lunch. But several youngsters soon got to hear of their presence and came autograph-hunting. They all got their idols' signatures. With mannerisms and facial expressions absolutely as per their films, Stan and Oliver had lunch, but even the flash of the Journal cameraman's photo equipment didn't interrupt Oliver's soup course.

Mr. Bill Batty, *mein host* at the Red Lion, and his staff, were introduced to the celebrities. A suggestion that they might be photographed at the hotel beer pumps was politely turned down on the score that a large proportion of their fun was for the benefit of children, but anything else – "It's OK by us".

WISECRACKS

Before departing for Barkston and the rendezvous with Mr. Jefferson, Laurel and Hardy caused roars of laughter with their comical expressions, antics and wisecracks, and as they entered the waiting taxi a final "so long!" was accompanied by the famed wiggle of Hardy's fingers.

Many villagers, principally the younger ones, were outside the Plough Inn when the party arrived, and they saw Laurel oblige with that amusing characteristic – finger-tips in his hair – which accompanies his screen performances.

Inside, the fun reached its peak, and at teatime Mrs. Healey's homemade pastry was particularly popular with Oliver!

Before returning to London the same evening the comedians joined with "the gang" in the *Plough* bar and issued plenty of challenges at darts.

They had evidently absorbed more of the instruction they received at lunch time on the Red Lion board from Mr. W. Gillison, well known Grantham darts player, than most of those present had appreciated!

It was obvious that Mr. and Mrs. Laurel and "Babe," as Hardy was nicknamed, had enjoyed their visit.

Once back in London, Stan sent a telegram to the Healeys:

"Again, Thanks Dears for the wonderful visit. Can't express fully our thanks. Arrived back an hour late but so happy we made the trip. Our best love to Dad, 'selves and all "The gang." Bye now and God bless" Stan, Ida and "Babe".

[AJM: The Plough Inn is still there, but has been converted back to flats. By combining the close-up on the 1947 photo, with a modern-day longshot, one can better imagine the scene in 1947.]

A more publicised event during the three-week run at the London Palladium was on Friday 21 March, when the comedy couple were invited to partake in the celebrations for the 21st Anniversary of the 'Romney, Hythe, & Dymchurch Railway,' and to open the new section of track between Romney and Dungeness.

Immediately after breakfast, Stan, Babe, Ida, and Harry Moreny left their London hotel and boarded a train bound for Ashford, in Kent, from where a car took them to Hythe Railway Station, on the Kent coast. There they were greeted by the Mayor of Folkestone – Ald. H.

Hughes, and the general manager of the railway, Major J.T. Holder, who accompanied them on the train to New Romney. Despite a constant drizzle, thousands of people had turned out, headed by the Mayor – Alderman J.A. Wiles, and the owners of the railway, Mr. & Mrs. J.E.P. Howey.

Mrs. Howey handed the Boys a key, which looked like it belonged to a giant clockwork train set, and directed them towards the tunnel in which the train engine was awaiting its unveiling. This afforded the couple ample means to improvise a comedy routine centred around the unlocking of the fake set of doors which had been placed over one end of the tunnel. Once the engine had been brought out onto the main line, raucous laughter accompanied the testing of the controls by Stan and Ollie, followed by further hilarity when Stan and Teddy Smith, son of the Dymchurch station master, tried to push Hardy's enormous frame into one of the third-scale Pullman Cars. Fortunately, two camera teams were on hand to capture the action. **[FILM]**

With the new line officially declared "Open," the train burst through the fake brickwork at the far end of the tunnel, on its way to Dungeness. Hot toddies served on the train were followed by lunch at the Jolly Fisherman pub in Greatstone; before reaching the turn-around point at Dungeness Lighthouse, and then back to Hythe for tea at the Light Railway Restaurant.

On the following Monday, as a "thank you" to Laurel and Hardy for giving up their day, Messrs. Holder and Howey turned up at the stage door of the Palladium and left no less than four hundred photographs for them to autograph. How thoughtful!

Fellow-professionals were also apt to drop in backstage at the Palladium. One was Dump Harris, a comedian and xylophonist who did his act in the guise of "Ollie." So good was Harris's likeness that, upon leaving, he was accosted by autograph-hunters wanting *Hardy's* signature.

On one occasion, Hardy set out on his own to witness some of the pomp and ceremony associated with the Royal Family (as he had done during the 1932 visit), of which he recounted in an issue of the *Weekly News*:

> I was determined to get a camera shot of the Changing of the Guard. It was raining that morning, but Stan assured me that, come rain, come shine, the full ceremony was always carried out. In actual fact, there were only about eight disconsolate guardsmen on parade. They did a brief curtailment of the full ceremony. In fact, the only thing not covered was yours truly, Oliver Hardy. My camera and film were ruined, and so was I. I was in bed for three days with flu. [AJM: Don't think so.]

In their dressing-room at the Palladium, Laurel and Hardy present pools' winner Edward Cross with a cheque for the enormous sum of £61,456 – more than sixty times their weekly fee.

Upon arrival at New Romney Station, the two stars are welcomed by a trio playing *The Cuckoo Song*.
[Two of the clarinettists are off right in this shot.]

[FILM]

Mrs. Howey presents Ollie with the giant key to open the train shed.

[If only Mrs. Holder were doing the presentation, I could have said he got it off "the key Holder."]

While Ollie tries to figure out why the key won't fit, Stanley opens the doors by hand.

Then it was time for the off.

Laurel and Hardy try to ensure it's not "Hat's Off" as they take over the controls of the locomotive "The Black Prince" from driver Tony Baker.

When the Boys try to push-start the engine, the Mayor of Folkestone and his entourage wisely stay well back.

Stan and Babe greeting their Coaster Box-Car waiter — ten year-old Teddy Smith, son of the Dymchurch Station Master.

[I hope he's not serving alcoholic drinks.]

One backstage visitor, sketch-artist Louis Valentine, was invited to bring his baby daughter with him next time, with the strange proviso that he also brought an empty suitcase. During that second meeting, after making a big fuss of baby Susan, Stan asked Louis to draw a sketch of him drinking coffee, and Babe drinking tea. It always amused Stan that the Englishman was the coffee drinker, and the American was the tea drinker. The sketch was much appreciated, and taken back to America where Stan proudly put it on display in his den.

A Louis Valentine sketch for a pools' advert

For payment, Stan told Louis to open his suitcase. He then proceeded to fill it with all kinds of goodies for Susan; plus tea, coffee, sugar, etc. for Louis and his wife Peggy. Some of the items they had brought with them from America, but most had been given to them by fans. There was so much, that the Boys couldn't possibly consume it all themselves. The problem now, was that Louis had to get home carrying a suitcase-full of contraband. He remained in a state of anxiety all the way back as, had he been stopped by the police and asked: "Where did you get all this contraband from?" it is doubtful if the reply, "Off Laurel and Hardy," would have got him out of trouble.

IDEAL HOME EXHIBITION

Jimmy Murphy, in the white mac, being told to get on his bike.

Another of Stan's friends was less fortunate where the law was concerned. Jimmy Murphy, from Newton-le-Willows, Lancashire, first met Laurel in 1940, when working as a pool cleaner at the San Francisco Exposition, and had then become his personal valet for a number of years. Now back in England after serving in the army, Jimmy contacted Stan at the Palladium and got his job back. His return was short-lived. Home Office officials located him backstage and issued him with an order to leave the country. Whilst in the US he had become an American citizen, and so had no work permit for the UK.

Having lost their tea-boy almost as fast as they had found him, Stan and Babe were invited to take tea with journalist Hannen Swaffer (*ibid.*) "the Dean of Fleet Street," at his tiny flat in Charing Cross Road. Also present were Billy Marsh and John Montgomery (prolific writer of biographies of comedians), all of whom enjoyed servings of toast, jam, cake, and tea served from a big silver teapot.

Swaffer was an eccentric person, to say the least. His appearance gave one the impression he had just dug his way out of a grave, using his finger nails. It was not always a pleasure to be a guest of his; but, as with Dorothy Parker and Hedda Hopper in America, to decline was to incur the wrath of a powerful enemy.

Stan was quite at ease in Swaffer's company, and able to discuss at length the merits of music-hall stars, past and present. Babe was lost in the conversation, having come from an entirely different background; but, being the polite gentleman he was, remained an attentive listener throughout. After a few hours of their company, during which Swaffer had constantly addressed Stan as "Ollie," and Ollie as "Stan," Billy Marsh noted with amusement that: "He didn't know the one from the other."

o-o-0-o-o

A LITTLE WISDOM

The Boys' next social meeting was at the 'Vaudeville Golfing Society Ball' on Sunday 23 March, at the Savoy Hotel. [The society consists of show business personalities who raise money for charity by playing in sponsored golf tournaments.] Amongst those present were English comedians Terry-Thomas, Bud Flanagan, Nat Jackley, Sid Field, and Gerry Desmonde; plus entertainers Donald Peers, and Bob & Alf Pearson.

On such occasions as these a kind of inverted snobbery occurs whereby protocol demands that, no matter how big the star guest is, he or she is treated as an ordinary person. The heady reaction which occurred upon Laurel and Hardy's entrance shows the ultra-high esteem in which these two gentlemen were regarded. Arriving late, and trying to sneak quietly to their seats, Stan and Babe were immediately converged upon by a swarm of people. Abandoning all decorum, men and women in evening dress hurriedly snatched menus from tables, and pushed and jostled each other to get them autographed. Sid Field made a plea for the honoured guests to be allowed to enjoy the evening in common with the rest, but it was forty minutes after the Boys had made their entry before the deluge stopped, and they were able to join him at his table.

Laurel and Hardy were also greatly admired by the 'Grand Order of Water Rats' (a fund-raising organisation made up of members solely from the entertainment profession), and were asked if they would consider joining the Order. Laurel was proposed by Fred Russell, and seconded by Talbot O' Farrell; whilst Hardy was proposed by Will Hay, and seconded by Bud Flanagan. The Boys accepted, and on 30 March went along to the home of the 'Rats' (the Eccentric Club, in Rhyder Street, London) for the secret ceremony. Will Hay presided in the absence of 'King Rat' Robb Wilton, and Fred Russell was 'Preceptor.' Also present at the meeting were: Peter Brough, Sid Field, Ted Ray, Albert Whelan, Nat Mills, Harry Tate Jr., Johnnie Riscoe, and Harry Moreny.

Of the theatre tour, Laurel and Hardy's run at the Palladium had ended on 29 March and so, having switched successfully from revue to variety shows there, Delfont next repeated the formula at one of his own venues, the Wimbledon Theatre, which Laurel and Hardy played week commencing 31 March. The *Boro' News* wrote:

> Following their great success at the Palladium, Laurel & Hardy come to the
> Wimbledon Theatre. Their sketch has been described as 'boisterously gay' and the

comedians at their best. The London critics were unanimous not only in praise, but in the opinion that, whereas most film artistes were disappointing on the living stage, Laurel & Hardy were even more riotously funny.

Just whether Laurel and Hardy were able to follow this build-up, wasn't told by the local newspapers, which totally ignored the two mega-stars, and so were are forced to move on – none the wiser.

The Wimbledon appearance was followed by a week at the Lewisham Hippodrome, where packed houses were the order of the day. One good reason for the high attendances is that one evening, two weeks earlier, Stan and Babe had shot over from the Palladium to the Lewisham Hippodrome and made a walk-on appearance to tell the theatregoers, in person, when they would be playing there. It is as well they did, for the *Borough News* thought the only interest lay in pianist Charlie Kunz being present at one of the shows. Why the press failed to react to Laurel and Hardy being in Britain, and attracting enormous business wherever they went, defies logic. On the 1932 tour the press coverage had been blamed for whipping up a wave of hysteria; but here in 1947 it didn't have the impetus to whip up lather in a washing-up bowl. But "still they came," and the crowds never dwindled.

Whilst at Lewisham Stan and Babe, taking a personal tip from a local greyhound owner, made a large wager on his dog. Norman Munro – who did a brilliant balancing act in the show, with his wife Vonnie – was sent along to watch the race. He reported back that the dog had set off at a fantastic pace but, upon coming to the first bend, had run headlong into the fence and was killed. The death of the poor animal upset the Boys enough to cure them of making further flutters.

On the Sunday following the week at Lewisham, Stan and Babe were back at the Eccentric Club to attend their first meeting as 'Honorary Water Rats.' Stan must have been in his element talking to Fred Kitchen, who for so long had been a principal comedian with the Karno Company (although they hadn't worked together). He also met stage and film comedian Lupino Lane who, like himself, had been a boy comedian during the early 1900s.

Monday 14 April saw the start of a four-week run at the London Coliseum. As at the Wimbledon Theatre this was again a gamble, as variety hadn't been staged there for nine years. In fact, there were no other variety shows then running in the West End. The show having been given this extended run added to the risk; so, for "insurance," a strong support bill had been put together. This included highly popular theatre, film, and radio personalities Elsie & Doris Waters (in their guise of 'Gert & Daisy'), and Rawicz & Landauer – world acclaimed piano duettists.

On the first day at any theatre, the acts have to report in early to give directions to the stage, sound, and lighting crews, plus of course the orchestra, after which there will be a run-through to ensure that everyone is synchronised. Hardy was bemoaning his bad luck in having to attend this first-day rehearsal as, that day, his wife Lucille was arriving from America. Her travelling companions on board the *Queen Elizabeth* were Russian-born Hollywood film producer Boris Morros, and his wife Catherine. Lucille had worked as script-clerk on Morros's film *The Flying Deuces*, on the set of which she first met Babe, but whether or not the three had planned to take the voyage together, or whether it was just chance, is not known.

The Hardys eventually met up at the Savoy, where one of the first things Lucille did was present Babe with a set of thick underwear he had left behind in America. At the time of his leaving it had been too tight, but now he thought it might fit him again.

The show became a smash hit, and *The Performer* noted:

> The Laurel & Hardy sketch now has additional gags and is much stronger than when they played the Palladium.

In 1983, journalist Derek Malcolm wrote a story of Laurel and Hardy's appearance, which shows that special affinity which the two stars had with their fans – especially children. The show played to full houses throughout its run, but the matinee he describes, was either an exception, or a trick of memory.

My mother took me, trembling with excitement to the Coliseum, but alas I went to a half-empty matinee. The audience sipped cups of tea, talked amongst themselves, and showed about as much enthusiasm for real artistry as a kipper for being breakfasted upon. I was very sad, and my mother knew it.

Accordingly, she sent a note round backstage, asking Stan and Oliver whether she could take me to see them. I could scarcely believe it at the end of the show when an usherette walked up to her and said: 'Mr. Laurel and Mr. Hardy would be delighted to see you and your son now'.

I was ushered into the not very plush dressing room in a state bordering on panic, to find Stan sitting at the mirror taking his make-up off, and Oliver in his shirt sleeves making a strenuous effort to bend down far enough to remove one of his boots. 'Oh hello', said Stan, 'Did you enjoy the show? Do you know I always watch Elsie and Doris from the wings. They're so good, aren't they?'

'Yes, and so are you,' I mumbled, 'I'm sorry there weren't more in to see you'.

'Oh well,' said Stan, 'You came, didn't you? How about a cup of tea and a bun? Would you like that?'

'Now then,' said Oliver, having finally got his boots off, 'I've got some sweets somewhere, unless Stanley's eaten them.'

Malcolm goes on to describe numerous bits of business which the two comedians performed for him, and concludes:

The point was, that after a tiring and, for them, disappointing show, they had bothered to entertain one small boy for half an hour before going on again for the evening show. Most stars, I've learnt to my cost, would only do that sort of thing in front of cameras to show how charming they are. With Laurel and Hardy it seemed a perfectly natural act.

With four straight weeks to play at the Coliseum, a little bit of tedium must have been creeping in, so Stan and Babe became tourists, and visited a few London attractions. At Tussauds they were caught in the Hall of Mirrors — amusing themselves looking at their distorted reflections.

They then moved on to entertaining themselves with the images of other stars — in the waxwork tableaux in Tussauds.

TUSSAUDS' TABLEAUX

A galaxy of stars – including Charlie Chaplin, Mary Pickford, Gracie Fields, and Tommy Handley – are complemented by the two life-like figures of Stan Laurel and Oliver Hardy.

Hardy breaking into a cold sweat, fearing that Laurel kissing the hand of Jane Seymour will get them beheaded by the man looking on.

Laurel trying to impress upon Clement Atlee and this cabinet of British MPs that "Honesty is the best politics."

Then on Tuesday 22 April they braved a look around what is commonly known as Scotland Yard's 'Black Museum,' which Laurel described some years later in a letter to a friend:

My Dear Earl Jr.

Another place we were invited to look around was Scotland Yard, was really interesting, especially the special privilege given us to look around their museum, which contains all kinds of paraphernalia used by well known criminals – all kinds of devices used in counterfeiting, murder weapons etc. that were actually used, the place is packed with all kinds of gadgets in glass cases, a card on each article, explaining the crime on which it was used. We were also taken on a trip on a police patrol boat around the Thames, that too was a very interesting trip.

The following night, Wednesday 23 April, the two Hollywood stars were guests of honour at the 'Daily Mail Film Awards,' at the Dorchester Hotel, where they themselves were filmed when turning up late and interrupting Lady Rothermere presenting an award to Margaret Lockwood. Lady Rothermere was the wife of the newspaper magnate Lord Rothermere (You know what a "magnate" is, don't you?), but it was another female dignitary who made a particular impression on Stan, as recounted in this letter some ten years later: **[FILM]**

Aug. 21ˢᵗ. '57

Dear Babe & I attended a large affair in '47. at the Dorchester Hotel, we were invited by a Lord & Lady Rothmere (think that was the name) they were in charge of the guest list dept.

It was a social function, I think everybody was there except Royal Family, it was certainly a lavish sight – furs & diamonds etc. waiters in knee britches, powdered wigs & all the fancy trappings. Being very formal, we of course had to wear white tie & tails (we never looked funnier!) anyway, we arrived quite late, due to our playing at the Palladium [AJM: No! Coliseum.

The party was in full sway, as we were being ushered in, an old Lady was leaving with an entourage, with a lot of formality, we were introduced to her – it was Princess Mary Louise (I think the Grand-Daughter of Queen Victoria) she looked like she had a snout full & was being escorted home – after the bowing & scraping was over she put on her lorgnette & thoroughly looked us over (slightly swaying) her eyes lit up, she said, 'Oh yes, I know you now – I've seen you on the radio" she then hiccoughed & was led out. Well champagne was flowing till the wee early hours, but we were too busy autographing menu cards for the Dukes & Earls to get in on the fun – however, remains a happy memory.

On Sunday 27 April, the 'Water Rats' staged a charity show, the *Rats' Revel*, at the Victoria Palace. One unknown comedian, after finishing his act on this show, did not remain unknown much longer. The reaction he received was ecstatic. His name – Norman Wisdom. Below, Norman takes up the story:

> I was in a show at the Hackney Empire. The producer asked me if I would do a charity concert on the forthcoming Sunday. I immediately said 'yes' as, at that time, I would have done anything to get on stage. I would have made the tea, if they'd asked me.
>
> On Sunday morning, I turned up for rehearsals, and there were all these big stars: George Doonan, Vera Lynn, Will Fyffe, and Laurel & Hardy. I did my rehearsal on about two foot of stage, and nobody took a blind bit of notice. Amongst all these stars, I wasn't known from Adam. In the evening, though – if I say so myself – I went extremely well, and had to take several bows.

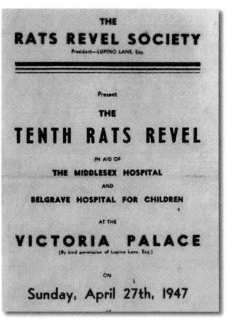

The reviews certainly bear out Norman's recollections. *The Performer* said:

> Then came one of the outstanding hits of the evening, young Norman Wisdom, who bounced himself up one more rung of the ladder towards stardom with yet another exhibition of uproarious foolishness.

The Stage said:

> Vera Lynn, Laurel & Hardy, and Will Fyffe all provided of their best in this half of the show, but it was newcomer, Norman Wisdom, who took the house by storm with some of the funniest business possible.

WISDOM

After the show, Stan and Babe told Norman that he was a brilliant performer. These weren't empty words, and to prove it, consider that, at two future meetings, it was Laurel and Hardy who went to see Norman Wisdom perform, and not the other way round. From this, Norman obviously gained a great deal of pride, and a whole lot of laughs. Stan's immediate response was to approach show business agent Billy Marsh and say: "You want to sign this man up. He's a great clown." Billy Marsh took his advice, and was Norman's manager for over forty years.

In 1932 Stan had wandered into the Holborn Empire where, by chance, Max Miller was playing. This time around he purposefully went to see Miller – as revealed in Miller's biography, by John M. East (*ibid.*):

MILLER

After we'd finished our booking at the London Palladium in 1947, I went to see Max Miller again. By that time Max's act was a work of art. His timing was perfect; he projected his personality as well, if not better, than any performer I have seen on either side of the Atlantic.

Yet another money-raising event Laurel and Hardy attended was on Tuesday 6 May, at a matinee performance of a play at the Apollo Theatre, in Shaftesbury Avenue, where the proceeds were going to the "Farmer's Disaster Fund." There, along with other stars of West-End theatre, they raised awareness by dressing in farmers' smocks and hats. Pathé Newsreels were on hand to capture the action, which shows Stan and Ollie with Sid Field, Tommy Trinder, George Robey, and 'The Crazy Gang' – selling programmes to patrons arriving at the theatre, and collecting donations in buckets. Others in attendance were Leslie Henson, Charlie Kunz, and Stanley Holloway. **[FILM]**

		Stanley Holloway	Stan Laurel	Tommy Trinder		
	Teddy Knox		Jimmy Nervo		Jimmy Gold	
Leslie Henson	Bud Flanagan	George Robey		Charlie Kunz		Sid Field

Sometime during Stan and Babe's stay in London, R.B. Marriott of *The Stage* interviewed Stan, with the main question on his mind being the reason for the longevity of the characters of 'Laurel & Hardy.' What emerged was a fascinating piece of original writing. The article states that Laurel had found after lengthy experiment, thought, and practice that:

> The basis of lasting success in team-comedy, no matter what the particular appeal of the comedians may be, must be built on always having a strong framework for individual gags, expressions and gestures. In other words, on a story or "situation." I do not think a pair of comedians can get very far and become popular over many years if they rely entirely on gags and mannerisms.

> Even during the average time on the stage of the star variety-turn, let alone in a full-length film, jokes and gags alone become tedious. But with a story or, if you like, with comedians in a "situation," such as the one Hardy and I find ourselves in, there is every chance of not only from time to time relaxing from gags and vocal and physical mannerisms associated in the public mind with the comedian's success, but also of enriching the act by "business" that would otherwise be impossible.

Marriott and Laurel agreed that the idiosyncrasies, for which a comedian had become known and loved, must always play a big part. Said Stan:

> It amazes me how much the public remember of apparently trivial things – a certain finger movement, a fleeting facial expression, and the like. Hardy and I noticed this especially since our return to variety here after many films. We have frequently been surprised at the response given to odd bits of "business" that we thought would have impressed only when seen in an actual film. Naturally, this sort of thing going on over the years enables us to build our act more and more securely, in detail as well as in its main structure. But again the value of a story or situation appears. In no other way can the act, as liked by the public, be kept fresh and varied.

Of the format of their act Stan believed that its power, with pathos and plenty of "human touch," remained undiminished:

> The sympathy for the little fellow who is knocked about and kicked around is as strong as ever. In my opinion it will always be one of the best liked things in comedy, simply because in the heart of so many of us, there is something of the little fellow himself.

Having read the above, one ought to now be able to understand why Stan Laurel and Oliver Hardy chose to retain the format of their stage act. Changing to "fast-patter merchants," or trying to reshape themselves into a more modern image, would have been denying the public what the public expected to see. By sticking with their old image Laurel and Hardy may have displeased some critics, but they certainly retained the love of the public.

o-o-0-o-o

Chapter 13

OLIVER-STAN IN ULVER-STON

The twelve weeks Laurel and Hardy had originally been booked for were now completed; but, owing to ecstatic reports causing a wave of demand from many provincial theatre managers, the 12-week extension clause on the contract was actioned The first to secure a booking were brothers Robert and Maurice Kennedy, who ran the Dudley Hippodrome. There, the appearance of Laurel & Hardy was rightly considered a great coup, and served to put not only the theatre on the map, but Dudley as a whole. Tickets were sold out well in advance, and all box-office records broken. The *Birmingham Post* missed the sense of occasion:

> The audience saw and loved, in reality, what it had so often seen at the cinema. Hardy administered rebukes to his partner; both by word and deed, and Laurel accepted them with the familiar tearful mien and much ruffling of the hair. The sketch gave them the fullest scope for their slapstick antics.

Mary Crettol, who worked at the Station Hotel, has fond memories of the overseas visitors:

> The Hippodrome was adjacent to the hotel, and huge crowds would gather to see them. When Laurel and Hardy had finished their performance they would return to the hotel and, after a few drinks, entertain the residents.

> They both liked English food, especially steak & kidney pie. After the war, when meat was rationed, we served pigeon pie. This was a favourite of Hardy.

> Hardy was a man with a great thirst. He drank large jugs of water with his meals and always ordered pots and pots of tea.

> Hardy always was the perfect gentleman, speaking almost in a whisper. We had difficulty accommodating him on a dining room chair. He seemed to find the ones we had uncomfortably small for his large frame.

> Laurel never ate breakfast in the dining room, preferring to eat in his bedroom with his wife. We were all young girls, and found it a great privilege to look after them.

The great time Stan and Babe had in Dudley was not just confined to the theatre and hotel, but also extended to visits to the Mintos Sweet Factory and Cape Hill Brewery, both in Smethwick, on the outskirts of Birmingham, where they were able to live out the fantasy many people harbour for being given the free-run of not only a sweet factory, but a brewery as well.

LOST PHOTO
Stan and Babe handing out treats to workers at the Cape Hill Brewery.

ABOVE: The Laurel and Hardy Family and Harry Moreny, being greeted by the manager at Mintos Sweet Factory — Rolfe Street, Smethwick.

At Mintos, the Laurels and the Hardys get to act out the expression: "Like kids in a candy shop."

From Dudley, the company took the train to Liverpool. Harry Moreny (the cop from their sketch) got aboard carrying a large parcel under his arm, which he took with him into the compartment he was sharing with Olga Varona and her husband Archie. In the next compartment were the 'Laurel and Hardy Family' (as they were referred to by Olga and Archie).

When the attendant came to ask what time they would like to book their meal in the dining car, Harry opened his parcel and said, "Can you do anything with this?" The attendant's mouth dropped open upon the revealing of a whole cooked leg of lamb, which a grateful theatregoer had donated to the party. "Don't move from there," said the attendant, "you have more food here than we have in the dining car." Sometime later he returned with cutlery, condiments, and tea, bread and butter, and the seven of them tucked into a very unexpected, and delicious, clandestine meal. A dog by the trackside then got an enormous treat when a lamb bone, thrown from a train window, landed at its feet, causing the perpetrators to laugh raucously at the astonished look on the dog's face, and its subsequent actions in trying to carry off the huge bone.

John Jones will never forget the week Laurel and Hardy spent in Liverpool, for he had the delightful daily job of chauffeuring the two stars from the Adelphi Hotel, along Lime Street, to the Liverpool Empire theatre.

On the Monday morning, John duly picked them up, and took them to rehearsals. In the evening there was one amazing difference: Lime Street was so jammed with people that mounted police had to be brought in to control them. Billy Marsh said: *"It was an unbelievable sight. Why! I'd never even seen a mounted policeman before."*

Inside the Liverpool Empire the seats and aisles too were packed, and remained so for the week's duration – with still hundreds left outside, nightly. The *Daily Post* revealed none of this:

> The stage act of Laurel & Hardy is cunningly simple – an introduction, a sketch, and a song and dance with some patter. But from the first note of the famous Cuckoo Song until they were reluctantly allowed to go, the pair kept the packed house in an uproar of merriment with all the tricks and antics that have won them a place amongst the world's great comedians.

Billy Nelson and Dougie Wakefield reminiscing about the time all four were making films at the Hal Roach Studios.

In his memoirs, in a 1962 edition of the *Liverpool Echo*, TV comedy writer Eddie Braben, (fondly remembered for the wonderful comedy sketches he wrote for the 'Morecambe & Wise' television shows of the 1970s) wrote a far more sentimental account of Stan and Ollie's appearance; an event which, he said, was to play an important part in his later years:

> The lights dimmed and a spotlight lit one corner of the stage; just five notes of a signature tune; the top of the bill act hadn't yet appeared but the ovation was thunderous. Then THEY walked onto the stage and the theatre trembled with clapping and cheering. The ovation lasted for fully two minutes. Now I saw 'Them'. It really was 'Them' – Laurel & Hardy. Stan smiled and scratched his head. Oliver wiggled his tie – they could have finished on that. Never before or since have I seen an audience show such love and affection. It was too much for Ollie, because he cried.

Sentiment, again, was to the fore in the episode of a Mrs. Mabel Yates, of Hartington Road, Liverpool. Mrs. Yates (born 1876) was at that time in life when all her bad fortune had caught up with her. Almost continuously since childhood she had suffered from rheumatoid arthritis. Ten years earlier she had been hit by a shop blind, and four years ago she had been involved in a tram accident. And now paralysis was taking a hold. When she heard that the two screen comedians were in town, she wrote to tell them that a great source of happiness in her life had been growing up watching the films of Laurel & Hardy. She ended the letter by wishing Stan and Ollie "Good Luck," and apologising that she was physically unable to come and see them.

To most stars the letter would have merited a signed photo being sent by return, but then Stan Laurel and Oliver Hardy were not your regular stars. They did write back, not to express their sorrow that she couldn't come to the theatre, but to offer something far more positive:

```
Dear Mabel,

Thank you for your letter. We were very sorry to learn of
your bad accident, and to know that you were no longer able
to visit the Cinema or the Theatre.

We could not let the occasion pass without you having the
opportunity of seeing our show, so we have made the
following arrangements to enable you to see the matinee
performance on Saturday afternoon May 24th.

A taxi with an attendant to assist you, will call at your
home at 1.30P.M. on Saturday, and bring you to the Theatre.
Attendants at the Theatre will help you to your seat, which
```

has been reserved, and a taxi will take you home again
after the show. So be ready at 1.30P.M. Saturday.

With Best Wishes, Stan Laurel, Oliver Hardy

In her time, Mabel had been a music teacher, and among her pupils, it is said, was Ivor Novello. She also used to play the piano for the silent movies, along with writing both music and poetry. So was it her CV that had earned her such VIP treatment from these two Hollywood movie stars? Well – no! The two stars knew none of this beforehand. Mabel Yates was obviously a very special lady; but, throughout this book, you will read similar stories of such kindness and thoughtfulness shown by Messrs. Laurel and Hardy – for they really were "the special ones."

Back to chauffeur John Jones: During their week in Liverpool John got to know Stan and Babe quite well, and reflected:

> I was an employee, but was not treated as such. I was often invited into their company, in the hotel. There they would buy me a half of beer, and a drop of dry whisky for themselves. They were clean living, definitely not boozers, and I never heard a swear word out of them in all the time I spent with them. They were kindness itself.

However, John did reveal a ruthless side, when it came to them defending their standards in the use of spotlessly clean material. At Monday morning rehearsals, a rather embarrassing scene was caused when one of the acts told what Laurel and Hardy considered to be smutty jokes, and so they exerted pressure on the theatre manager to have him removed from the show. They explained to John:

> We would never appear in any theatre that allowed any sort of rude joke. We have never had any need of it ourselves, as we use good, clean, slapstick fun.

At the end of each evening's performance it was not a simple matter of the comedy duo putting on their coats and strolling out of the stage door, for outside would be hundreds of autograph hounds. The crowds that week were not only huge, but exceptionally physical and, as a result, the Boys had begun to dread their nightly confrontation. Come the third night they were delaying as long as possible, when Babe suddenly pointed to the door and said, "Well! who's going first?" which "broke up" the whole company. On the fourth night, it was Stan who got the big laugh when he announced: "I'll just pop outside to see what's happening." Everyone knew if he had ventured outside, the crowd would have "torn him to pieces."

On the Sunday morning, with their week in Liverpool ended, John went along to the hotel to pick up the Laurel and Hardy Family and take them to the next stop-over. The police had cordoned off the area to keep back the vast crowd so, getting into character, Stan and Ollie were able to pause for a moment on the hotel steps. Standing there in their raglan overcoats, Stan took off his trilby and scratched his head, and Ollie twiddled his tie. A roar went up, as if the Liverpool football team had scored a goal, and the crowd surged forward. John quickly ushered them into the awaiting silver-blue Rolls Royce, for fear

ALDELPHI HOTEL
Lime Street

they would be mobbed. What happened next was witnessed by no-one else but John.

As we pulled away, Oliver Hardy asked me if I wouldn't mind driving them around Liverpool a little. He particularly wanted to be shown some of the bombed areas. I drove them around the worst of these: Church Street, Whitechapel, Vauxhall Road, Derby Road, and up the Dock Road, where many buildings were now just rubble. After a time I happened to glance at Ollie, who was sitting beside me in the passenger seat, and saw that tears were rolling down his cheeks. Ollie said he would never know how the poor British had put up with this.

Laurel, who was sitting in the back of the car, slid back the window and said to me, 'This is one of the things we wanted to see for ourselves. Otherwise, living in America, we couldn't have known what it must have been like.'

John certainly wasn't exaggerating when he later said: "They had an awful lot of feeling for the British people."

After going through Aintree, the journey was continuing along the country roads towards Preston when, at Longton, Stan asked if they could stop at the village pub, as he wished to savour some good olde English beer. John advised the Boys: "Keep your heads down and, whatever you do, don't speak."

The pub was practically empty but, whilst pouring the beers, the landlord asked who the VIPs were. "Just some people I'm taking to Morecambe," replied John. "They don't half look like Laurel and Hardy," said the landlord, who insisted on taking the drinks to the table. As he entered the back bar, Stan and Babe turned away, but the restricted view of the pair sent him away dissatisfied.

Next minute his wife entered with a tray of bread and cheese. "Excuse me, but we haven't ordered that," Babe politely pointed out. "It's free," said the landlady. "Gee thanks," responded Stan, to which the landlady, unable to withhold her feelings any longer, enquired: "You *are* Laurel and Hardy, aren't you?" With that, the pub magically filled with people, and they ended up getting a huge send-off from the whole village. So much for a "quiet drink."

Upon reaching their destination in Morecambe, John felt very sad that he was dropping them off for the last time. Understandably, he had grown very fond of them:

> Stan seemed really pleased to be home, and I found him such a nice guy to be with. Off stage they were like brothers, often asking each other questions, and were all the time concerned about each other. For example, Stan would offer Ollie the front seat of the car, as he felt Ollie would be more comfortable there. Sometimes I was up with them till 2a.m., but I never once heard a sharp word, never mind a cross word, between them.

Of the Boys' humour away from the public, John said:

> They couldn't help but be funny off-stage as well – it came so naturally to them. It was just the little things. They only needed to look at one another and everyone would laugh. I'm sure they could read each other's minds. They knew exactly what the other one was doing, and what they were going to do next. They were so close.

And of the tour he said:

> Their lives were not their own. It was as if the whole of Britain just wanted to get to know them, to meet them. They seemed so nice and approachable, and they did have an awful lot of feeling for the British people.

With the characteristics John described, which are all very faithful to the general consensus, is it any wonder? His last memory of them was an emotionally charged farewell, as he shook their hands outside the Elms Hotel, in Bare, Morecambe.

Later that day the Boys decided to go for a stroll along the prom, prom, prom. Before the brass band could play: "Tiddly-om-pom-pom," Stan and Ollie were surrounded by a crowd of onlookers. After a while the situation became hopeless. Those who had been given attention wouldn't leave, whilst others kept joining the melee. Eventually the two comedians gave way to the futility of their efforts, and retreated to the sanctuary of the hotel.

Harry Smirk, manager of the Winter Gardens, visiting his headlining
act in the sanctuary of the Elms Hotel garden (pictured above).

On Tuesday, Stan took Ida and the Hardys on a forty-mile car journey north, to Ulverston, to show them the house he was born in (16 June 1890) and in which he spent the first five years of his life being brought up by his grandparents – George & Sarah Metcalfe (his mother's parents). But firstly, the Mayor and Councillors wanted to present the local-lad-cum-Hollywood-star to the townspeople of Ulverston, as Stan reveals in this letter:

```
In 1947 I returned to my home Town Ulverston - just for a
quick visit & was given a Royal welcome by the Town
officials & Citizens, I was presented with my birth
certificate on the balcony of the Town hall in front of all
the inhabitants, then a parade headed by the Mayor & taken
to the house where I was born, even to the room, they
treated me like I was a hero, needless to tell you I broke
down & shed a few tears. I was then taken to the beautiful
Golf Club for a lunch in my honor by the Dignitaries of the
Town, then another parade to the outskirts when I left -
must have looked like I was being run out of Town!!
```

If you are wondering what the crowd in County Square, Ulverston, is looking up at, see below!

It's Laurel's big day, in his hometown, but that man Hardy is mightily due some of that adulation as well.

[Coronation Hall balcony, overlooking County Square.]

When Counc. Simpson presents Laurel with a copy of his birth certificate, Hardy snatches it away, to check that his partner was actually born here.

Up till then, he thought Stan had been made in Taiwan.

[FILM]

TOP
Balcony
Coronation Hall

MIDDLE
Outside 3 Argyle Street

BOTTOM
Doorway of
3 Argyle Street

Luncheon at the Golf Hotel was followed by a stroll around the grounds, after which the party left to allow time to make the evening shows in Morecambe. Once safely in his dressing room at the Pavilion Theatre, in the Winter Gardens complex, Stan wrote in a letter to his cousin Mary:

> Dear Mary,
>
> Delighted to receive your sweet letter. Funny you should mention Ulverston, just back from visiting there today – quite a turn out. I was presented to the folks at the Coronation Hall and was given a copy of my birth certificate on the balcony outside. Then went over to 3, Argyle Street, went through the old house, brought back many memories. Had lunch with the officials at the golf club, a wonderful time, was thrilled to death.

[AJM: It was the *Golf Hotel,* in Ulverston town centre where they had lunch.]

Stan also wrote a thank you letter to Counc. Simpson, which read:

> Just a line to express my deep appreciation for the wonderful reception accorded me on my return to 'Lile Oostan' ['Little Ulverston']. The sincere kindness of you all will never be forgotten.
>
> Please accept my humble 'Thank you' also to all concerned for bestowing upon me the biggest thrill of my life in the true Lancashire spirit.
>
> My love and fondest thoughts always – Stan Laurel.

On Wednesday afternoon the comedy couple adjudicated at a Bathing Beauty Competition, at Morecambe's open-air swimming stadium. Caught out by an uncustomary British climate of 29°C, they had to endure the heat dressed in suit and tie, whilst most of the four and a half thousand spectators relaxed in swimwear.

Amongst the dignitaries in attendance were the Mayor of Morecambe – Herbert Willacy MBE; the Earl of Sefton and Lady Sefton; and the Mayor of Lancaster. Popular as the comedy duo were, the crowd were quick to show dissension when they felt that the girl in second place ought to have won.

On Thursday evening, Stan and Babe were interviewed in their dressing room at the theatre, for an 'on-air' broadcast during the BBC radio programme *Morecambe Night Out*; but what they said will have to remain a mystery, as it went out 'live', and there is no known recording.

Above shows where the two
Hollywood stars were seated.

Sat in the shade,
but still shining lights.

LOST PHOTOS

ABOVE:
A contestant posing on the
dais in front of the judges.

RIGHT
The three winners get to be
immortalised with the
Hollywood comedy stars.

BBC presenter Reg Smythe interviewing the Hollywood legends
for the radio programme *Morecambe Night Out*. **[AUDIO]**

Laurel, BBC man Reg Smythe, manager Harry Smirk, Hardy, unknown –
posing by the doors leading backstage.

Come Sunday, the Laurels and the Hardys checked out of the Elms Hotel and had only a forty-mile car journey south to their next destination – Blackpool. But it is at this point in the narration, that I am going to take a gamble and place a previously unpublished event on this day.

Harry Moreny — Roy Murray — Laurel — Leslie Murray — Hardy — Will Murray

Here we see Stan and Babe at a private luncheon at the home of mill owner George Henry Taylor, in Clitheroe Road, Whalley. Taylor had arranged entertainment during the war years, for wounded soldiers being treated at Calderstones Hospital, Whalley, and so had made useful contacts within show business.

The Taylors and the Murrays had other guests, all of whom were treated to a snippet of Stan and Ollie's stage act. It would seem that supper isn't the only meal you have to sing for.

Hardy comparing girths with Roy Murray (aka: Roy Leo).

So NOW on to Blackpool where, in 1932, the comedy couple had experienced the full force of the vast number of holidaymakers it attracted. This time, to prevent being held siege in a hotel on the Blackpool Golden Mile, they chose the Clifton Arms Hotel, in Lytham St. Annes, a few miles south of Blackpool – from where they took a taxi to the Palace Theatre each night.

Behind the railings supporting the CINEMA, DANCING, and VARIETIES signs is a balcony. In the next photo, Stan and Ollie are believed to be standing beneath the PALACE sign – directly overlooking the beach in the foreground.

Oliver-Stan in Ulver-ston

Monday morning, after rehearsals at the Palace, located on Blackpool's central seafront, the Boys stepped out onto the balcony and gained instant response from passers-by, and those on the beach opposite. Hats, caps, and handkerchiefs were waved, and shouts of the familiar "Good old Stan – hi-ya Ollie" were heard high above the passing traffic. A *Blackpool Evening Gazette* reporter recorded their comments:

'Stanley,' said Ollie, twiddling his tie, 'we are in Blackpool.'

'Don't lean on the railing, Ollie,' said Stan, 'or we'll all end up on the Promenade.'

'Don't take any notice of him' said Hardy, his chubby cheeks wreathed in smiles, his eyes twinkling. 'In any case, it's an exaggeration. I originally weighed 22 stone, but I've lost 40 pound since coming to England. Mind you, hard work in doing thirteen shows per week – not dieting – is the cause.'

With comments still being shouted up from the sea of happy smiling faces below Hardy urged Laurel: "Give the folks a big hand, Stanley" and together they clasped their hands, raised them above their heads and, shaking them with appreciation, shouted back expressions of goodwill.

'You know, Ollie,' said Laurel, 'It's nice to make people happy.'

'Brother,' echoed Hardy, "You said it. – I like Blackpool.'

'Me too,' says Laurel, as they retired inside with the crowd still cheering and waving.

The press certainly weren't going to be blamed for instigating another "siege" like the one in 1932, as it was only the *Evening Gazette* which gave them coverage:

> If you are a Laurel & Hardy picture fan you will get full value for money at the Palace Theatre, Blackpool, this week, where the famous Hollywood comedians are making their second appearance in fifteen years.
>
> You will laugh, as packed houses did last night, not so much at the words of the script as at the stars themselves. Ollie calls their sketch a 'spot of nonsense.' It is just that, with a dialogue that is always wholesome and in line with the Laurel & Hardy tradition of uncoloured fun.

The latter point stood out so strongly in the reviewer's mind that, a few days later, he took it up again:

> Why are Laurel & Hardy so triumphant on their tour? The answer is surely because their humour is simple, unsophisticated, and clean. People like it. At a time when the dirty joke, the sly innuendo, the double meaning, are far too prevalent, these two veterans show that mirth does not solely depend on references to sexual aberration, procreation, or the lavatory. It is comforting to find that comedians like these two can be so successful and so clean.

Sometime during the week, a Mr. Lowndes – secretary of the British Limbless Ex-Service Men's Association – came up with an enterprising idea for raising money to help the war-wounded. Through a connection (possibly George Henry Taylor, *ibid*) he arranged a recording session with Laurel and Hardy. This is thought to have taken place at the Palace Theatre, where Stan and Babe read from a script, and their voices were then recorded onto a 10-inch, single-sided, steel disc. It is thought the recording was then played, pre-show and/or during the interval, to audience members at the Palace, and possibly other venues in Blackpool. This was probably followed by charity volunteers going around the audience, collecting donations in buckets.

On Thursday Stan and Babe were invited to a luncheon, given by the Grand Order of Water Rats. Although most of the events and activities organised by the 'Water Rats' were held in London, it was acceptable, when many of their members were away from the capital doing summer shows, for the splinter groups to host their own events.

After cocktails at the Fleece Hotel, they all adjourned to Hill's Restaurant, where a number of the leading entertainers from the Blackpool shows, and others who lived in the area, had turned up, including Josef Locke, Nat Jackley, and Frank Randle.

Among the Water Rats' members are: Josef Locke, Albert Burdon, Harry Moreny, Roy Murray, Nat Jackley, Hardy, Tom Moss, Laurel, Will Murray, and Frank Randle.

A few "shandies" later and lovable maniac Frank Randle felt sufficiently courageous to go to George Formby's house and tackle his wife Beryl, who had forbidden George to keep company in "a room-full of drunken men." An inebriated Frank Randle turning up on his doorstep was the last person Formby wanted to fight his case; but, somehow, he was reprieved and allowed out of the house. On strict instruction not to enter the premises, Formby had to stay by his car, and Stan and Babe were brought out to meet him. After exchanging pleasantries, he returned home. Not to have done so would have brought on an onslaught bigger than the one Laurel and Hardy had next to face – a return to Glasgow.

o-o-0-o-o

Chapter 14

LAUREL WHERE'S YER TROOSERS?

On Sunday, heading north on the train from Blackpool, Stan spent part of the three-hour-plus journey gazing out of the window as the train passed through the Lake District. And then, when nearing Glasgow, he went into the corridor to obtain a better view, and was joined by Archie Collins – a now familiar travelling companion. Although Archie's wife Olga was Australian, he himself was from the Glasgow suburb of Pollokshaws, near Cathcart – where Stan's mother was buried. The train went on through Rutherglen where, knowing the area well, Archie said casually to Stan, "That's Rutherglen." "Archie, you have gone quite up-stage," replied Stan, "it is Ru'glen. I went to school there." This astounded Archie as he had no previous knowledge of Stan's background in Scotland. Needless to say, in future company, the two of them were to spend many happy hours comparing notes.

Still on the train, Laurel and Hardy must have had a forewarning of the huge reception they were about to receive, for here, miles out from Glasgow, children had turned out in their hundreds to wave flags as they sped by. To see the look of sincere glee on the children's faces had the Boys almost fit to burst into tears before they even reached Glasgow. When they did arrive it was like another step back in time, for there at the Central Station was pretty well the same scene they had witnessed fifteen years earlier. Although five thousand was considerably less than the numbers then, the station area was still crammed tight, and the returning heroes were given the most enthusiastic welcome of the tour so far. The *Evening Citizen* had had more than a little to do with the turn-out, as two days earlier they had advertised:

> Laurel & Hardy are due to arrive in Glasgow on Sunday. Their train from Blackpool gets in at 4-15 p.m. A hint for the fans: watch the first-class carriage nearest the engine.

Railway police and civil police, backed up by mounted policemen, had turned out in force, and all were needed to escort the two idols from the platform to the Central Hotel. Even so the events of 1932 were almost repeated when an ugly scene began to develop. As the party made headway, the crowd closed in behind them, shunting them forward like a human train, until eventually the duo were shoved through the hotel doors. People then began to congregate by the front entrance in such great numbers that mounted police were needed to clear them; and it was only after Stan and Ollie had made an appearance on the hotel balcony that the crowd did finally disperse.

There to meet Hardy on Platform 2 at Glasgow Central Station, is his old golfing nemesis Sir Alex King.

To cater for the expected audience demand, the Glasgow booking was for two weeks — with several visits, both official and private, also having been planned. The first approach was by Sir A.B. King, well-known local cinema magnate and theatre impresario. It may be remembered that on Laurel and Hardy's 1932 visit to Glasgow, Sir Alex (when he was 'plain' A.B. King) had challenged Hardy to a game of golf, and was still the proud owner of the half-a-crown he had taken off him in the rematch.

Whether Sir Alex asked Babe if he still had the tartan umbrella he had given him during the 1932 match is not known. If he had, it would have caused Hardy some embarrassment as, in December 1941, Hardy was dining at a Hollywood restaurant when a blackout was announced. In his haste to get home, he had rushed out – leaving the brolly behind. Friends reported him to be heartbroken, to the extent that he lodged an appeal for its return through the Hedda Hopper newspaper column.

Now, in 1947, asked if his handicap was still four [*sic*] Babe replied: "My handicap is twenty-one stone, and about seventeen, I should imagine." In mentioning his weight Babe had forgotten that in Blackpool he had stated that he was twenty-two stone when he arrived in England, but had since lost forty pound – which would make him making him a much slimmer nineteen stone. When asked of the food situation by a reporter from the *Evening News*,

Ida and Lucille looking pleased to meet local chocolate-maker Alf Ellsworth, or could it be they are just pleased with the boxes of chocolates he has given them?

Hardy revealed he was feeling much better for his weight loss. Laurel added, tactfully:

> I know it's tough to have such rationing after all that Britain has gone through, but people can still laugh, and it amazes us to hear their capacity for enjoyment. Many of them must have lost everything they had during the war and are starting from scratch again, but still they can laugh. It shows they have a lot of guts.

Of the near future, Laurel admitted that prospects of making a film were remote. The bookings for their world tour had piled up at such a rate that he didn't even know when they would be returning to America. The proposed visits were to Scandinavia, Belgium, France, and Switzerland. After this would come visits to South Africa and Australia. They would then be back in time to do *Babes in the Wood* for the Christmas season of 1948-49, at another of Delfont's venues, the Saville Theatre in London. As it turned out, the latter three places were never visited, and the pantomime was never played.

Eddie Campbell of the *Daily Record*, wrote of his personal feelings towards the two comedians:

> Stars of the cinema make frequent stage appearances these days. All too often the reception they get for their boosted 'personal appearances' springs less from appreciation than from an audience's charity. And what a relief to find two screen performers who are not less worth looking at on the stage, but more. Meeting Laurel & Hardy on Sunday and watching five thousand people milling and crushing round

Central Station for a glimpse of them, I felt that no stage artiste deserved such adulation. Watching them on stage, I had to agree that there was at least something to be said for it. For these two are master dispensers of the world's most precious commodity – laughter. They really are genuinely and truly funny. Behind the make-up you get a glimpse of two blokes genuinely embarrassed at the warmth of public approval.

The critic from the *Evening Times* was obviously fond of the Boys, but didn't go overboard:

> Every seat was occupied for the triumphant appearance of Laurel & Hardy. In their sketch, one realises that their jokes and dialogue are not so very funny at all – it's the actions that count. Papers are thrown in the air, shoulders are pushed, lapels brushed, faces made, and all the other known tricks of the comic pair are produced one after another. There is only one complaint – we could have done with a lot more of their happy clowning.

Archie Collins and Olga Varona, as artistes in the show, felt more cause to celebrate than did the newspaper critics:

> Never to this day, in any theatre in the world we have played, have we heard anything like the reception given to Laurel & Hardy on their entrance. We thought that the whole of Hampden Park [football crowd] had come to the Empire.

Considering the waves of euphoria which had greeted Laurel and Hardy – from the children by the rail side, the thousands at the station, and the packed audiences at the theatre – it is hard to comprehend how blasé the critics remained. Seeing as how the Glasgow Empire held the most dreaded reputation of *all* British theatres for giving the cold shoulder to comedians, especially non-Scottish comedians, one would have thought such an amazing success story deserved some critical acclaim. It was only the *Evening Citizen* which conveyed some of the hysteria of their stage appearance:

> No wonder Oliver Hardy blew most of his 'Thank you' kisses to the gallery at the Glasgow Empire last night. The whistles, yells, and cheers of welcome were loud enough to be heard at Charing Cross [London], and the audience just wouldn't let them go. Taken critically, the sketch is quite ordinary and some of the jokes are very familiar. But who wants to be critical with old friends like Laurel & Hardy?

Once again, the public's enthusiasm outshone that of the critics and the "NO SEATS AVAILABLE" sign was up for the entire fortnight. Robert Hewitt, of the *Evening Citizen*, added the following, personal, observations:

> If there's one thing I dislike it's snobbishness. And I'm sorry to say I've seen it shown by quite a few stars, some of whom refuse to mix with other artistes on the bill, and walk past stage crews as if they didn't exist. It is an attitude I have always deplored. Let me therefore tell you what a pleasure it is to meet Laurel & Hardy. Backstage I've found them to be probably the most unassuming, modest and friendliest top o' the bill stars who ever walked through the stage door. For them the stagehands would do anything. Every evening before they go on, the Hollywood pair wander around at the back of the stage chatting to the lads. As one stagehand says: 'They're just a couple of regular guys.'

On Tuesday, Sir Hector McNeil, the Lord Provost of Glasgow, invited the Boys to the Glasgow City Chambers. There he presented them both with a copy of C.A. Oakley's book, *The Second City*, in which Laurel is mentioned in the section which deals with Glasgow-born celebrities. This was meant as a tribute to Stan, but may well have turned out an embarrassment, seeing as how he was not born in Glasgow, nor even in Scotland for that matter.

Present also, and undisputedly Scottish, was legendary entertainer Harry Lauder – accompanied by his niece, Greta. Harry watched the Boys' show that evening, then went backstage to pay his respects. After spending an hour chatting, he invited them to his home, and left them, quite unnecessarily, with the advice, "Keep it clean!" (Their act, that is – not, his home!)

Of the stay in Glasgow, the undisputed highlight for Laurel was Thursday's visit to his beloved Metropole Theatre. Right from stepping into the foyer — where he was welcomed by the owner, Alec Frutin, and the manager, Peter Hart — Stan's eye started to roam over the decor, and he began a non-stop narration which lasted until he left. His running commentary took on a literal meaning, when he began to race through the building in his haste to re-acquaint himself with his boyhood haunt. No cornerstone was left unturned: "There used to be a wide pend* there, but these steps were always there, and the pay-box is still the same ... and the staircase is still the same ... and that's the office ... ," are some of the phrases he addressed to his, by now, breathless followers. [*"Pend" is a colloquial Scottish term for the arched entrance to a corridor, or staircase.]

METROPOLE
Stockwell Street
Glasgow
As in many cases, the theatre building is fronted by shops. To gauge the size of the theatre, look above the shops. The entrance is under the canopy. The building, on the corner, to the right is the Scotia pub.

In his father's former office, Laurel signs his "X" in the visitors book, watched over by owner Alec Frutin and manager Peter Hart.

This lucky lady recognised the face in the box-office, but was unaware he was playing out one of the roles he had had there forty years earlier.

In the office Stan recalled where the safe used to be, then sat down at the desk and reminisced about the times he had sat there as a boy whilst his dad was "out front." Leaving the office, he raced up the staircase to the gallery and, going into the pay-box, re-enacted his role as ticket boy. From there he went to the circle, and then wound his way backstage via the maze of passages in this near-century-old theatre. Having been in every dressing room, he walked out onto the stage, and recounted the story of the morning he had stood in that very spot and decided to become a comedian. On leaving the Metropole, one could see that Stan had been through a very emotional experience, and the crying face was not the pretend one seen on the screen.

This might well have also been the day when Mr. Laurel took Mrs. Laurel to one of his former Glasgow schools. The event was recollected by former pupil Irene Piazza:

> In the summer of 1947, our school held their annual sports competition, and we had an unexpected visit from one of our famous alumni – Mr. Stan Laurel and his wife. This was Queen's Park Secondary School, in Langside – a suburb of Glasgow.

I remember standing there in my regulation knickers, being amazed by the pair of them [The Laurels – not the knickers]. Stan was quiet and inconspicuous, but his wife was pure Hollywood. The whole school was disappointed that his visit was so short, and we had no time for an indoor assembly.

In the early-60s I wrote to him, recalling his visit to our high school. He immediately wrote back a four-page letter, with the information that he had not attended Queen's Park for very long, but he remembered playing hooky by climbing the same six-foot-high wrought-iron fence that I had also climbed.

On Friday both the Laurels and the Hardys were guests at a luncheon given by the 'Glasgow Stage and Screen Memorial Club,' at which Stan was reacquainted with Albert Pickard, the former manager of the Britannia Theatre, where Stan had made his debut as a boy comedian.

At the end of the dinner, all three hundred guests stood up and sang *Will Ye No' Come Back Again*, and this time both comedians were moved to tears. Babe jollied things up by sitting at the piano and leading everyone in a sing-song.

One has to wonder if Hardy is singing: "*You Are the Ideal of My Dreams*" — especially when you compare it to this still from *Beau Hunks*. [Pictured are the wives of the President and Vice President of the Cinema Club, Messrs. Breckenrigde and Tamplin].

Not previously having seen at close quarters the beautiful lakes, mountains, and greenery for which Scotland is famous, Stan and Babe, and their wives ensured seeing as much of it as they could this time around. As soon as the Saturday evening show at the Glasgow Empire finished, the Hardys were picked up and driven to the home of Sir Alex King, to stay the night. Meanwhile, the Laurels were receiving the same hospitality from Alec Frutin – the manager of the Metropole. This was done so that the two parties could make an early-morning start on Sunday, for what was to be a guided tour of 'the five Lochs' by Alec and Sir Alex.

Following their drive, the parties retired to the Inversnaid Hotel, on the North-Eastern shore of Loch Lomond. This beautiful hotel faces onto its own harbour and jetty, but is surrounded on the other three sides by sixty-five acres of wooded grounds. After the consumption of copious amounts of liquid refreshment, Hardy again treated the company to a sing-song at the piano before (so one unconfirmed report has it) the party slept the night there. Lucille and Ida were to say of the trip: "We'd looked forward to seeing Scotland, but it surpassed all our expectations."

On the Monday morning, 16 June, after making the forty-four mile journey south from Inversnaid to Glasgow (if indeed they did stay the night there), the Laurels and the Hardys drove on a further twenty-five miles south, to Strathaven, to take up Harry Lauder's invitation to visit him. At his beautiful residence, Lauder Ha' (House of Lauder), they found Sir Harry dressed in full Scottish regalia, whilst the visitors did their part by donning diced-Balmoral hats.

After a stroll through the grounds, the party retired inside for a typical
Scottish tea, for which Lauder charged them only 3/6d per head.

The three stage performers arming themselves, in case any
hecklers from the Glasgow Empire are hiding in the bushes.

Lauder making sure to kill any stinging insects, before they get a chance to fly under his kilt.

Stan and Babe were thrilled to be in Lauder's company, as every American artiste knew of him through his having played over twenty tours in America. Laurel's conversation was of the Glasgow Metropole, which both had played in their earliest days (Lauder's being pre-1899, when it was known as the Scotia Music Hall). Laurel and Lauder's conversation then moved on to the Karno productions Lauder had seen, and the ones Laurel had performed in, between 1909 and 1914.

Hardy could not resist requesting Lauder to sing the songs which had made him famous during the thirty-plus years he had been one of the greatest box-office attractions around, on both sides of the Atlantic – a performance to which Lauder readily acceded and Stan and Babe were only too happy to join in. The Boys must have later reflected how privileged they had been, as 1947 marked Lauder's last official performance, in Glasgow.

Over at the Glasgow Empire, that very evening, Laurel was puzzled when MacKenzie Reid, one of the support acts, walked on stage playing his accordion at the end of *The Driver's Licence* sketch. It was only when Stan recognised the tune *Happy Birthday* that he realised what was going on. The full company then came on stage and, with the audience joining in, wished Stan a "Happy 57th Birthday."

On the Tuesday night, it was the audience who were given the surprise, when Laurel and Hardy came on stage wearing kilts, sporrans, and tartan stockings. In an interview given during the 1932 visit to Glasgow, Stan had revealed that, as a boy, he had sometimes gone to his Glasgow school wearing a kilt, and had learned the sword dance. So wearing a kilt on stage was an attempt by Stan to show he had not forgotten his roots, and for both he and Hardy to show how much they loved Scotland, and respected Scottish tradition. The Scottish audiences loved them in return, as they had done when the Boys wore kilts in their film *Bonnie Scotland,* a film (perhaps not so co-incidentally) being shown that week at one of the local cinemas. Thankfully, no-one asked Laurel to demonstrate the sword-dance.

On the final Saturday of their stay, the two comedians opened the 'Eastwood Gymkhana' on Lord & Lady Weir's estate, at Giffnock. Wearing their now familiar diced-Balmorals, the Boys ascended a specially erected dais and addressed the crowd over the P.A. system. It was as late as 2010 before footage of Laurel and Hardy's walk-on was rediscovered. Sad to say the footage is silent, but a contemporary newspaper report does give us an idea of the flavour of Stan and Ollie's speech:

'What are we here for?' asked Stan.

'We are here to open the gymkhana,' replied Ollie.

'How can I open it? I haven't got any openers.

Lady Weir clapping in appreciation of Laurel and Hardy's speech, while Lord Weir bows out.

Having opened the gymkhana, the two stars were not able to remain and watch many of the events as they had to rush away to get to the 4 o'clock matinee at the Glasgow Empire. I can think of no other stars, past or present who, having three shows to do in one day, would put themselves out to make an unpaid guest appearance. But to Stan Laurel and Oliver Hardy this was par for the course in giving back to the people, what the people gave to them, and similar gestures were frequent.

The following day the fortnight came all too rapidly to a close – and so, having gasped with awe at the beautiful Scottish scenery, and cried at the sentiment expressed by the Scots, and with the sounds of *Will Ye No' Come Back Again* forever etched in their memories, the "McLaurels and the McHardys" bid a sad farewell to the city and the people of Glasgow.

o-o-0-o-o

Chapter 15

HOLIDAYS ARE JOLLIDAYS

The Butlins Holiday Camp at Skegness (opened in 1936) was the first of many similar camps built and run by South Africa-born entrepreneur Billy Butlin. Amongst the wooden chalets and steel-and-plaster entertainment venues it housed its own theatre, where a Variety show, with "Star Attraction," played twice-nightly. One of Butlins' advertising slogans was "Butlins Jollidays." Well now it was to become a "Stan and Olliday" as Laurel and Hardy were about to play six nights there, commencing Monday 23 June 1947.

On their way through from Glasgow to Skegness, on the Sunday, the celebrities stopped off at Grantham to change trains. A small crowd of locals had gathered to welcome them, and were surprised to find the two film stars wearing the kilts and complementary Scottish regalia they had acquired in Glasgow.

It was lucky for Stan's sister Olga and husband Bill that their pub was only four miles away, and so they were able to meet up at Grantham station. After some refreshment at the Red Lion Hotel, in Grantham, the now six-strong party headed for the Butlins Skegness Holiday Camp, next to Ingoldmells, on the Lincolnshire coast.

Of one incident at the Butlins Camp, Olga later told her son, Huntley Jefferson Woods:

> When we arrived, the holidaymakers were outside - shouting for Laurel & Hardy to come out of their accommodation on to the balcony. Mr. Hardy declined as he said he was too tired, and so I volunteered to accompany Stan. But Stan insisted that Mr. Hardy come with him, saying: "When the fans are no longer there, that's when we're finished," so Hardy reluctantly went with him onto the balcony.

Olga had made Stan a birthday cake. It was a week late, but neither comedian was complaining. [Note the Butlins plate – inset.]

This wasn't the first time, or the last, that Hardy railed about the fans' demands and, each time, Stan would pitch the same spiel.

Unlike most of the other entertainment venues on the camp, the Butlin Theatre, at the south end of the camp, was a brick-built building. Its pedigree was that it had featured in the Empire Exhibition, hosted by Glasgow in 1938 — was dismantled, and then reconstructed brick-by-brick at its present location. With a capacity of eighteen hundred, and with twelve shows to be staged, the theatre was going to take some filling. But as holiday camp residents, and outsiders alike, were able to attend, the two Hollywood comedians played to full houses at every show:

The Butlin Theatre – facade, stage, and auditorium

Of Laurel & Hardy's opening-night show, the critic for the *Skegness Standard* enthused:

Those two great comedians, Stan Laurel and Oliver Hardy, who have clowned their way through countless films, received a tremendous welcome when they made their first appearance at the Butlin Theatre on Monday.

The cheering and applause started, in fact, even before the two actually appeared, for it commenced when Alec Lerner and the Theatre Orchestra played the first bars of the signature tune which prefaces all the Laurel and Hardy films. And, as the curtains parted to reveal two inimitable figures, the cheering changed to laughter, which continued almost uninterrupted throughout their side-shaking act.

Dressed in the clothes known to millions of cinema goers, the diminutive, rather pathetic Laurel, and the gargantuan, dignified Hardy, assisted by Harry Moreny, ran the gamut of expressions which made their names–and faces–two of the best known in the world to-day.

The sketch, in which Hardy, aided and abetted by Laurel, tries to renew his driving licence, is one of the funniest turns with which the two have yet raised a theatre or cinema roof. The pair manage to get into–and out of–every conceivable tangle and, at the end, the policeman on duty in the licencing office has been driven to the verge of madness, whilst the audience is even nearer to hysteria.

Butlin Theatre stage crew and other acts on the show.
On Harry Moreny's left is Alec Lerner MD.

Ron Kerr, stage electrician at the *Gaiety*, revealed in later years what the audience didn't see:

Each night, just before Laurel & Hardy's sketch was due to start, Mrs. Laurel would leave the dressing room, and stand in the wings. Next to her she would place a silver tray on which was a bottle of whisky and a glass. Whenever Stan got the chance, he would pop off into the wings and have a quick shot.

[Mmm! Not sure about that. But it does explain why he never got the driving licence].

The entertainment programme on a holiday camp runs from 10am till midnight, seven days a week, with a non-stop barrage of outdoor games and sporting tournaments; plus numerous indoor games and competitions – complementing the attractions of the extensive entertainment facilities, ballrooms, bars, and sports venues. Laurel and Hardy, though, were booked solely for their show, and were quite at liberty to sneak into and out of the theatre each evening, to avoid contact with the holidaymakers. But not our Boys – no hiding for them. They relished mixing with the public, and took every opportunity to show up on camp to participate in activities.

On Monday afternoon, in the Empress Ballroom, both comedians judged the 'Holiday Lovelies' competition; and, whilst the Boys were keeping their eyes on the girls, Lucille and Ida were keeping their eyes on the Boys, by making up the rest of the judging panel.

There was less beauty to behold in the competition which followed, namely the 'Knobbly Knees' competition – in which men, with their trousers legs rolled up, were subjected to a series of humiliating exercises.

EMPRESS
BALLROOM
Top Left:
The three winners of
the Holiday Lovelies.
Top Right.
Winner of the
Knobbly Knees.
Left
Neville O'Brien,
Entertainment Manager,
assisting the judges.

On Tuesday afternoon the Laurel and Hardy Family were to be found on the Gloucester Green, judging different competitions for boys, girls, and toddlers. Note the British flag has now been supplemented by the American one. [The people behind are standing in a boxing ring.]

At other times, the Hollywood legends were photographed participating in other activities, such as roller skating, and riding around on one of the Butlins' fun-bikes.

In one appearance, Stan and Babe were called upon to show more of an intellectual aptitude when Billy Butlin himself invited them to participate in an edition of *The Brains Trust*. The Boys had played this game before with Billy Butlin (back in February, at a Water Rats' meeting), but not with such a distinguished panel of "brains."

The Brain's Trust panel:
Clay Keyes, Hardy, Professor Joad, Laurel, Billy Butlin, Commander Campbell

Upon leaving Skegness, the following Sunday, Stan and Babe firstly had Olga and Bill dropped off at the Plough Inn. However, as they had a little time to spare, they stayed on to spend some time with Stan's dad. It was late afternoon, therefore, when the Laurels and the Hardys caught the train from Grantham, to alight at Edinburgh's Waverley Bridge Station shortly after 8pm.

The doors to the station were locked, to keep out the fans, and only the official reception party had been allowed onto the platform. The Laurels were dressed for the occasion, with Stan again looking dapper in his diced-Balmoral hat, and Ida sporting a Glengarry bonnet.

Reception Committee at Edinburgh Waverly Station – Sunday 29 June.
Jimmy Whitelaw, Hardy, James Hill (Manager of the Empire Theatre), Lucille Hardy,
Mrs. Hill, Laurel, Ida Laurel.

Knowing what to expect, and seeing no point in avoiding the confrontation, Hardy said impatiently: "What are we waiting for? – Let's get going." With that, a squad of twelve policemen ringed the party and shepherded them into the street. The ensuing scene resembled a department store at the opening of the January sales. Thousands of people rushed forward, jostling for leader position. Those who reached the target first, were easily able to slip under the linked arms of the now 40-strong police cordon, and come face to face with their idols. With these restrictions it took several minutes for the foursome to travel the few yards from the station doorway to the awaiting 4-car convoy at the Waverley Bridge exit.

The sanctuary of the cars was limited, for they now had to manoeuvre them through the ten thousand people congregated on the bridge. The idea had been for the onlookers to line up on the pavement, with the children nearest to the roadside, and wave to the celebrities as they went by. Less-caring adults, though, removed the barriers and entered the roadway – thus not only impeding the cars' progress, but also totally obscuring the view of the stars. Taking a firm hand, the police who were walking alongside the motorcade shoved the offenders back towards the pavement. This had the disastrous effect of forcing the people in the roadside onto the children who were lining the pavement. Many of the children were bowled over, and the crowd found themselves playing a dangerous game of hopscotch to avoid stepping on them. Fortunately, no hospital cases were recorded, but what should have been the happy sight of the world's two funniest men turned, for some of the children, into a tearful encounter – having seen nothing.

Ten minutes later the car pulled up outside the Caledonian Hotel, in Princes Street, where fans were standing five deep; and it again took some strong-arm action from the police to stop them breaking through the cordon. Once safely inside the hotel, the Laurels and the Hardys retired to the safety of their hotel rooms. Following an announcement that they would not be making an appearance, the fans gradually began to disperse, and fifteen minutes later Princes Street returned to normality.

But the arrival was just the beginning of the fans' determination to set eyes on the Hollywood screen stars. The following night, an huge gathering awaited them outside the Empire Theatre. Inside, the show was summed up by the *Evening News* as follows.

> The moment the orchestra struck up their signature tune and Laurel & Hardy strode on to the stage, each arrayed in a kilt of startling hue, they were welcomed by a gust of laughter from the packed-audience. It was a fine tribute to two great comedians, and for the next half hour they fanned this favourable breeze into a veritable gale of merriment by an exhibition of supreme artistry. The very contrast in styles is sufficient to make an audience laugh without a word being spoken. And when they speak and clown together the appeal is irresistible. It was pantomime at its best, for which they earned and received a great ovation.

On Tuesday the Laurel and Hardy family were more than happy to attend a Luncheon, hosted by the Cinematograph Exhibitors Association, at the North British Station Hotel, a short drive along Princes Street. Any mention of food and drink, and Stan and Babe would always be there. And it was second-time mention of food and drink, which drove them to the museum in Chambers Street, to re-stock their ration vouchers.

Another visit was to the "Enterprise Scotland Exhibition" at the Royal Scottish Museum, in Dryden Street. There the manager, Mr. Donaldson [pictured behind Laurel], found himself being entertained by two Scottish pipers who looked suspiciously like Laurel and Hardy. With six thousand props to choose from, it was a certainty that the comedy couple would find something amusing to play with.

Ida Laurel was a professional singer, with a trained ear.
Unfortunately, Stan and Babe played the bagpipes like trained seals.

During his stay in Edinburgh, Hardy tried hard to trace the Scottish part of his ancestry. His grandmother, on his mother's side, was Irish; but his grandfather, Thomas Edward Norvell (from whom he took his middle name) was Scottish; and Hardy was convinced he had been a graduate of Edinburgh University in the 1840s.

When asked, by a reporter, about the name "Norvell," Hardy replied:

> I quote the lines in 'Douglas': "My name is Norval [sic], on the Grampian Hills my father feeds his flocks," and everyone says the Grampian Hills are not in Scotland. But they are. I have dozens of maps.

Even now Hardy's ancestry is hazy, so we will do what he did – move on, little the wiser.

After yet another sell-out week, the Boys travelled down the North-East coast to the fishing port of Hull, on the River Humber. Considering the distance, and the number in their party, five, they unwisely chose to go by car, and ended up paying the price. At Woodmansey, a little village less than three miles north of Hull, they broke down and had to seek assistance at the local pub, the Dixon's Arms. This story only came to light some four decades later, when local Laurel & Hardy fan and researcher Ken Owst obtained the account from one of the pub residents.

You may not consider a car breaking down newsworthy, but at least it would have been a mention that the world's

DIXONS ARMS — Landlady Mrs. Porter

greatest funnymen were in town, whereas, out of four local papers, only the *Hull Daily Mail* gave any coverage whatsoever, and that was the obligatory Monday night review. Even then, it was the tiniest of entries:

> Few film stars will achieve such success with a personal appearance as Laurel & Hardy at the New Theatre this week. They are everything their public hoped for, natural buffoons and as lovable as ever. Children shrieked and adults roared, yet it wasn't the slick wisecrack, just The Thin One and The Fat One happily awkward. The twiddle of a finger from Oliver, the chalky smile of Stan in his endearing simplicity and their battered bowlers were enough. After 20 minutes, which included a typical sketch, and a song from each, they left to terrific applause.

On Wednesday, the Laurels and Hardys attended a luncheon given by the local cinema managers, at the Royal Station Hotel, but this too did not contribute to advertising the presence of the two Hollywood stars in Hull, seeing as how it was a private affair, behind closed doors.

Never in a million years could the cinema managers of Hull and District ever have imagined that they would get to sit down with the two men behind the comedy legends whose films they had been showing for the last two decades.

They say "No news, is good news," but that wasn't true of the stay in Hull, as this comment Stan wrote to show business friend Lorraine and his assistant reveals:

```
Dear Lawrie and Jeanette,
Note you wrote from Hull. We played the New Theatre there
in '47. Even tho' we did good Bus. was glad to get out,
being just after the war. The place was really a mess.
```

[AJM: The "mess" was not in reference to the theatre, but to Hull in general. Being a major shipping port, it had suffered devastation from eighty-two German bombing raids. The worst of these occurred in 1941, but there was one as late as March 1945.]

Although Laurel did not enjoy Hull, one would have to believe that the people of Hull enjoyed having these two mega-stars bringing such laughter and happy memories to enlighten the terrible tragedies they had recently suffered, and hopefully giving them re-newed motivation to get on with the big clean-up and regeneration which Hull so badly needed.

o-o-0-o-o

Chapter 16

NORTH COMES SOUTH

Any semblance of a pattern in the travel plans of the tour was well and truly broken when, from Hull, the company had a journey of over two hundred miles to Bristol, in the South West of England. Coming in to Bristol by train, Hardy remarked how magnificent the English countryside was, and how proud it made him feel to be of British heritage. Tragically, Bristol, like Hull, had been badly bombed during the war, because of the importance of the docks as a major supply post, and several buildings of note had been damaged or destroyed.

The people of Bristol knew exactly when to expect Laurel and Hardy as the *Evening World* had announced: "Fans please note: Stan & Ollie arrive at Temple Mead Station from York, at 6:26 on Sunday evening." Consequently, they were met by an estimated one thousand people, whom Stan described as being, "good humoured, but a bit boisterous."

This number may seem rather small after some of the crowds the Boys had encountered, but one thousand people can do an awful lot of damage to two men. In fact, one person can do an awful lot of damage, as was proved when Hardy got a very painful dig in the back from an umbrella. The incident was passed off with good humour at the time; but, once inside the hotel, Babe began to feel the effects. Apparently, the metal ferrule on the brolly had poked him in the exact spot where, just a few weeks before leaving the US, he had had an operation in which two ribs had had to be removed. After minor treatment from a doctor and a hot bath at the Royal Hotel, he felt a little better. This was the second occasion on which Hardy had become unwell from post-op symptoms. In Glasgow, a Red Cross nurse had attended to him backstage, until a doctor arrived and treated him for a high temperature.

At this stage of the tour the farcical claim about Laurel and Hardy making a film had now been dropped. The reason for this was given as: "due to weather uncertainty and Continental commitments." This leaves one wondering if a film crew, plus producer, actors, costumes, millionaire-backer, and a finished film script, would have suddenly materialised if the sun had chosen to shine.

Both Babe and Stan had made a note to go on a sight-seeing trip of the surrounding countryside, plus to visit some of Bristol's historic buildings; but they knew from previous experience that they wouldn't get ten yards if they attempted a walkabout. Hardy, especially, couldn't go anywhere without being recognised. He was so big, and stood out so much in a crowd; he simply had nowhere to hide; and so, many times, ended up having to stay in the hotel — or stick to touring by car. Laurel was luckier in that, if he wasn't with Hardy, he could sometimes escape notice. Taking advantage of this, on Monday morning Laurel "changed partners" and ventured out with Archie Collins to find a theatre he had appeared at in the early 1900s. With collar pulled up, and hat pulled down, Stan wound his way unerringly to where he remembered it to be. Although his memory was faithful to him, the years weren't — for the theatre (formerly the Broadweir Hall) was now used as an engineering workshop.

Stan still wanted to look around but, in doing so, was spotted. Within five minutes the whole of the labour force had turned out, and were fussing around him as if he were an old mate. Invited inside, he was shown over the premises and, after much hand-shaking, finally allowed to leave; but not before he had extracted promises from all those present that they would attend the show.

That evening, John Coe of the *Evening Post* said of the opening night at the Bristol Hippodrome:

Come the sketch in which Mr. Hardy wants to obtain a driving licence. How do they handle it? By provoking the traffic officer into a paroxysm of rage with their misunderstandings of his simple purpose and intent. Mr. Hardy puts on the bold front, while Mr. Laurel meekly sits back and blows up a balloon, plays with a fingerstall, oblivious of the situation which is about to explode.

Their technique is of course, superb. The timing to the split second of the hilarious gag is as good as the economy of their script and patter. And the sketch builds up into a wildly funny climax which is in the best slapstick tradition.

Laurel had obviously been adding new bits of business, as the bit where he blows up a balloon is not to be found in any known copies of the sketch, nor in previous reviews. John Bennett of the *Evening World* was also very complimentary of the improved sketch:

Laurel & Hardy's perky signature tune was the signal for a full minute's applause. It was three minutes before Ollie spoke his first words: those minutes were packed with miming fun that convulsed the huge audience. If, as they say, it cost £1000 to bring them to Bristol for a week, Bristol is having its money's worth ... with even some elephantine dancing from Ollie and some 'Sinatra-like' crooning from Stan, to the end of the show.

But to gather what the atmosphere was like to a child, we have the benefit of an account from D.C. Marshall, who was ten at the time:

By the time the interval arrived I was becoming a little worried. "When are we going to see them Gran?" "Soon," came the reply. I probably asked the question a hundred times. At last something seemed to be happening. There was a distinct air of anticipation sweeping through the theatre. I sensed that everyone else felt the same as I did: "Never mind all these jugglers and dancers – let's get on with what we've all come to see." At last the lights dimmed, the orchestra struck up with that familiar tune "The Dance of the Cuckoos," and the curtain began to rise. We were confronted with the scene of a police officer seated behind a desk, idly shuffling through his paperwork. "But where were they?" I thought. Perhaps they weren't going to be here after all. But my fears did not last long.

A loud knock on the door, stage left, made everyone's head turn in that direction. The policeman called: "Come in," and the door was thrown open by Oliver [followed by Stan]. He started to speak his first line, but was drowned out by the thunderous applause from the audience. The whole building came alive. Never have I heard such applause in my life. It seemed to go on for ages before it died down enough for Ollie to continue.

Seeing them standing there, Ollie in front and Stan, peering with a bemused expression, beside him, I remember two thoughts going through my mind. Firstly: "Isn't Oliver huge." I knew from their films that he was a big man, but nothing had prepared me for this. And secondly: how much older they appeared, compared to their film images. But this in no way prevented me from enjoying the wonderful experience of being seated only yards away from these fun-loving characters, and splitting my sides with laughter at the acts of mayhem they rained down on the poor police officer.

They were my idols then, as seen through the eyes of a ten year-old boy, and with the passing years I have come to love and admire them all the more.

On Thursday, both Laurel **and** Hardy, plus their wives, were driven from Bristol to Weston-super-Mare, twenty-two miles away. On arrival at the outdoor swimming stadium they were greeted by a very large and enthusiastic crowd. A tussle ensued, during which the police cordon failed to keep the fans away from their car. Eventually, the VIPs were led through three huge queues of people, to be officially welcomed at the entrance by the Mayor & Mayoress – Alderman G.E. Bosley and his lady wife. Inside the pool area a further six thousand gave them a rousing welcome. [**FILM**]

Ollie keeping Stan at bay, to get an unimpeded close-up view
of the lovely ladies in the Modern Venus competition.

Babe's Babes

After the foursome had judged the "Modern Venus" beauty competition, Lucille and Ida were presented with bouquets by the Mayoress; and then, thanks to a number of fans who had generously donated sweets coupons, Stan and Babe received a 1lb. box of chocolates. If this weren't enough, an anonymous donor, who had heard of Hardy's weight loss, tried to replace it all in one go by having the Mayor present him with a 4lb. juicy steak. Having used up Glasgow's supply of clothing coupons to purchase kilts, it would seem that Laurel and Hardy had now exhausted Weston-super-Mare's supply of food coupons.

In the film *Any Old Port*, Hardy requests that his steak be "smothered in onions." Laurel's preference would seem to be tomato ketchup, if this letter from a fan is anything to go by:

> Dear Mr. Hoggett,
>
> The bottles of Tomato Ketchup which you so kindly sent us have been safely received, and both Mr. Hardy and myself very much appreciate your kindness.
>
> We have already sampled it, and find it most excellent and palatable. I will most certainly let you know if at any time we run short, and will take advantage of your kind offer.

Never has the saying, "The gifts that keep on giving" been more aptly quoted.

On the Friday there was a Speedway meeting at the local Knowle Stadium — with the Bristol Motorcycle team competing against one from Wigan. At the last minute, the stadium manger, Reg Witcomb, plucked up the courage to invite Laurel and Hardy to attend, and to officiate at the *Bathing Beauty* competition being staged between races. The meeting was to commence at 7:30 p.m. Meanwhile, over at the *Hippodrome*, Laurel and Hardy had two shows to do, one starting at 6:15 and one at 8:25pm. Even though there was little to be gained for future publicity (as they had only the Saturday shows to do before leaving Bristol); coupled with the pressure of fitting in the speedway appearance between shows – Stan and Babe readily agreed.

As this was a flying visit, there was no press present. Luckily for us, the stadium photographer was on hand to take some snaps, three of which we are privileged to present here:

The manager, Reg Witcomb, welcoming the two comedy giants to the Knowle Stadium.

Upon being shown to the Royal Box, the visiting VIPs decide they'd rather stand.

Photographs by Stan Vickers — courtesy of Colin Greenwell.

In conversation with Laurel in the early part of the week, Archie had described the beautiful cottage he and Olga were renting whilst in Bristol. Stan liked what he heard and suggested that Archie invite the Laurel and Hardy family over. A few days later the invite was taken up, and the family was driven to the Marlborough Hill district and dropped off at the gate of Kozy Kot Cottage – a beautiful two-storey building, with a lovely view over the Bristol Channel.

During afternoon tea, Stan returned the invitation for Archie and Olga to have tea with the Laurels and the Hardys at the Royal Hotel. On subsequent viewing of the starch and starkness of the hotel, Archie said: "If this is what you get for being top of the bill, I'm glad we're only a support act." This was taken in the spirit in which it was meant, and all looked back with fond memories of Bristol, and especially Kozy Kot Cottage.

OXFORD STREET, MANCHESTER.

After the crowd scenes during Stan and Babe's 1932 visit to Manchester, and the hysteria they had been experiencing on this tour, one would have thought the Manchester press might have made something of Laurel and Hardy's two-week run at the Palace Theatre. Amazingly the *Evening Chronicle* offered only a critique, and even that suffered from a severe case of word deficiency:

Beyond applying unavailingly for a driving licence, Laurel & Hardy do nothing in particular. But they do it so well that a co-operative audience end by being surprised at the passage of time and asking for more. The screen is the famous pair's best medium, but it is a pleasure to see at close quarters Stan Laurel back in the city where he first joined Karno's show to understudy Chaplin. Apprehensive, self-deprecatory, able to hold an audience by the movement of a finger, he is, in his own way, a consummate actor.

The *Evening News* also went in for paper rationing:

Laurel & Hardy – like Marks & Spencers and fish and chips - are a natural pair. Straight from stage to screen* they bring the familiar trappings of the elfish and elephantine buffoonery. When not tormenting each other, they combine forces to torment a hapless police officer. Last night's packed audience enjoyed every minute.

[*Shouldn't that read: "from screen to stage"?]

Fortunately, one particular member of that audience found the experience totally unforgettable and, over forty years later, was able to recall his feelings for inclusion here. Then he was a young boy, but during the 'sixties he became a household name himself and star of countless radio and TV series – ace impressionist, Peter Goodwright:

I remember the almost tangible murmur of anticipatory whispers which filled the auditorium as the first few notes of the Cuckoo Song were played. They walked onto the stage and the suppressed excitement and pleasure at their appearance erupted into a never-to-be-forgotten roar of welcome. The applause was deafening as the audience rose to its feet to greet the two men. They stood centre-stage – Ollie twiddling his tie, and Stan removing his hat and scratching his head.

In the 'evening' of their career in America – having been ousted out of position by Abbott & Costello – here they were being afforded the honours usually only conferred on heroes. Still the ovation continued and so great was it, that it became very emotional to realise what high esteem these two comedians commanded. In retrospect, I think the audience were saying: 'Thank you for making us laugh during the dark days of the war. And thank you for coming to England to see us. And thank you for being Laurel & Hardy.' Whatever it was, the approbation afforded to these two men – containing as it did, a mixture of love; admiration; delight; and laughter – was one I had never experienced before – nor heard of since.

Eventually the audience subsided into their seats, with men and women alike, wiping away tears of emotion. During the sketch, laughter and applause rang constantly around the theatre, and at the end of the show I remember feeling very privileged to have been there to see these two gentlemen perform

Alma McKay ran theatrical digs in Longsight (a suburb of Manchester), and was looking after some of the support acts in the show. Apparently Stan and Babe weren't too happy with the food at the Grand Hotel, and wangled an invite over to Alma's, at Astra House. Although she too was feeling the pinch, she treated them to cakes and sandwiches, after which they were quite happy to stay on a while, merrily chatting. Mrs. McKay, however, wasn't very happy as, when they left, she voiced the opinion that Laurel & Hardy were typical of show business stars in that they never offered to pay, but just thought that their presence was payment enough.

MIDLAND HOTEL MANCHESTER

The food situation at the Grand probably also prompted the following amusing incident: One evening when Hardy fancied some "good old fish & chips," Laurel decided to have tripe & onions – a traditional Lancashire dish he hadn't had for years. Popping out of the theatre to a local cafe, Stan gave the order to the girl and waited at the counter. On bringing out the order, the girl chanced to give him a second glance, and with dawning recognition said, "Oh no!" to which Stan said, "Oh yes!" – and she promptly dropped the lot on the floor.

On the Sunday between the two-week engagement, Stan took advantage of not having to pack up and move on, and attended a long-awaited family reunion with a party of close relatives – most of whom were living in close proximity to each other in Yorkshire. Stan's Uncle John (Shaw) and Aunty Nant from Leeds Road, Woodkirk, had spent four days with Stan during Laurel and Hardy's recent appearances in Blackpool; but now joining them at this Manchester meeting were Stan's cousin Jack, cousin Mary (Jennings) of East Street, Batley; cousin Nellie (Beaumont) of Newsome Street, Dewsbury; and cousin Charlie (Shaw) of Mount Pleasant, Batley; plus their spouses and children. John Shaw reported:

> We all had a great time together. Stan has a serious outlook on life – he couldn't have got where he is if he hadn't. He knows show business inside out, but we don't talk shop with him.

Nancy Wardell, daughter of Laurel's cousin Mary Jennings, who had first met her famous uncle during his engagement in Morecambe, further revealed of the most-recent meeting.

> Stan's cousin Jack met Stan & Ida at the Dewsbury Empire and took them back to his home. After an early lunch they went on to cousin Nellie's house in Newsome Street, Dewsbury, where his cousin Mary (my mother) and the rest of the family welcomed him. He was totally at ease and fell in with all the family's fun-and-games. It was hard to realise he was so famous. Sadly the time passed all too quickly, and though at the time everyone promised to have another get-together, it never happened.

Dates were still being added to Laurel and Hardy's tour without the luxury of being able to choose the venues in geographical order. From Manchester in the North West, the touring company had to make yet another two-hundred-mile-plus journey, to the South Coast, for their next engagement — Southsea, near Portsmouth. The press was again in a coma, and reported nothing whatsoever of the celebrities' stay there. Nevertheless, the public were well aware, and the box office at the *Kings Theatre* did great business.

A rather touching event happened that week which modesty, on behalf of the participants, forbade the story being told publicly. Olga Varona related the circumstances of her husband Archie's chance meeting as follows:

> Laurel and Hardy's driver for that week asked Archie if he knew his brother, 'Hector St. Clair,' who was in show business. It turned out that Archie had known him very well, right up to the time of his death. The driver then asked Archie if he wouldn't mind visiting his sister, who lived near the theatre but was bed-ridden. Archie gladly obliged, and entertained the lady with tales of her late- brother, and some of his songs. This made her very happy, but later she was even happier when having been told of her plight, Laurel, Hardy, and Harry Moreny paid her a visit.

The bad weather which had plagued the company earlier on, was now well behind them, and they enjoyed another week of glorious sunshine, during which Stan took a look over *HMS Dolphin*, a dry naval base, in Gosport, where he was *forced* to sample some of the King's rum.

You might think those billy-cans are just for getting the rum out of the barrel, but then no-one is looking around for wine glasses to drink it from.

Courtesy of
Lt. Commander Richard
Swift (pictured)

On Sunday morning, the touring party took a pleasant drive through the New Forest, on their way through to Boscombe, near Bournemouth, for their next engagement. The press made nothing of their stay, before, during, or after – except for the compulsory first-night review:

> Those first class slapstick comedians, Laurel & Hardy, had the large audience at the Boscombe Hippodrome rocking with laughter from the time they made their appearance until their exit. For the majority of people it was the first time they had seen those popular screen comedians in person, and the event was regarded with some importance by both young and old. For nearly half an hour Stan and Oliver delighted the audience with their simple but cleverly timed actions.

> (*Bournemouth Daily Echo*)

HIPPODROME
An F.J.B. Theatre
BOSCOMBE
Manager & Licensee: J. LONSDALE
6.35
Twice Nightly
MONDAY, AUGUST 11th
Box Office Open Daily 10 to 9.0
8.45
BERNARD DELFONT presents
PERSONAL APPEARANCE OF
HOLLYWOOD'S GREATEST COMEDY COUPLE
STAN
OLIVER
LAUREL
AND
HARDY
Assisted by
HARRY MORENY
in "GETTING A DRIVING LICENCE"
OLGA VARONA
AUSTRALIA'S QUEEN OF THE AIR
READING & GRANTLY
FUN ON A TRAMPOLINE
Scotland's B.B.C. Ace Accordionists
MACKENZIE
REID
And DOROTHY
SLIM
KOMEDY KAPERS
RHYDER
THE SPARK AND HIS FLAME
LEN
CLIFFORD
and FREDA
THE
Dancing to Delight
THREE REDHEADS
IVOR E. KEYS
Assisted by BETTY ROSS
KEYBOARD COMEDY

The Boys spent most of the week in the *Chine Hotel* – owned by Fred Butterworth, who also owned the *Boscombe Hippodrome*.

[Butterworth proved to be a good contact for, on the 1953-54 tour, Laurel and Hardy were to play a further six of his theatres.]

Gerald Warr J.P. visited the hotel that week and recalled:

Laurel and Hardy seemed to enjoy their own company within the hotel where they kept themselves privately, but separately. I met them both, though not together, and throughout the talks they were most cordial and entertaining.

I attended one of their shows, but was a little disappointed, as the stage did not reflect their film performances. The best part was some very memorable singing and some dance steps. The reception given them was very warm, as this was considered a tremendous booking. The audience came from Dorset as well as the greater part of Hampshire, and the theatre was sold out at nearly all performances.

Babe with baby Butterworth

Remaining on stage after their sketch on the Monday night, Stan and Ollie had the pleasure of crowning seventeen-year-old Pauline Ashdown as "Carnival Queen." Stan rushed up to Pauline with a hammer, but Ollie got there just in time. Said Stan, "Well, they told me to crown her."

The carnival itself was held mid-week in King's Park, where fifty thousand spectators turned out. Laurel and Hardy stayed indoors. They might have acted daft, but they weren't stupid!

o-o-0-o-o

Chapter 17

DOUBLE TROUBLE

Having had two weeks of sunshine and sea air it was to be three in a row when, after travelling along the 'sole and heel' of England, the show members booked into the Kent holiday resort of Margate. On arrival at the St. Georges Hotel, in Cliftonville, Babe presented his party's ration cards to a surprised young lady called Dorothea Neal. Each evening from behind the reception desk, Dorothea would observe the two comedians as they waited in the foyer for their car. Stan struck her as being morose, whereas Babe was always very outgoing and pleasant. What she was probably witnessing in Stan was the nerves which most comedians experience before a show, wherein they totally withdraw and notice little of what is going on around them. Babe's nerves however, didn't show themselves in the same way. He never classed himself as a comedian, but saw himself only as acting as a foil to Stan. That he was totally wrong in his estimation, is a sign of the man's immeasurable modesty. "After the show, Laurel would be in a more relaxed mood, and would stay up for a 'nightcap' with the others," revealed Dorothy.

On the Monday evening, Bill Evans, reporter for the *East Kent Times* met the Boys backstage between houses:

> Laurel & Hardy stepped onto the stage at the *Winter Gardens*, and received a great ovation. But what are these two characters like off stage? Very simple and philosophical, and great in the tradition of their calling. It is not often Americans find our weather as hot as of late, and Oliver Hardy, mopping his brow, was in his shirt sleeves. 'It's been 93 [34C] where I've just come from', he said, 'and it seems hotter than California's 105 degrees [40.6C]. It's a different kind of heat'. Oliver used to be a first-rate golfer with a handsome handicap though he has not played for four years.

John Eddols, resident drummer at the Winter Gardens, remembers having to make sound effects during Laurel and Hardy's sketch. One particular piece of business required a loud cymbal crash, and one night, as the drumstick hit the cymbal, the head broke off and flew across the stage. Stan observed it, picked it up, leant over the edge of the orchestra pit, and with considerable aplomb said to John, "Is this what you're looking for?" This may not seem funny in writing, but the audience, who were witness to the way in which Stan brought magic to such a simple act, dissolved into laughter.

For one little girl, the thrill of meeting the two great stars was still fresh in her mind some forty-plus years later when she wrote:

> I and my mother were enjoying a week's holiday at Margate. Money was tight, but we managed to see the show and I was determined to get their autographs. The next day I waited with my book at the stage door, but was sent away by the stage door keeper. I crept near enough to the door to hear the applause which signalled the end of the performance, and then took up a position at the door.
>
> Ollie was first to come down the stairs. He saw me – turned and said: "Stanley, I do believe there's a little lady here, just waiting to see us." Stan scratched his head and, with his famous wide grin, replied: Is there, Ollie? That's wonderful." And indeed it was – for me.
>
> They invited me into their dressing room, and put their famous bowlers on my head and, whilst signing my book, told me all about filming in Hollywood. I was with them for something like twenty minutes; thoroughly entranced and totally forgetting my, by now, frantic mother waiting for me.

(Aileen S. Scott – Maidstone 1989)

I know of big-name stars who would almost literally run out of the stage door as soon as the curtains closed at the end of a show, just to avoid fans, so for these two mega-stars to show such caring hospitality to just one small fan, who would have been happy with a scribbled signature in her autograph book, shows just what lovely men they were. Also bear in mind that they weren't out to impress the press.

On 24 August the Laurel & Hardy Company left Margate by train, to travel the one-hundred and sixty-miles-plus to Coventry. This beautiful Midlands' city had been badly bombed during the war but, even so, the people of Coventry had kept up morale, and life went on as normally as possible. Most theatres and cinemas had stayed open during these troubled years, and did good business, but the shows had started and finished much earlier. One cinema which didn't survive the bombing was the local Rex which, legend has it, was blown to pieces during the run of the film *Gone with the Wind*.

To cater for demand, it was decided that Laurel and Hardy should play two weeks there. The decision was well taken and, from the outset, one could see that the visit was going to be a success. The crowd waiting to greet them at the station was so great, it was impossible for the two comedians to get through the main exit. They were therefore led out of a back exit, which hadn't been used for years, and were able to get into their waiting car with not a fan in sight.

Coventry Station.

This advert in the *Evening Telegraph* had more than a little to do with the turnout:

Hollywood's Greatest Comedy Couple — STAN LAUREL & OLIVER HARDY
ARE ARRIVING AT COVENTRY STATION TOMORROW (Aug 24) AT 6-30 p.m.
WHY NOT BE THERE WITH US TO WELCOME THEM?

It was a nice change to see the press taking an interest in the Boys, but a little misguided as, after many previous scares, Laurel and Hardy had had enough of greetings at railway stations.

Of the show, the *Coventry Standard* wrote:

> Laurel & Hardy head a tip-top show at Coventry Hippodrome, and their buffoonery – simple, but clever – keeps the audiences thoroughly amused. In a short sketch they apply for a driving licence. Hardy explains he cannot read and that Laurel cannot write, and later Laurel says that though he can read he cannot read writing! But even if they remained completely silent their clowning is sufficient to keep folks roaring with laughter.

The *Telegraph* revealed nothing of the on-stage action:

> And so one is drawn to Laurel, the classic clown, and his perfect foil, the amiably pompous Oliver Hardy, upon an irresistible wave of nostalgic reflection. The skit ends characteristically in a riot of knockabout retribution. This is excellent fun, but many will prefer the gentler sequel, when the couple face the audience in an intimate frolic, sometimes at the expense of their Hollywood contemporaries [Referring to the send-up of Crosby, Sinatra, and Astaire]. Incidentally, it gives Hardy an opportunity to air a surprisingly well-pitched tenor voice.

What is surprising about the last comment is that Babe was suffering from a sore throat that week and, to alleviate the problem, had requested George Cockayne, the sound operator, to "lift" the sound during his song.

Although Babe didn't lose his voice that week, he had since the beginning of his stay in England lost 23lbs. Of this, he commented:

> I don't blame your Mr. Strachey [Minister of Food]. It's all due to hard work. Rationing doesn't worry me. I'm a light eater anyway, and I never touch breakfast or lunch. I brought two small trunk loads of canned food with me from the States, in case of emergency, but I have only dipped into six tins. I intend to give the remainder to a newly-married couple in London.

Considering the amount of dinners to which Hardy was invited, and the contraband gifts of food which were lavished upon him, it is not surprising that he hardly needed to raid his tuck-box. The *Standard* reported that Hardy had lost 46lbs. since arriving in England, which, if both reports are correct, would mean that he had lost 23lbs. in the last five days. Laurel said he knew Hardy's weight very well, "because he often treads on my foot."

COVENTRY HIPPODROME staff
courtesy of George Cockayne (seated front right)

Of their on-stage comedy, Stan said he was convinced that there was still a great future for slapstick comedy, because ...

> ... it had universal appeal. Peoples of different nations might not understand the finer points of English, American, or French humour, but they shared equally with Europeans in their delight at seeing a man receiving, for instance, a blancmange full in the face.

Whilst in Coventry the comedy partners uncharacteristically stayed at separate hotels – and even in different towns. Stan stayed at the Abbey Hotel, Kenilworth, whilst Babe stayed at the Clarendon, Leamington Spa. A *Morning News* reporter upon enquiring after Hardy at his hotel was told:

> He won't see anyone. He was pestered to death – that's why he's here. He really has so many demands on his time, he doesn't take telephone calls, and all arrangements are made through his agent.

Persistency paid off, and the reporter secured an interview. Asked of his impressions of Leamington, Hardy replied:

> We [Mr. & Mrs. Hardy] have only walked a few blocks, but this is one of the cleanest and prettiest towns we have seen.

He went on to tell the reporter how chance had brought him to Leamington – and how glad he was at the outcome:

> In another district, some accommodation difficulty arose and the closest bath was a block away. But here at the Clarendon, this is one of the nicest places we have been in. The service and the people have been an absolute revelation. We have been continually on the go since February, but the peace and quiet we found here – that is something.

With memories of the severe winter still fresh in their minds Babe and Lucille were very much surprised that an English summer could follow such weather. Of their trips around the countryside, the reporter concluded that Mr. & Mrs. Hardy had decided upon Warwickshire as their favourite part of England. Said Texas-born Mrs. Hardy:

> Your little villages are absolutely fascinating. Anything written, painted, or said about England in the spring is not half enough. It is so entirely different from anything we have.

Asked about sightseeing, Hardy told the reporter they had been to Stratford-on-Avon, where he deplored the modernistic appearance of the Shakespeare Memorial Theatre:

> "It looks so out of place to represent something with so much tradition behind it." He added that he first saw the theatre after a visit to other places of interest at Stratford which were more in keeping with the Shakespearean setting, and consequently the theatre came as a surprise.

Guests at the hotel saw little of Hardy as he usually remained in his apartment till afternoon. Twice he and Lucille went for a short walk in town where, whilst wearing his horn-rimmed glasses, he was recognised by only a few people. A shopping trip in Leamington Spa though, where he met up with Laurel, had to be curtailed when a walk around Woolworths resulted in the shop becoming jammed with sightseers, and ended with the manager expelling the two stars with the humorous command: "Never darken Woolies' doorstep again."

On another outing, the Boys did manage to get out to a private dinner, the circumstance of which demonstrates the total openness which Laurel and Hardy afforded their fans. Arthur Brearley said:

> Instead of dreaming of meeting them, I wrote to them at the theatre and invited them to tea. To my amazement and delight, they came. My children were not old enough to enjoy their company as much as I did, but Laurel and Hardy put themselves out to entertain them. It is something I will always remember and I was the toast of the neighbours for months.

The next visit was to the Triumph Standard Auto Works, in Canley. The day must have started off chilly, as the Laurels and the Hardys were well wrapped up. As the day wore on it got hotter and hotter and, inside the metal building, the party began to cook. Subsequently, they all retired to the canteen, where Babe had two large mugs of tea to top himself up. (Maybe he should have drunk some radiator coolant.)

While still in Coventry the two comedy stars made a gesture to one fan, similar to the one they had made to Mabel Yates in Liverpool some weeks earlier. It started when a lady living just outside Coventry sent a letter thanking Laurel and Hardy for the wonderful job they had done in boosting the morale of the British people, during the war. She regretted being unable to attend the show and thank them in person but, since the war, she had gone blind. The letter closed with her wishing them every success possible. Sincerely touched by this tribute, Stan and Babe sent a car to bring her to the theatre. Given a seat in the front row, she was later led backstage for tea with the two stars themselves, before being driven home. Once again, Stan Laurel and Oliver Hardy had shown utter sincerity and genuine concern for the welfare of their fans.

The company next found itself in the Lancashire cotton mill town of Bolton. Bolton had remained untouched by wartime devastation (the nearest bombing having been on Manchester), but had deemed it safest to close some of its cinemas and theatres during the war years.

The Laurel & Hardy show was being staged at the Lido, which was to open its doors for just the one week, then close them again. There were better suited venues in the town, but these would have been booked up long before Laurel and Hardy's tour was conceived. One must remember that the tour was originally planned for twelve weeks only, so all the later bookings were being done at short notice. As their booking agent Billy Marsh told me:

Laurel and Hardy were put into theatres which would normally not be considered. There just weren't theatres around to satisfy the demand.

Ida Laurel recollected to biographer John McCabe:

It was a really dirty, drafty [sic] old theatre. Stan wanted to send out for some fish & chips. Stan adored fish & chips. But the stage-door keeper protested – he said indignantly fish & chips would smell up the place. Stan just looked at the man, and took a deep breath, getting that backstage air in his lungs:

'*Bring the fish & chips please,*' he told the man politely. '*They'll be like perfume to the air floating around in here now.*'

Bolton journalist Joe Rothwell visiting, backstage.

Nora Chadwick, a Bolton resident, said of the show:

I remember the occasion with great happiness at actually seeing Laurel & Hardy in person. I never thought it possible. We had seats on the front row of the stalls, and were amazed at how agile Hardy was able to dance, and so quietly, too – such a big man. I well remember the part of the sketch when Laurel answered the telephone and on Hardy enquiring, 'Who was that?' Stan replied, 'Long distance from Glasgow'.

[This is a reworking of the gag: "It's a long distance from Atlanta, Georgia" – from the Laurel & Hardy film *The Fixer-Uppers*. It would have gone like this: The phone rings. Stan picks it up, listens, and then tells the caller: "It sure is." When Ollie asks, "Who was that?" Stan replies, "Oh! just some joker. He said, "It's a long distance from Glasgow," and I said: "It sure is."]

Up till being informed by Nora about this gag, I had no idea it was included in the 1947 *Driver's Licence* sketch, but **was** aware that it was included in the sketch Laurel and Hardy were to play in 1952.]

Although there were hotels in Bolton at which Stan and Babe could have stayed, they chose to stay at the Brooklands Hotel, in Sale, Manchester.

A retro article, in the *Sale & Altrincham Messenger*, included some comments which some may not wish to hear. However, "Honesty is the best politics!" Schoolboy Peter Moiseeff got to observe Laurel and Hardy at close quarters, as his dad was the hotel's head-waiter, and his mum also worked there. Peter, who was 13 at the time, has vivid memories of the visit.

BROOKLANDS HOTEL

I recall the frequent comings and goings of the two comics with their wives, always signalled by a large limousine drawing up. Oliver Hardy was stunningly pink-skinned and, most of the time, he was taciturn, unsmiling and rather unpleasant – though he always had the knack of projecting affability when a camera appeared.

Stan Laurel was very different, a much warmer and genuine person. My parents got on well with the two couples. Stan Laurel's wife was Russian, as was my father, and so the two would have long chats together.

Also, on one occasion, when the group arrived in the early hours of the morning, long after the evening dinner service was finished, mother obligingly agreed to go down to the kitchen, at their request, to fix some flap-jacks – before they turned in.

Both of the comics had been married previously, and were working, principally, to pay off alimony awards.

In Hardy's defence, I would say that it is difficult to be "affable" in the early hours of the morning, when one is both tired and hungry. Conversely, it is easy to be "smiling" when one has had a good night's sleep, enjoyed a hearty breakfast, and then been invited into the morning sunshine for a photo-shoot. I think most of us would react similarly in these two situations, without being thought upon as being of bad character. Strange, though, when you compare Peter's character assessment with that given by Dorothea Neal, in Margate (at the beginning this chapter), as he gives a total reversal of the two partner's attributes.

Meanwhile, the support acts from the Laurel and Hardy Show *were* staying in Bolton. One meal cooked for them that week in their "pro' digs" was tripe and onions. This was thoroughly enjoyed by all; so much so, that a full description of it was relayed to Stan. Not being one who could resist the taste of tripe and onions, he charged one of the acts with coercing the landlady, a Mrs. Wotherspoon, into sending some round to the theatre. The following evening Mrs. Wotherspoon duly obliged, and the Boys were able to savour for themselves the delights which the other acts had enjoyed. The follow up to this is that every time Stan cooked the dish, once back in America, it was from Mrs. Wotherspoon's recipe.

On the last day of their week in Bolton, Saturday 13 September, Laurel and Hardy made a personal appearance which pretty-well duplicated the one at the speedway track in Bristol. This one was in Wigan, eleven miles west of Bolton, and the arrangement to go there had almost certainly been made in Bristol, back in July, when the Wigan Speedway Racing team were the opposition.

So, after doing their spot in the second-half of the 6:10 show, Laurel and Hardy were driven the eleven miles to the Poolstook Stadium, in Wigan. There, they were paraded around the track on the back of an open-topped car, and given a rousing welcome by eight thousand people there to watch the Speedway Racing. They then presented a trophy to speedway aces Oliver and Ronnie Hart, on which was the inscription:

> An appreciation of two grand fellows who had the courage to educate the folk of Wigan to the sport of speedway racing. Presented by Hollywood's greatest comics – Stan Laurel and Oliver Hardy.

The two comedians themselves then had to speed away, in order to get to Bolton for the second show of the evening, which commenced at 8:20 (although, to get it right, L&H wouldn't be on till the second-half). On a day when they had also performed a matinee, one would again have to ask why Stan and Babe burdened themselves with this extra appearance, when they had absolutely NOTHING to gain from it. Had the speedway stadium appearance been on an evening earlier in the week, there was a chance they could have persuaded some of the eight thousand crowd to come and see their show; but here, on a Saturday evening, the bike fans would be staying rooted, while Laurel and Hardy went to the theatre to make their *last* Bolton appearance.

The following day the Boys and their wives made the two-hundred-mile journey from Bolton to Swindon by road, but sent the company's forty pieces of luggage by rail. As the tour was now taking its toll, they chose accommodation well-away from the theatre – at the Bear Hotel, Hungerford – where they would not be pestered by over-zealous fans.

Of the show at the Swindon Empire, the *Evening Advertiser* reported:

> The question that comes to mind is whether Laurel & Hardy live up to their reputations as two of the finest comics the screen has produced. The answer is: 'They do.' Their sketch provides full scope for their mimicry and will even further endear them to their fans.

Stan had played the Swindon Empire twice before, with the Levy & Cardwell Juvenile Pantomime Company – in *Sleeping Beauty*, back in October 1907, when it was known as the Queen's; and then in *The House That Jack Built*, in January 1909. His combined memories of the two visits, though, was only that: "*It was winter and, as we were kids, we played snowballs.*"

The Boys' gambling habit, which their wives thought they had been cured of, after the greyhound incident at Lewisham, returned when a tipster put them on to a horse called 'Stuart.' Having been convinced it was a 'cert' they instructed Billy Marsh to place a considerable bet on it, and to keep doing this as long as funds lasted. There then followed such a run of wins that, as a postscript to the story, the Hardys and the Laurels were back in America when Billy Marsh phoned Stan:

> 'What are you going to do with all this money, Stan?' enquired Billy.

> 'What money?' puzzled Stan.

> 'The money from the horse. It kept winning. I got over fifty quid here,' explained Billy.

> Without a moment's hesitation, Stan said: 'Give it to the Water Rats.'

Come 22 September, Laurel and Hardy were back in London for the last theatre engagement of the tour. If they'd been hoping for an easy week on which to finish, they were soon disappointed, for they ended up working twice as hard – *literally*. A few weeks earlier, Bernard Delfont had brought over the American singing quartet 'The Inkspots' to do the whole of September at the London Casino. Come the third week, Delfont had arranged for the Inkspots to double at the Chiswick Empire – i.e. play the two theatres on the same night. This they refused to do, and returned to America prematurely, leaving Delfont without a name act at the Chiswick Empire.

The ever-obliging Stan and Ollie agreed to stand in and, on Monday evening, by changing the running-order, played two houses at Finsbury Park, and two at the Chiswick Empire. If this weren't a big enough labour in itself, Laurel was given a further handicap when a foot-rule used in the sketch flew back off Harry Moreny's desk and struck him on the forehead, causing a cut. After having a stitch inserted, Stan was able to carry on, and the rest of the week went off without further incident, despite the complicated timing needed to switch between the two theatres – twice.

The Stage said of the show at Finsbury Park Empire:

> Are Laurel & Hardy as funny on stage as in films? Realising how some have sadly failed to adjust themselves, one went prepared for disappointment – and got a surprise. They are funnier. At least, seeing them in the flesh brings home more forcibly than photography the inborn sense of clowning of this most lovable couple. They have the advantage of good material here in their sketch, which with its cinema technique of action going on all the time – knockabout scattering of papers and exchange of hats – gives constant laughter.

Of the same show, *The Performer* observed:

> Young folk more than usual in evidence in big audience this week, with Laurel & Hardy giving the fullest satisfaction. In short they were a riot.

> [Short – indeed!]

The *Chiswick Times* was equally short:

> What good showmen Laurel & Hardy are! Without doing anything in particular, they can stand in front of a microphone for ten minutes at a time and keep the audience rocking with laughter.

On the eve of the London appearances, Stan and Babe had attended a banquet given in their honour by the Water Rats, at the Savoy Hotel, where they were staying. Amongst the three hundred male guests were: Will Hay, Wee Georgie Wood, Bud Flanagan, Fred Russell, Jewel and Warriss, Sid Field, Billy Butlin, Val Parnell, Bernard Delfont, Billy Marsh, Lupino Lane, Louis Valentine, Archie Collins, Hannen Swaffer, Harry Moreny and, rather surprisingly, Ben Shipman (secretary of "Laurel & Hardy Feature Productions") who had come from L.A. to negotiate an extension to the tour.

Bud Flanagan, in proposing a toast, pointed out: *"One of the guests is English, and one is American. After seven years of rationing, it's not hard to tell which is which."*

This tongue-in-cheek statement was followed by a sincere acknowledgement to the fund-raising and troop entertainment done by the Boys during the war. He went on to say: *"Laurel and Hardy aren't finished. With their comic abilities they will never be finished as performers."*

Tribute was then paid to their guests' generosity in presenting the then colossal amount of £1,100 towards the purchasing of new premises for the 'Rats.' (The money raised was from the fees given to Laurel and Hardy for appearances, outside of their theatre work.)

As a thank you, Stan and Babe were each presented with a leather-bound volume containing the history of the Order, and inscribed by all their 'Brother Rats.' When the cheering had died down, Laurel was first to stand and reply to the toast:

> I can scarcely find words to express our appreciation of the grand way in which we have been received. Everyone has made us wonderfully happy, and our visit has been made a memorable one. I am particularly grateful to the "Water Rats" for extending so warm and brotherly a feeling to us, and we are proud to have been admitted into their ranks. The beautiful book I will treasure all my life.
>
> Our hearts are full of love and affection for all of you. We hope to return to this country, and when we do, we hope to see the new clubhouse well under way.

Babe then stood up, and replied:

> I don't think I have sufficient words to express my appreciation of the hospitality and friendship extended to Stan and I since our arrival in Britain. I would like to start by thanking Bernard Delfont and Billy Marsh for having the courage to bring us over.

At this, cheering broke out. Babe continued:

> I must also extend thanks to Harry Foster and Leslie MacDonnell; and to Val Parnell for his friendly pat on the back at the start of our tour. We are also very grateful to the people of Scotland for the wonderful receptions they afforded us.
>
> We must thank all the theatre managers for the way they have treated us; and most of all we must give a special thank you to Harry Moreny for his assistance in our act.

Praise for the latter was well deserved, as was echoed by theatre critics and newspaper reviewers throughout the tour. Of Moreny, Archie Collins said: *"He was more than just a foil to them – he was a terrific back-stop in every way."* Babe closed by thanking the Rats themselves, and ended with: *"Please don't ever forget us, for we shall always remember you"*.

The evening was a fitting tribute to Laurel and Hardy, and the sentiments expressed by all were genuine and heart-felt affection for these two lovable men.

Like a scene from *The Hoosegow*, the Boys finding everyone has a seat at the table – except them.

Between Laurel and Hardy is Fred Russell. Also Identified are:
Will Hay, Bud Flanagan, Bernard Delfont, Billy Marsh, Harry Moreny,
Wee Georgie Wood, Stanley Holloway, Sid Field, Jimmy Jewel, Ben Warriss.

One week later, 30 September, the Boys attended their last lodge meeting, before leaving Britain. As if they hadn't already given enough, they presented the GOWR with accessories to a silver desk-set (which is now housed in the Water Rats Museum), and 'the egg.' This is an actual egg, diamanté-studded and suspended on a ribbon, which is placed around the neck of a Rat as a penance for telling a really awful joke. Stan invented the idea as an addition to the Rats' existing ritual, and the same egg is still in use, today.

Having paid their dues to their supporters, and their supporters having paid their respects to them, it was time for Laurel and Hardy to move on. But, although they were leaving Britain, they weren't ready to return home just yet. There were other countries to conquer.

o-o-0-o-o

Chapter 18

A RIGHT ROYAL DO

Word of Laurel and Hardy's popularity and box-office success had spread eastwards across the North Sea, and the English Channel, for which dates and venues were rapidly being booked in Denmark, Sweden, France, and Belgium – and where the mob scenes at public appearances, and the packed audiences in theatres, would be repeated at each location. These were booked by Harry Foster, and not Bernard Delfont.

From the minute they arrived in Copenhagen, the two lowly comedians were treated like royalty. Here, they are being carried in style from the station to their hotel, aptly named "The Palace."

The sailing to Denmark occurred on 1 October, and the bookings in Copenhagen, Sweden, and back to Copenhagen, took them up to 27 October. **[AUDIO]**

The following day, Laurel and Hardy were in Paris. Their booking at the Lido de Paris showbar was scheduled to run from 7 November to 9 December; but shortly before opening night they had a very special show to attend – back in England. At just ten days' notice, Stan Laurel and Oliver Hardy had been invited to appear on the *Royal Variety Performance*.

Although L&H were currently only in rehearsal at the Lido, the manager, Pierre Louis-Guérin, stipulated that they (with their wives) had just forty-eight hours leave of absence. And, to make sure they didn't overstay, Guérin went with them. **[FILM]**

Doing the show meant a return to the London Palladium, a venue they had conquered earlier in the year. This night though (Monday, 3 November 1947) would prove to be a whole new challenge:

Monsieur Guérin – backstage, London Palladium

Firstly, it was to be in the presence of King George VI and Queen Elizabeth (the Queen Mother), and their younger daughter – Princess Margaret. The occasion was further marked by the first public appearance, after the announcement of the engagement, of their older daughter, Princess Elizabeth, to Lieutenant Philip Mountbatten (later Queen Elizabeth II and Prince Philip).

Secondly, the audience would not be regular theatregoers, drawn from the public, but mainly dignitaries, famous faces, and other acts, agents, and promoters from show business.

Thirdly, instead of Laurel and Hardy being the star attraction, with hand-picked support acts around them to complement their act, they were to be only one of many top-class acts. The audience may not have regarded the show as a competition, but there is no doubt that most of the performers did, and each would be striving to achieve the greatest acclaim.

The audience too would not be easy. Because it was a charity show, tickets prices were well up on the usual admission charges, and so the patrons expected only the best. Val Parnell, the show's producer, admitted to *The Stage*:

> The audience at a Royal Variety Performance is hard-boiled, and there's nothing worse than for an act to be received in stony silence. I don't say that variety is exactly on trial at this show, but it is a test of performance.

These then, were to be difficult conditions under which the duo were to be tested, and they were going to need the head start given to them by their film status, if they were to survive on the London stage amidst its most revered and popular performers, and theatreland's hardest critics.

Tea-break during rehearsals, backstage at the Palladium, with singer Dolores Gray.

In a 1957 radio interview, Arthur Friedman asks of Stan, regarding the *Royal Variety Performance*: "Were you [Laurel & Hardy] the only representative from this country [America]?" to which Stan replies: "Yes, I believe we were." As it happens, American acts were

154

well represented with Dolores Gray & Bill Johnson; Jack Durant; Borrah Minevitch's Harmonica Rascals; and Wally Boag, to name but four.

Of the competition between the British and American acts, the *Birmingham Mail* commented:

> By the interval, it was obvious that British and American acts on the bill were fighting for honours. The English artistes may or may not have been a little hurt at the trans-Atlantic emphasis in the programme. But from the moment they came on, they were determined to persuade the Royal Family that music hall is still something we can do better.

The *Evening Standard* offered their opinion of who ultimately won in the honours stakes:

> It was the Britons and not the Americans who dominated the show.

Having established that Americans were in proliferation, consider Friedman's next statement:

> According to the information I have, Laurel & Hardy received perhaps the greatest ovation that any act had received.

To this Stan makes the irregular reply, "We did – yes, we did." I say "irregular" as Stan was not wont to make false claims. In this instance, though, it must be presumed that Stan replied in the affirmative to discourage Friedman from further questions on the subject. For if truth be told, Laurel and Hardy had, to put it kindly, a rather mixed reception. The *Birmingham Mail* wrote of the show:

> There was also a failure: Laurel & Hardy in a humourless sketch about motoring.

The *London Evening Standard* was a little kinder:

> Laurel & Hardy struck me as a little over-awed and too subdued.

The Stage, which is noted for being kind to show business artistes, pointed out:

> Their first appearance in front of the curtain was the signal for a burst of cheering, and the Royal party seemed to know their work and worth.

After describing the plot of the sketch, the review finished with:

> The two popular comedians kept the house in the merriest of moods.

In a letter to the author, Laurel & Hardy biographer John McCabe (now deceased) holds the view given by *The Stage*, and refutes this author's claim that: "they wouldn't say anything unless they could say something nice." Although McCabe wasn't present, he had the benefit of testimony from three people who were – Stan, Ida and Lucille. These three were unanimous in declaring Laurel and Hardy a hit. Their opinions were strengthened by Charlie Henry (Chief of Production at the Palladium), who told Stan he had observed the King: "laughing long and loud at Laurel & Hardy, throwing his head back while laughing in great appreciation." Note, though, that both Henry and *The Stage* credit the laughter as emanating from the royal box only.

> "WE haven't laughed so much for years," was the King's comment to Harry Marlow at the close of the Royal Variety Performance on Monday, and the Queen added, "It's the best show we can remember." Comedy was the keynote of the performance, although spectacle was not forgotten, and the Royal Party sat enraptured at some beautiful scene, or merrily enjoying some clever piece of comedy. There was plenty of enthusiasm in the Royal Box, as one of the party turned to the other to enjoy mutually some of the humorous sallies.

But then we have some counter-evidence. Billy Marsh and Bernard Delfont had not only booked the 1947 Laurel & Hardy tour (and the two which would follow), but also went on to produce thirty *Royal Variety* shows, so knew more than a little bit about gauging how well acts were received. Both were present on the night, and had the comedians' interest totally at heart; but, when interviewed by the author, could not raise their review to more than lukewarm. Billy Marsh's comment was more of a defence than a commendation:

> They were a very tough audience – even infamous for being hard – because they'd paid their money, and said: 'Come on – show us.' They weren't very good audiences at all. The acts only did it for the honour.

Having stated the case for the artistes, Marsh then presented the case for the audience:

> You have to bear in mind that Laurel and Hardy weren't a sophisticated act. They couldn't go out and fight an audience, if things weren't going well. They were considered to be only a 'light' act. [Tommy] Trinder could go out there and have a go – but not them. They were successful on their own shows, but that night wasn't one of their best.

When pushed, by the author, the then Lord Delfont commented on Laurel and Hardy's acceptance, "They got by, nicely." When asked what he meant by that, he again remarked, "They got by." Then added: "They were a hard audience."

When a despondent Babe Hardy asked backstage the possible reason why they hadn't scored with the audience, Charlie Henry jokingly replied: "Don't worry! They're always hard first house on a Monday."

A possible answer is that the Boys' mental preparation and, ultimately, their usual faultless timing, was affected by two main factors: firstly, the sketch was cut from twelve minutes to just eight; and secondly, the act who were to go on before them, Dolores Gray & Bill Johnson, failed to arrive in time from their show at the London Coliseum. This unnerved Stan and Babe who, instead of following a singing act, had to follow a strong comedy act – ventriloquist Bobbie Kimber. Billy Marsh puts down this reshuffle as the major contributory factor in their less-than-usual enthusiastic reception

The debate over the *Royal Variety Performance* should not be taken too seriously. The only issue at stake is whether the audience were too hard, or Laurel and Hardy too weak. After the comedians' track record earlier in the year at the Palladium, it should be obvious to everyone which option is correct. This one-off, egotistical audience, whose main aim on the night is not *to see* but *be seen*, should not be allowed to detract from the fact that Laurel and Hardy were asked to entertain the Royal Family, and can rightly feel the utmost pride for having done just that.

King George VI was moved by the singing of: *God Save the King*.
Laurel and Hardy were RE-moved, for singing: *We Are the Sons of the Desert*.

Stan and Babe's personal disappointment was not in their performance, but in missing the opportunity to be presented to the Royal Family – for they had to dash from the theatre to make the train connection for the ferry back to France.

In two letters, written some ten years later, Laurel's only topic of comment on the show was regarding the Royal party:

```
The Command Performance was a thrilling experience, don't
know if the Royal Family laughed or not, as we were not
permitted to look at the Royal Box. Only at the finish were
you allowed to look at the King & Queen and make a special
final bow to them.
```

The follow-up expounded a little bit:

```
I really don't know why foreigners are not permitted to
look at the Royal Family at a Command Performance. Maybe
it's a tradition. I doubt if it would affect the artist in
any way, even if they are at attention when appearing
before Royalty, they still retain the "Show Must Go On"
attitude, regardless of anything. Frankly, I think it's
ridiculous to enforce this rule. A little peek wouldn't
hurt anybody. I know it because I did.
```

As to whether the show was recorded, here is a statement made at the time:

> The Royal Variety Performance will not be broadcast, as the BBC would not compensate for the loss of revenue incurred by the theatres.

From the presence of royalty at the Palladium it was, for Laurel and Hardy, straight back to the peasantry in the Lido de Paris. This is not an unkind statement, as Paris in wintertime is out of season, and many of the people who make it a cultural meeting place have vacated.

Stan hated every minute, at the Lido, and regarded their run there as a flop. Contemporary reviews, though, would suggest that the flop was in Stan's eyes only.

The show then moved on to Belgium where, between 10 December 1947 and 8 January 1948, they played shows and made appearances in Brussels, Antwerp, Charleroi, Verviers, Liege, and Ghent.

[AUDIO]

Laurel and Hardy's provisional *twelve-week* engagement had lasted *eleven months*, but finally the two film-stars-turned-stage-stars were able to return home.

The Hardys sailed from Antwerp on 15 January on board the *MV Bastogne*, bound for New York. The Laurels, mean-while, popped over to England to spend a few nights in London.

At the Lido, it wasn't possible to dress the stage for their sketch. Going off this picture, one would have to surmise they worked on a bare stage, with just a table and chair for the cop to sit at.

Stan Laurel wasn't the only major Hollywood star in London at that time. Sex-symbol and controversial actress and playwright Mae West was opening in her brand new stage show *Diamond Lil* – and Laurel was invited along.

```
Dear Betty Healy :-
I met her in London in '48 at a party after her opening in
"Diamond Lil" at the Prince of Wales Theatre, I saw the
show too, she was really sensational.
```

After the show (Saturday 24 January 1948), the agents Harry Foster and Leslie MacDonnell threw a party at Ciro's Club. [Harry Foster was the agent who had booked Laurel and Hardy's European tour, possibly along with Leslie MacDonnell.]

Back row) Leslie MacDonnell, Sam Preager, Edwin Coleman, Lou Wilson, Eddie Duckof, Val Parnell, Ben Conte, Harry Foster, Jim Timony, Clem Butson, Sam Stixyel.
Mrs. Laurel, Mrs. MacDonnell, Miss Marsden, Mrs. Parnell, Mrs. Conte, Miss Mae West, Miss Arnold, Mrs. Arnold, Mrs. Coleman.
Mickey Rooney, Tom Arnold, Danny Kaye, Stan Laurel.

Publicity revealed the aims of the party to be threefold: 1) to celebrate the opening of Mae West in *Diamond Lil*. 2) to welcome Danny Kaye on his arrival in London. And 3) to bid "bon voyage" to Stan Laurel and Mickey Rooney. Also present were Sid Field and Arthur Askey.

An unconfirmed attendance was that of Stan's father, Arthur Jefferson. It *is* confirmed that Laurel's sister Olga, and husband Bill, came down from Barkston to spend time with Stan, but in two extant photographs he isn't featured. If Stan did not get to see him it was a great shame, as Arthur Jefferson passed away just one year later (15 January 1949), during which period Stan paid no further visits to the UK, and so would have missed the opportunity to say a final 'Farewell.'

Bill Healy seems to be saying: "That's his *sister* he's kissing. I'm married to her, and even I don't kiss her that passionately."

Laurel had been away from his California home now for almost exactly a year, and must have been desperate to get back. However, he would have to wait just a little while longer than planned, as the crossing of the *Queen Mary* from Southampton to New York, leaving 28 January, took two days longer than scheduled, owing to rough seas.

Although glad to be home, both Stan *and* Babe were most concerned that job prospects for the future looked extremely bleak. After their one-year absence, they had to face being treated with indifference by most of the American public, and also come to terms with a younger generation who didn't even know them.

In November 1947, while the comedy duo were in Paris, Hollywood columnist Erskine Johnson had announced: "Stan Laurel and Oliver Hardy will return to the screen in a series of comedy shorts, when they return from Europe." But, come the end of 1948, neither this nor any other projects had borne results. 1949 was bound to bring something – wasn't it?

Come May 1949, sixteen months after their return from Europe, Laurel and Hardy had still not had any film offers; done any radio shows; nor made any personal appearances. But then Hal Roach, after making a personal fortune out of selling most of the Laurel & Hardy back-catalogue of short films, seemed to believe his two former comedy stars might still have some mileage left in them to make a few new ones. It wasn't to be:

> If you are wondering about those Laurel and Hardy comedies you've been seeing on television, here's the inside: Hal Roach sold the TV rights for $750,000. The buyer expects to make about $250,000 on the deal.

> Roach tried to talk Stan and Babe into making a series of 14 shorts, running 12 minutes each, expressly for television, but they turned him down, saying the price wasn't right.

(Erskine Johnson – 11 May 1949)

Meanwhile, just as it appeared things couldn't get any worse, Laurel was diagnosed as having diabetes. While Stan took things easy, Hardy side-tracked his career and appeared in a stage play – *What Price Glory?* A short time afterwards, John Wayne – who had also been in the stage cast of *What Price Glory?* – asked Hardy to appear in his next film, *The Fighting Kentuckian*. The result was a very creditable performance from Babe, in a straight acting role, from which he was next invited to play a cameo role in the Bing Crosby film, *Riding High*.

Then, before there were thoughts of a permanent solo career, both Hardy *and* Laurel were offered a deal to make a film in France:

'The deal sounds like the best we've had in years,' Hardy said today (17 March 1950).

'We have a good story, and that's important.'

'We've had many Hollywood offers, but none have included good stories. Producers feel that all we need to do is some slapstick and that's enough.'

To be fair it was a lucrative offer, and one which they were more than happy to grasp with both hands. But there would be a price to pay, and that price was twelve months of frustration, anger, embarrassment, despair, and life-threatening illnesses. Had the two ageing comedians not had so much debt to pay off, by way of back-taxes and alimony, they might well have opted to remain in the US – which, hindsight reveals, would have kept them out of another unfunny mess.

Stan and Ida set off first, sailing from
New York on the RMS *Caronia*,
and arriving in Paris on 13 April 1950.

Babe arriving at St. Lazare – 17 June

Using the Prince de Galles Hotel as a base, Stan spent several weeks with two other writers, trying to knock out a working script for *Atoll K*. The task was almost impossible, as all three had different ideas, and had to try to communicate in three different languages – English, Italian, and French. A later change to English-speaking writers did little to improve the script.

Babe and Lucille Hardy joined Laurel in Paris in mid-June, nearly ten weeks after work had first started on the script – but still it wasn't ready.

So, while the other writers stayed in Paris to continue work on the script, the two star comedians went on a publicity tour of Italy – to promote a film that had not even been written. But the fans didn't know or care about that, and at every stopover – Marseilles, San Remo, Genoa, Milan, and Rome – the Boys were mobbed.

Of the Milan visit, Laurel later wrote in a letter:

```
The L&H film version of 'Fra Diavolo' is still shown every
year in Italy, it was showing in Milan when Hardy and I
were there in 1950, the English was 'dubbed' in Italian
language, I got a big kick out of L&H speaking Italian just
like the natives!
```

Marseilles Harbour

The Boys were back in Paris before June was out, where Laurel had to make major alterations to the rubbish the writers had written in his absence. It was 5 August before the script was deemed workable, at which point everyone set off for Marseilles to start filming. The next seven or eight days were spent shooting outdoor scenes in Marseilles Harbour.

From Marseilles, cast and crew moved to St. Raphael, on the Côte d'Azur, where shooting commenced on 16 August on a peninsula called Cap Roux. But the film was ill-fated right from the off. The two comedians found themselves unable to fight against the insurmountable odds of having actors of several different nationalities in the cast, each speaking their native language; plus a production crew which was totally inefficient. And then, the hardships of the daytime shooting began to cause both actors severe health problems. Hardy was now around 330lbs (23st 8lbs), and the excess weight he was carrying, combined with the intense heat he was exposed to daily, caused him to develop heart fibrillation.

As for Laurel, he was rapidly losing weight, and eventually hit a low of 114lb (8st 2lb). His diabetes, coupled with another illness, rendered him so weak he was unable to film for more than a few minutes at a time. He struggled gainfully on and, like the old trooper he was, managed to complete the location scenes, plus those done over the weeks which followed at a studio in Nice.

A scene from *Atoll K*, in which the marked difference in bodyweight can clearly be noted.

No filming was done between the end of October and the first two weeks in January, owing to Laurel's continuing illness and eventual hospitalisation, and it was mid-January 1951 before filming recommenced, in Paris. Both stars struggled on with filming till the end of March, before finally hearing, what was for them at the time, the most glorious four-letter word in the English language – it's a "WRAP."

Suzy Delair, Max Elloy, Simon van Collem (journalist) Adriano Rimoldi, Michel Dalmatoff

In February 1951, while Stan and Babe were still shooting *Atoll K*, there had been a deal pending for them to go to Australia to make another film but, by now, all they wanted to make was *their bed*, and to lie in it for several months.

The Boys had come to France expecting to spend just twelve weeks there. This had turned into twelve MONTHS – twelve months of sheer torture. Laurel wasn't going to extend it by one more day than was absolutely necessary. He and Ida left France on 17 April, aboard the RMS *Queen Elizabeth*, and sailed for home. The Hardys, meanwhile, were happy to stay on for a short holiday, before departing from Belgium on 23 April 1951, aboard the MS *Washington*.

Having waited six years to regain credibility as film stars, Stan and Babe had been dealt the cruellest of blows. From now on, the stage would be the only medium in which they were to work. On the film-making front, Laurel and Hardy had made the final cut.

o-o-0-o-o

To find out what happened next, treat yourself to a copy of:

LAUREL and HARDY – The British Tours

Part 2 – 1951 to 1954

The Last Stage

ACKNOWLEDGEMENTS

[N.B. The majority of those acknowledged here gave their assistance during research for the First Edition, between 1987 and 1993. Sad to say that a number of them will have since passed on since, but I have no way of checking just who. Only those I have personal knowledge of are marked with an asterisk to signify "deceased."]

[KEY: "*" indicates "deceased"]

-----0-----

My sincere thanks to all those whose valued contributions made the story of "The British Tours" as near to definitive as one could hope it to be.

A Special Mention to:

Roy Sims – whose assistance with the book, from birth to maturity, was invaluable; to Bruce Crowther – for guiding me on my first, faltering steps; to Billy Marsh* – who gave me credibility, and whose memory is astounding; Jean Darling*; Jeffrey Simmons; and Eric and Joy Dalton – for their encouragement and guidance; to Norman Wisdom* – who realised my life-times ambition; to Olga Varona* and Archie Collins – who put aside illness to write a loving documentation; John and Jean Cooper; Jefferson Woods*; and Nancy E. Wardell* – who so kindly allowed me family insights; taxi driver John Jones – for the heart-touching story; Shirley Davies – who painted such poetic pictures; and Eric Nicholson; Ray Alan*; Peter Goodwright; Billy Barron*; Dorothea Birch*; Bill Butler MBE; George Cockayne; John Eddolls; Sybil C. Henderson; Audrey Jenkins; Robert F. Kennedy*; Francis J. Mavin OBE; Nancy Jane Reid; and Ronald Thomson* – for their personal eye-witness accounts.

Many thanks also to:

Dr. Kathleen Barker*; Mrs V. Bolton; Estelle Bond; Allen Bromley; Charlie Brooks; Rod Byrne; Frank Carson*; Nora Chadwick; Perce Champin; B.D. Cook; L. Crane; Mary Crettol; Mike Davie; Freddie Davies; Norma Devitt; Kim Drinkwater; Joe Ellis; Peg Francis; Alec Frutin*; R.R. Fry; John Galloway; Elizabeth M. Gammage; Malcolm Gilbert; Chris Hawes; Kevin Henriques; Mrs. S.M. Hess; Emily Hopper; Terry Johnson; Liddell Johnston; Ron Kerr; George Knox; Edward J. Laker; Brian Lazarus; Jack Leighton; Jimmy Logan*; Billy McCaffrey; Veron McGinley; Ron Mason; John Mullinder; J.S. Myers; Mrs. R.J. Nendrick; Mrs. V. Osmond; Dick Pearce; Ron Pearson; Les Pudney; Dereck Riddell; Johnnie Riscoe; Billy "Uke" Scott*; Arthur E. Shorter; Giles Squire; George Strzodka; Valerie Sturges; Mrs. L. Swindells; Carole Thomas; Herbert D.G. Tinkler; Patrick J. Trainer; Jack Twells; Peggy Valentine; Max Wall*; Gerald H.A. Warr JP; Ben Warriss*; Elsie Waters*; Jock M. Whitehouse; George Wilkinson; Mrs. Willis; Bea Winterburn; Ken Woodward; Mrs. Wotherspoon*; David Guy-Johnson; Hazy Paul; Leo Roberts; Derek Sculthorpe; Leslie Melville; Penny Corner; Gordon Bailey; Patrick Vasey; and Jason Allin. And to Ethel Challands* for her extreme generosity.

The "Sons of the Desert" — UK

Rob Lewis; Stephen Bolton; Laurence Reardon; Mike Jones; Graham McKenna; Dave Walker; Derek Ward; Philip Martin Williams; and David Wyatt; who unselfishly shared what they had. And to Peter Brownlow; for his valued assistance.

The "Sons of the Desert" — Europe

Chris James (Sweden); Michael Ehret (Germany); Bram Reijnhoudt (Netherlands); Gunther Mathias; Siep Bousma (Netherlands); Peter Mikklesen (Denmark) Marc de Coninck (Belgium)

To the Societies:

Concert Artistes Association – Jimmy Perry*; Entertainment Artistes Benevolent Fund – Reg Swinson; Grand Order of Water Rats – John Adrian* and Charlie Chester*; Northamptonshire Police – Tom Paintain and Jack Spiller; Scotland Yard (Black Museum); West Mercia Constabulary – A. W. Sykes.

ACKNOWLEDGEMENTS

To the Libraries who were helpful in the extreme:

BELFAST – Jennifer Grant; BIRMINGHAM – Patrick Baird; BLACKPOOL – James K. Burkitt; BOLTON Department of Education – Brian Hughes; BOURNEMOUTH Local Studies – Mrs. R.M. Popham; BRADFORD District Archives – Gina L. Szekely; BRIGHTON – Stephanie Green; BRISTOL – Miss D. Dyer; BURY – Mrs. R. Hirst; CARLISLE – Stephen White; COVENTRY – A.J. Mealey; DUDLEY Archives – Mrs. K.H. Atkins; DUMFRIES – John Preston; DUNDEE – J.B. Ramage; DUNFERMLINE – John Jamieson; DURHAM County Library – J. Main; EALING – Miss A. Terre; EDINBURGH – Norma Armstrong; GLASGOW Mitchell Library – Elizabeth Carmichael and Anne Escott; GLASGOW University – Miss E.M. Watson and Claire McKendrick; GREENOCK Watt Library – Mrs. L.E. Couperwhite; HARTLEPOOL – Miss M.E. Hoban; HULL – Peter J. Ainscough; KENILWORTH – L. Alexander; LEAMINGTON SPA – Gary Archer; LEEDS – Mrs. A. Heap and Mrs. J.H. Horne; LEWISHAM Local History Centre – Richard A. Martin; LIVERPOOL Brown, Picton and Hornby – Janet Smith; LONGSIGHT – Hilary Pate; NEWPORT – Mrs. S. Pugh; MANCHESTER – Helen Foster and David Taylor; NEWCASTLE – F.W. Manders and Patricia Sheldon; NEWCASTLE Blandford House – Bruce Jackson; NEWCASTLE James Joicey Museum – Joe Ging*; NORTH SHIELDS Local Studies – Eric Hollerton; NORWICH – C. Wilkins-Jones; NOTTINGHAM – Dorothy Ritchie; OLDHAM – Deidre L. Heywood; PETERBOROUGH – R.W.E. Hillier; PLYMOUTH – J.R. Elliott; PORTSMOUTH – John Thorn; RHYL – Rona Aldrich; ST. ANNES – P. Shuttleworth; SALFORD Local History – Royston Futter and Tony Frankland; SHEFFIELD – J.M. Olive; SHREWSBURY Local Studies – Anthony M. Carr; SOUTH SHIELDS – Rod Hill and T. Graham; SOUTHAMPTON – H.A. Richards; SOUTHPORT Atkinson Library – J. Hilton; STAFFORD William Salt Library – Ms. P. Davies; STALYBRIDGE Tameside Local Studies – Alice Lock; STOCKPORT – Mrs. M.J. Myerscough; STOKE on TRENT – N. Emery and Miss A. Ormsby; SUNDERLAND – D. Hinds and Jeffrey Devine; SUTTON – Mary Batchelor; SWANSEA – Brian Thomas; SWINDON – D.M. Allen and Roger Trayhurn; SWISS COTTAGE – Malcolm Holmes; WAKEFIELD – John Goodchild; WALSALL Local History – Cath Yates; WIGAN Record Office – N. Webb; WOLVERHAMPTON – Elizabeth A. Rees; YORK Archives – Mrs. R.J. Freedman; YORK – Elizabeth A. Meline; and LONDON – Abbey Road Studios.

[Unless otherwise stated, all the above are "Central Libraries."]

PLUS: British Film Institute – Tony Widdows and Sue Wilson; Cinema Theatre Association – David Jones; Leslie Bull; R. Benton; Donald Hickling; Bill Flockney; Fred T.P. Windsor; Barry R. Stevenson; Huntley Archives – John Huntley*; Scottish Film Council – Janet McBain; Stoll Moss Archives – George Hoare*; Theatre Museum – Jonathan Gray; The Theatres Trust – D.F. Cheshire; Writer's Guild of Great Britain – Nick Dalziel.

The Public Records Department, Kew; and the Cunard Archives, Liverpool University – for the shipping data; and Scott T. Rivers (for the Australia news clips).

And a massive thank you:

To the staff of the British Newspaper Library, Colindale, who, with unquestioning service, supplied me with literally thousands of newspapers during one hundred and fifty-five visits.

Sincere Thanks Also:

To the Newspaper Companies – who printed my appeal and supplied photographs:

Accrington Observer; Bir*mingham Post & Mail* – Richard Edmonds and Carol Evans; *Bolton Evening News*; *Bournemouth Daily Echo*; *Bradford Telegraph & Argus* – Mike Priestley; Bristol *Evening Post*; *Cumberland News* – Dick Allen; *Daily Mail* – Nigel Davies; *Eastern Evening News* – Derek James; *T. Bailey Forman* – Ralph D. Gee; *Glasgow Evening Times*; *Grimsby Evening Telegraph*; *Edinburgh Evening News*; *Irish News Ltd* – Martina Stewart; *Isle of Thanet Gazette*; *Newcastle Evening Chronicle*; *Northampton Chronicle & Echo*; *Portsmouth News* – Keith Ridley and Alan Montgomery; *South Wales Evening Post*; *Southern Evening Echo* –

ACKNOWLEDGEMENTS

Alison Tilley; *Shrewsbury Chronicle* – Alan Godding; Solo Agency – Danny Howell; Staffordshire *Evening Sentinel*; *The Stage* – Graham Ireland and Peter Hepple; *Sunday Sun* – Robin Etherington; *Sunderland Echo* – Chris Storey; *Blackpool Gazette* – Robin Duke and R.P. Officer; *Wolverhampton Express & Star*; *Yorkshire Evening Post* – John Thorpe; *Yorkshire Express*; *Doncaster Free Press* – Chris Page; *Left Lion* – Gav Squires; *Grantham Journal* – Graham Newton.

And to the Hotels:

LONDON, Savoy – Peter Crome and Rosemary Ashbee; TYNEMOUTH, Grand – Mrs. J. Richardson; EDINBURGH, Caledonian – Allan G. Blest; RHYL, Westminster – Mrs. A.M. Qureshi; SOUTHPORT, Prince of Wales – John Barrington-Fortune; CARDIFF, Park – Doris McIntyre and Frank Bois; SOUTHAMPTON, Polygon – Anne Midgely; BRISTOL, Grand – Christopher Skidmore; SCOTLAND, Gleneagles – Ian Wilson; DUDLEY, Station – Mrs. E. Stephenson.

For the kind use of photographs – from their personal collections:

Roy Sims; Rob Lewis; Paul E. Geruicki; Randy Skretvedt; Tyler St. Mark; Siep Bousma; Bernie Hogya; Cliff Sawyer; Scott MacGillivray; Bill Cubin*; John Ullah; Marc de Coninck; Bram Reijnhoudt; Harry Hoppe; Willie McIntyre; Tony Traynor; Huntley Jefferson Woods*; Nancy E. Wardell*; David Tomlinson; Stephen Neale; David Crump; Ronald Thomson*; Phillippe Petit; and Camillo Moscati.

Colin Greenwell; Cliff Temple*; Olga Varona* and Archie Collins; John and Jean Cooper; Billy Barron*; Charlie Cairoli Jnr. & Claudine; Ron Kerr; George Cockayne; John Eddolls; Sybil C. Henderson; Audrey Jenkins; Francis J. Mavin OBE; Mike Davie; A. Nesbitt; Nancy Jane Reid; Lt. Cdr. Richard Swift (R.N.Rtd.); Mrs. Willis; Norman Wisdom*; Kenny Baker*; Richard Townend; Gordon Bailey; Lynda Gocher; Carole Anne Williams; Alan Parsons; John Pinchbeck; Ron Roper; and Roy Baines.

IMAGE SOURCES

Back Cover Colour Photo – The British Tours part 1 — Nick Wall

Back Cover Colour Photo – The British Tours part 2 — Aimee Spinks

Getty Images – Morgana Gooding; Alamy; Cine-Variety (Mike Lang); Carl M. Cole; Autographs Inc.; Blackpool Gazette; Madame Tussauds; London – Undine Concannon; Google images; Author's Collection.

[Every effort was made to trace the present copyright holders of the photographs and illustrations contained within these pages. Anyone who has claim to the copyright of any of those featured; please make representation to the publisher, who will be only too pleased to give appropriate acknowledgement in any subsequent edition(s).]

It isn't that long ago when the only way to receive photographs was by negatives or prints being sent by post. Nowadays, with email, and especially with tens of thousands of related images available to download from the Internet, keeping tabs on the source is nigh on impossible. My sincerest apologies, therefore, to anyone I may have omitted to acknowledge as source.

And with much Gratitude to:

John McCabe* – for his encouragement, appraisal of the manuscript, and loan of photographs.

And to Bob Spiller, and Alison Grimmer – by whose brilliant perceptions, and much appreciated suggestions, the text of the First Edition was greatly enhanced.

And lastly to Lord Delfont* and Billy Marsh* – who revived the career of two neglected comedians, and without whom there would be no story.

o-o-o-0-o-o-o

ACKNOWLEDGEMENTS

BIBLIOGRAPHY

John McCabe — The Comedy World of STAN LAUREL (Robson)

John McCabe — Mr. LAUREL & Mr. HARDY (Signet USA)

John McCabe — BABE – The Life of Oliver Hardy (Robson)

Pawson/Mouland — LAUREL BEFORE HARDY (Westmorland Gazette)

Jack Read — EMPIRES HIPPODROMES & PALACES (Alderman Press)

Randy Skretvedt — LAUREL and HARDY – The Magic Behind the Movies (Moonstone)

Ken Owst — LAUREL & HARDY in HULL

Scott MacGillivray — LAUREL & HARDY – From the Forties Forward (iUniverse Inc.)

Simon Louvish — The Roots of Comedy

And to the Authors and writers:

Dave Bradshaw* – Press Officer Butlins, Skegness, and ex-journalist.

Bill Ellis – Seaside Entertainers: 100 years of Nostalgia.

Bill Evans – Ex-Journalist – East Kent Times.

Leslie Frost – Thanks for the Memories.

John Montgomery – Comedy Films; and others.

Douglas Salmon – Ex-Journalist and Ex-BBC Television producer.

Tony Wheatley – TV and Radio Scriptwriter.

David Robinson – Chaplin biographer.

Reference works:

CURTAINS!!! — (John Offord)

London Theatres and Music Halls — Diana Howard

Writers & Artists' Yearbook — (A & C Black)

-----0-----

ARTICLES

LAUREL & HARDY MAGAZINE – Rob Lewis

Glenn Mitchell — HARRY WORTH (Laurel & Hardy Magazine)

BOWLER DESSERT – Willie McIntyre

John Land — The Jeffersons in Bishop Auckland (Bowler Dessert)

-----0-----

WEBSITES

Laurel & Hardy Magazine (Rob Lewis, Howard Parker) – www.laurelandhardy.org

Letters From Stan [Laurel] – www.lettersfromstan.com – hosted by Bernie Hogya

Queen Street Arms, Keighley – www.valendale.myby.co.uk/pubs

Ellis Island Foundation – www.ellisisland.org

o-o-0-o-o

FILM FOOTAGE

1932 Jul 27 LONDON – Screen Artistes Federation Social Club (book 1 page 16)
Laurel and Hardy make an appeal for the "Cinema Trade Benevolent Fund."
[They *are* talking, but the sound is considered lost.]
It was screened in British cinemas on 3rd November. The footage is undated, but the author has placed it here as that is when L&H were at the Screen Artistes Federation Dinner.

Universal Talking News

1932 Jul 28 TYNEMOUTH – Grand Hotel, and Tynemouth Plaza (book 1 page 22)
After leaving the Grand Hotel, Tynemouth, the Boys relocate to the veranda of the Plaza Cinema, overlooking the beach. There they sign autographs, make speeches, clown for the crowd of thousands, and give out presents to 600 children.
Filmed silent, but with title cards. Amateur footage. (J. G. Ratcliffe)

1932 Jul 29 EDINBURGH – Edinburgh Castle, and Playhouse Theatre (book 1 page 26)
L&H shown disembarking at Waverley Station, and being escorted along the platform. Second scene is a walk around the Castle grounds; and third is a lengthy sequence at the Playhouse showing the cinema and its large number of pageboys, the huge projection room, and then Stan and Babe on stage. (Alan J. Harper)

A second version contains a longer sequence of the Edinburgh Castle walkabout, along with the arrival and departure, by car, at the North British Station Hotel.

1932 Aug 8 EALING – Stan Visits His Father (book 1 page 49)
Stan filmed with his father Arthur Jefferson and stepmother, Venetia, outside their home at 49 Colebrook Avenue, Ealing. London W13. Most of the footage is shot in the doorway, with both father and son mugging to the camera.

1932 Aug 10 PARIS – Champs Élysées (book 1 page 52)
Gaumont's "CAR OF THE COMEDY STARS." – Stan and Ollie board a chauffeur-driven Renault; the car crosses Paris with the Boys waving to the camera; they arrive at Claridges, in the Champs Élysées; do some business with a policeman checking their passports; and finally enter the hotel.

1932 Aug 31 NEW YORK CITY, Broadway (book 1 page 60)
Considering this was done on location, in ONE-TAKE, it emerges as a delightful piece of footage.
Hardy is engaging throughout, staying within character and seemingly ad-libbing.

At one point, when the cop says he wants to speak to the driver, Hardy utters the killer line: "I don't think the driver can talk. In fact, I don't think the driver can see."

Hearst Metrotone News

1947 Feb 10 SOUTHAMPTON – On board the Queen Elizabeth (book 1 page 67)
(Monday) Interviewed by John Parasols on arrival. They talk about the forthcoming tour and the proposed film *Robin Hood*, then do the "You're standing on my foot" routine. Robert Taylor and Barbara Stanwyck are also interviewed.

(Pathé Newsreels)

1947 Mar 14 LONDON – Daily Mail Ideal Home Exhibition, Olympia (book 1 page 84)
(Friday) Entertainer Tessie OShea and actress Vera Pearce sitting on Hardys knee, at the Stak-a-Bye tubular tables and chairs stand. Stan grins, and is kissed by Tessie.

(Pathé Newsreels)

1947 Mar 21 KENT – Romney Hythe & Dymchurch Railway (book 1 page 92)
(Friday) Laurel and Hardy are welcomed at New Romney Railway Station by Mr. & Mrs. Howey – owners of the line. They do business of opening the tunnel doors with a huge key; fool about on the engine; then get into a Pullman Car and set-off for Dungeness along the section of line they have just re-opened.

(Gaumont, Movietone, and Paramount)

1947 Apr 28 LONDON – Daily Mail Film Awards, Dorchester Hotel (book 1 page 99)
(Monday) Laurel and Hardy arrive late and interrupt Lady Rothermere presenting an award to film actress Margaret Lockwood. There is then some improvised comic business, instigated by Hardy, with flowers plucked from a nearby vase.

(Pathé Newsreels, and Gaumont British News)

1947 May 6 LONDON – Comedians at the Apollo (book 1 page 101)
(Tuesday) Laurel and Hardy, Sid Field, The Crazy Gang, Tommy Trinder, and George Robey, dressed in farmer's smocks, selling programmes outside the Apollo Theatre, prior to a matinee benefit performance for the "Farmer's Disaster Fund."

(Pathé Newsreels)

1947 May 27 ULVERSTON – Coronation Hall, and 3 Argyle Street (book 1 page 110)
(Tuesday) L&H appear on the balcony of the Coronation Hall, overlooking a packed crowd in the square below. Laurel is presented with a copy of his birth certificate, which Hardy snatches away from him. Next they visit the house where Stan was born, and then are seen in the grounds of the Golf Hotel, before being driven away.

1947 Jul 17 WESTON-SUPER-MARE – Outdoor Swimming Pool (book 1 page 134)
(Thursday) Stan and Babe are seen entering the open air swimming pool. Inside, they and their wives judge the 'Modern Venus' beauty competition in front of 6,000 people.

[continued]

1947 Nov 2   "Aboard the French Boat train bound for London"   (book 1 page 153)
(Tuesday*)   "The Laurels and the Hardys en route from Paris to London to attend the *Royal Variety Show*," is on the catalogue notes, and also on the soundtrack, for this footage — but this is incorrect. It was actually shot during the train journey from Jeumont to Paris on **28 October 1947***, wherein they are seated at a dining table, and attempt some comedy business with the cutlery and menu. The end sequence shows the comedy couple disembarking at the Gare du Nord station.

                                                                (Pathé Newsreels)

1952 Jan 28   SOUTHAMPTON – Arrival Aboard the 'Queen Mary'   (book 2 page 4)
(Thursday)   Laurel and Hardy are interviewed on the quayside, as they come off the gang-plank at Southampton. They interact with two local girls dressed as hula-dancers. Hardy quickly excuses himself, and Laurel is left to try to ad-lib some comedy business. Unable to do so, he 'kills' time by treating the girls to lollipops.

                                                                (Movietone, and Gaumont)

1952 Jan 31   LONDON – Variety Club Luncheon, Empress Club   (book 2 page 7)
(Thursday)   L&H are first seen seated at a charity dinner, at which boxer Freddie Mills, comedian Charlie Chester, and CoCo the clown are also present. Later, Eamonn Andrews interviews them, and then they do the, "You're standing on my foot" routine with CoCo.

                                                                (Pathé Newsreels)

1952 Mar 14   GLASGOW – Opening of the Stage and Screen Memorial Club (book 2 page 26)
(Friday)   Present is Albert Pickard – former owner of the Britannia Theatre. Hardy does a quick gag with Pickard's customised car. [colour]   (Colonel A.E. Pickard)

1952 Jul 28   BRADFORD – Alhambra Theatre   (book 2 page 60)
(Monday)   Stan's second-cousin, Nancy Wardell, and her mother are seen visiting Stan and Ida, in his dressing-room at the Alhambra Theatre, Bradford. Stan, in costume, chats with his visitors, kisses Nancy, and mugs for the camera.
                       (Shot by Nancy's sister-in-law on 9.5mm. Lasts only a few seconds.)

1953 Oct 22   NORTHAMPTON – New Theatre   (book 2 page 97)

(Wednesday)   Laurel and Hardy's taxi is shown arriving at the stage door. They do business of getting in and out on the wrong side. Once in their dressing room, Laurel brushes Hardy's coat and catches his chin with the brush, then traps Hardy's coat in a trunk. The latter sequence is almost certainly what the Boys did on the *Face the Music* television show, five days earlier.   (Pathé Newsreels)

-----0-----

RADIO

1932 Jul 26   NATIONAL – on air broadcast from the BBC London Studio. (book 1 page 15)

1947 May 29   NORTH – *Morecambe Night Out* – live on air BBC interview by Reg Smythe in the dressing room of the Victorian Pavilion, Morecambe.   (book 1 page 113)

1952 Jun 17   BBC BELFAST – broadcast from the Grand Opera House, Belfast – link up with an "on air" Talent Show at the Tonic Cinema Bangor, for which Laurel and Hardy acted as judges.   (book 2 page 51)

1953 Oct 10   DUBLIN – interviewed for radio by a Mr. Boden regarding the debut performance of their stage sketch *Birds of a Feather* the following day at the Olympia Theatre. [No recording was made, but the script is extant.] (book 2 page 94)

1953 Oct 23   MIDLAND – *What Goes On* – interview by Philip Garston-Jones, backstage at the New Theatre, Northampton.   (book 2 page 102)

TELEVISION

1950 Jun 10   SHIP'S REPORTER SERIES – Oliver Hardy Interview.   (book 1 page 160) Babe Hardy is interviewed aboard the RMS. *Caronia*, bound for France, prior to the shooting of *Atoll K*.   National Television Guild

1952 Feb 20   BBC – *Picture Page* – interview by Leslie Mitchell   (uconfirmed* [page 8])

1953 Oct 17   LONDON – BBC Studios: *Face the Music*, hosted by band leader Henry Hall, and featuring music mixed with Variety entertainers. Laurel and Hardy did a short scripted sketch, which involved Henry Hall introducing them to the "audience at home," followed by a short slapstick routine in which Stan traps Ollie's tie while he is packing a suitcase, and Stan struggles to free him.

    [No recording was made, but the script is extant.] (book 2 page 95)

GRAMOPHONE

1932 Aug 18 *Laurel & Hardy in London* (Columbia CAX 6488 DX370)   (book 1 page 53)
Recorded at the Columbia Studios, Abbey Road, London.

o-o-0-o-o

Page 1 of Laurel's script for the taped radio interview
DUBLIN – 10 October 1953

TAPE INTERVIEW....BODEN – LAUREL & HARDY.

BODEN.   WELL MR. HARDY, I'D LIKE TO ASK YOURSELF AND

            YOUR PARTNER MR. LAUREL ABOUT YOUR CAREERS.

HARDY.   WE'LL BE HAPPY TO ANSWER ANY QUESTIONS,

            WHAT WOULD YOU LIKE TO TALK ABOUT?

BODEN.   WELL, COULD I TALK TO YOU BOTH....IS MR. LAUREL

            AROUND?

HARDY.   YES, HE'S OVER THERE TALKING TO THE STAGE MANAGER.

            YOU SEE WE'RE DOING A BENEFIT MATINEE HERE AT THE

            OLYMPIA THEATRE TOMORROW AFTERNOON, FOR THE IRISH

            The new Catholic church in

            RED CROSS AND DONNYBROOK PARISH.

BODEN.   YES, SO I UNDERSTAND. THAT'S A VERY WORTHY CAUSE.

            BUT DO YOU THINK WE COULD TALK TO MR. LAUREL FOR

            JUST A MOMENT?

HARDY.   CERTAINLY. I'LL CALL HIM. STAN.....STANLEY!

LAUREL.   (off mike) YES....YES.... WHAT IS IT?

HARDY.   THIS GENTLEMAN HERE WANTS A RADIO INTERVIEW.

LAUREL.   HE DOES?

HARDY.   YES, AND I THINK WE OUGHT TO HELP HIM.

LAUREL.   SURE, WHY NOT..... WHAT'S YOUR NAME?

BODEN.   BODEN.

LAUREL.   WELL, MR. BODEN, WHERE WERE YOU BORN?

BODEN.   WELL, MR. LAUREL, THAT'S NOT EXACTLY.....

HARDY.   NO, NO, STANLEY, THAT'S NOT THE IDEA.

LAUREL.   IT ISN'T?

HARDY.   NO. CERTAINLY NOT.

LAUREL.   ALRIGHT, WHAT ARE YOUR HOBBIES, MR. BODEN?

AUDIO TAPE

1947 Jun   BLACKPOOL, Palace – tin plate recording   [Extant] (book 1 page 116)

1952 Apr   NOTTINGHAM, Empire – *A Spot of Trouble* sketch   [Extant] (book 2 page 40)

1952   WARRINGTON, Ritz Cinema – message to ABC MINORS.   (book 2 page 46)
[No known copy of the recording]

1953 Oct 19   NORTHAMPTON, New Theatre – *Birds of a Feather* [Extant] (book 2 page 102)

1954 Dec   NOTTINGHAM, Empire – *Birds of a Feather* sketch   (book 2 page 116)
[Location of recording not known]

EUROPEAN RECORDINGS

1947 Oct 1   COPENHAGEN, Radio interview   (book 1 page 153)

1947 Oct 04   COPENHAGEN, K.B. Hallen   (book 1 page 153)
Short amateur recording of the opener to Laurel and Hardy's act, before launching into *The Driver's Licence* sketch. Hardy makes reference to Esbjerg. Stan corrects him and Ollie says "Odense," but then goes on to mention Copenhagen.
(So which is it?).   [Recorded on the 4 or 5 October] (2 mins 10 secs)

1947 Nov 2   PARIS, Gare du Nord Station.   (book 1 page 153)
The Laurel and Hardy party leaving Paris by train, from the Gare du Nord, to attend the Royal Variety Performance, the following day.

1947 Dec 10   BELGIUM,   (2 mins 59 secs) (book 1 page 152)
Recorded at a press reception, the day after their arrival.

1947 Dec 19   BELGIUM, Alhambra Theatre   (2 mins 20 secs) (book 1 page 157)
Short extract of *The Driver's Licence*, recorded sometime between 19 December 1947 and 1 January 1948.

o-o-0-o-o

THE BRITISH LOCATIONS

KEY:

The theatres which Laurel and Hardy played, and the hotels at which they stayed are listed on the left. In brackets is the capacity of each theatre, followed by the address.

Their current state, or whatever now occupies their former sites, is on the right-hand side.

The date in brackets is the year the venue was demolished, where applicable.

-----0----

CUMBRIA

ULVERSTON, 3 Argyle Street.   occupied house

  County Station Hotel, Court Square, CARLISLE.   Hallmark Hotel

Demolished:

CARLISLE, Her Majestys (1,300) Lowther Street.   (1970s) Iceland

SCOTLAND

GLASGOW, Britannia Music Hall, 115 Trongate.   [Grade A listed] working theatre

GLASGOW, La Scala (1,300) 155 Sauchiehall Street.   gutted – clothes shop

  Central Hotel, Gordon Street, GLASGOW.   Grand Central Hotel

EDINBURGH, Playhouse (3,131) 18-22 Greenside Place/Leith Walk.   musicals and concerts

  North British Station Hotel, Princes Street, EDINBURGH.   Balmoral Hotel

EDINBURGH, Empire Palace (2,016) Nicholson Street.   [refurb' 1992] Festival Theatre

  Caledonian Hotel, Princes Street, EDINBURGH.   Waldorf Astoria Caledonian

Demolished:

GLASGOW, Metropole (2,000) Stockwell Street.   (1961) offices

GLASGOW, Empire (2,500) 31-35 Sauchiehall Street/West Nile Street.   (1963) shops

THE BRITISH LOCATIONS

NORTH EAST

NEWCASTLE, Stoll Picture House (1,389) Westgate Road.	Tyne Theatre & Opera House
Royal Station Hotel, Neville Street, NEWCASTLE.	working hotel
Grand Hotel, Percy Gardens, TYNEMOUTH.	working hotel
NORTH SHIELDS, Gaumont Cinema (1,790) Russell Street.	bingo
Town Hall, Saville Street, NORTH SHIELDS.	Grade II listed
SUNDERLAND, Empire (1,550) High Street.	working theatre

Demolished:

TYNEMOUTH, Plaza (713) Grand Parade.	(1996) restaurant and shops
NEWCASTLE, Queens Hall (1,400) Northumberland Street.	(1983) shopping arcade
NEWCASTLE, Empire Palace (1,849) Newgate Street.	(1963) Swallow Hotel
Albion Assembly Rooms, 19 Norfolk Street, NORTH SHIELDS.	(1985) wasteland
Ayton House, Ayres Terrace, NORTH SHIELDS.	new houses
Gordon House, 8 Dockwray Square, NORTH SHIELDS.	new houses

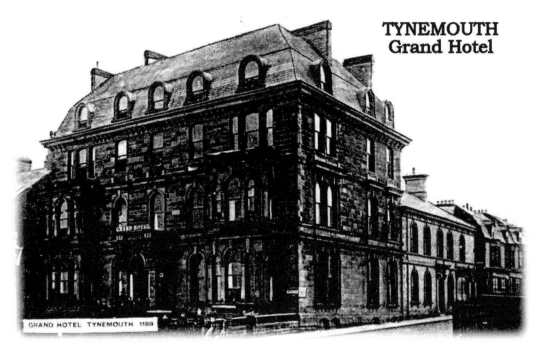

**TYNEMOUTH
Grand Hotel**

YORKSHIRE

YORK, Empire (1,000) Clifford Street.	Grand Opera House
Royal Station Hotel, Station Road, YORK.	Principal Hotel
HULL, New, Kingston Square.	working theatre
Royal Station Hotel, Ferensway, HULL.	Royal Hotel
Dolphin Hotel, Alexandra Road, CLEETHORPES.	Smoke Shack
LEEDS, Majestic Cinema (2,392) City Square.	2018 – £40 million refurb into office spaces
Queens Hotel, City Square, LEEDS.	working hotel [built on site of old one – 1937]
Midland Hotel, Cheapside, BRADFORD.	working hotel
BRADFORD Alhambra, (1,480) Morley Street.	working theatre
BRADFORD, Exchange Station Hotel, Bridge Street.	Great Victoria Hotel

THE BRITISH LOCATIONS

Demolished:

HULL, Palace (1,800) Anlaby Road. (1965) flats

GRIMSBY, Palace (1,509) Victoria Street. (1979) Palace Court and car park

LEEDS, Empire Palace (1,750) 108 Briggate. (1962) Harvey Nicols – Empire Arcade

Queens Hotel, City Square, LEEDS. [1935 - see earlier entry]

SHEFFIELD, Cinema House (763) Fargate. (1961) Fountain Precinct - shops

SHEFFIELD, Empire Palace (3,000) Charles Street. (1959) shops

Grand Hotel, Church Street, SHEFFIELD. (1974) Fountain Precinct – shops

SHEFFIELD
Grand Hotel

MANCHESTER

Midland Hotel, Peter Street. working hotel

MANCHESTER, Palace (2,000) Oxford Street. working theatre

Grand Hotel, 8 Aytoun Street. working hotel

SALFORD, Opera House (2,070) Quay Street. Grade II listed

Demolished:

ARDWICK GREEN, New Hippodrome (2,100) [former Empire]. (1964) roadway

New Oxford Picture Theatre (1,150) Oxford Street. (2017) office block

LANCASHIRE

BOLTON, Lido (1,800) Bradshawgate. (2005) (façade only) converted to flats

MORECAMBE, Victoria Pavilion (2,960) Winter Gardens, Marine Road. renovated 1992

BLACKPOOL, Tower Ballroom, Promenade. restored 1956

BLACKPOOL, Empress Ballroom (3,000) Winter Gardens. restored 2017

BLACKPOOL, Baronial Hall, Winter Gardens. preserved

Metropole Hotel, Princess Parade, BLACKPOOL. working hotel

Clifton Arms Hotel, St. Annes Road West, St. ANNES. working hotel

SOUTHPORT, Garrick (1,600) Lord Street. bingo

Prince of Wales, Lord Street, SOUTHPORT. working hotel

Demolished:

Elms Hotel, Princes Crescent, BARE. (2012) luxury flats

BLACKPOOL Palace (2,012) Central Beach. [ground] Poundland and Harry Ramsden's

BLACKPOOL, Picture Palace (1,972) Central Beach. (1961) [above] Viva Cabaret

THE BRITISH LOCATIONS

LIVERPOOL

LIVERPOOL, Empire (2,293) Lime Street.	working theatre
Adelphi Hotel, Lime Street.	Britannia Adelphi Hotel

IRELAND

DUBLIN, Olympia (1,750) 72 Dame Street.	restored 1974
Gresham Hotel, OConnell Street, DUBLIN 1.	working hotel
Royal Marine Hotel, DUN LAOGHAIRE.	working hotel
BELFAST, Grand Opera House (1,050) Great Victoria Street, B12.	restored 1980
Midland Hotel, Whitla Street, BELFAST, BT15.	Midland Building - offices

NORTH WALES

RHYL, Queens, Promenade.	Amusement arcade
Westminster Hotel, East Parade, RHYL.	working hotel

SHROPSHIRE

SHREWSBURY, Granada (1,456) Castle Gates.	bingo
Demolished:	
Raven Hotel, Castle Gates, SHREWSBURY.	(1960) Marks & Spencer

STAFFORDSHIRE

HANLEY, Royal (1,800) Pall Mall.	(gutted) nightclub
North Stafford Hotel, Station Road, STOKE.	working hotel

WEST MIDLANDS

Demolished:	
WOLVERHAMPTON, Hippodrome (1,960) 34 Queen Square.	(1956) Yate's Beer Garden

WOLVERHAMPTON
Hippodrome

NOTTINGHAM/LINCOLNSHIRE

Plough Inn, West Street, BARKSTON.	converted to flats
Bull Inn, 5 Market Street, BOTTESFORD.	working pub
GRANTHAM, Guildhall, St. Peter's Hill.	working theatre

Demolished:

NOTTINGHAM, Empire (2,200) South Sherwood Street.	(1969) Royal Centre
County Hotel, Theatre Square, NOTTINGHAM.	(1975) Royal Centre
Red Lion Hotel, GRANTHAM, 22-23 High Street.	(1963) Nationwide
SKEGNESS, Butlin Theatre (1,800) Butlins Funcoast World.	(1998) go-kart trak

CAMBRIDGESHIRE

PETERBOROUGH, Embassy (1,500) Broadway.	Edwards Nightclub
Great Northern Hotel, Station Road, PETERBOROUGH.	working hotel

NORFOLK

Royal Hotel, Prince of Wales Road, NORWICH.	(Grade II) offices

Demolished:

NORWICH, Hippodrome (1,836) St. Giles Street.	(1966) car park

MIDLANDS

Clarendon Hotel, The Parade, LEAMINGTON SPA.	Clarendon Court – flats
Abbey Hotel, Priory Road, KENILWORTH.	[converted 1982] flats
Chesford Grange Hotel, Chesford Bridge, KENILWORTH.	working hotel
BIRMINGHAM, Hippodrome (2,000) Hurst Street.	working theatre
Midland Hotel, New Street, BIRMINGHAM, B5.	Burlington Hotel
DUDLEY, Hippodrome (1,500) Castle Hill.	derelict
Station Hotel, Castle Hill, DUDLEY.	working hotel

Demolished:

COVENTRY, Hippodrome, Trinity Street.	(2002) Millennium Place

COVENTRY
New Hippodrome

THE BRITISH LOCATIONS

BIRMINGHAM, Gaumont Cinema (2,200) Steelhouse Lane.   (1983) Wesleyan

Queens Hotel, New Street, BIRMINGHAM.   (1966) Pallasades – part of Grand Central

ASTON, Hippodrome (1,800) Potters Lane.   (1981) Drum Art Centre (closed)

NORTHAMPTONSHIRE

Plough Hotel, Bridge Street, NORTHAMPTON.   working hotel

Demolished:

NORTHAMPTON, New Theatre (2,000) Abington Street.   (1960) Primark Store

NORTHAMPTON
New Theatre

SOUTH WALES

CARDIFF, New (1,600) Park Place.   working theatre

Park Hotel, Park Place, CARDIFF.   Park Plaza Hotel

Demolished:

SWANSEA, Empire (963) Lower Oxford Street.   (1960) Primark Store

Mackworth Hotel, High Street, SWANSEA.   (c.1971) Oldway House Arcade

AVON/WILTSHIRE/BERKSHIRE

BRISTOL, Hippodrome (2,000) St. Augustines Parade, BS 1.   working theatre

Royal Hotel, College Green, BRISTOL.   Marriott Royal Hotel

Grand Hotel, Broad Street, BRISTOL.   working hotel

Bear Hotel, Charnham Street, HUNGERFORD.   working hotel

Demolished:

SWINDON, Empire (1,470) Clarence Street.   (1959) Lloyds Chemists

THE BRITISH LOCATIONS

LONDON

"Drayton House", 49 Colebrook Avenue, EALING, W13.	occupied house
WIMBLEDON, Wimbledon (1,700) The Broadway, SW19.	working theatre
Burford Bridge Hotel, Box-Hill, DORKING.	Mercure Hotel
Victoria Palace (1,600) 126 Victoria Street, SW1.	working theatre
LEICESTER SQUARE, Empire (3,226) WC2.	[facade, only, is original] cinema
Drury Lane (2,283) Catherine Street, WC2.	refurbished 2019
Coliseum (2,400) St. Martins Lane, WC 2.	London Coliseum
Savoy Hotel, 189 The Strand, W1.	working hotel
London Palladium (2,300) Argyll Street, W1.	working theatre
Washington Hotel, Curzon Street, W1.	Washington Mayfair Hotel
Dorchester Hotel, Park Lane, W1.	working hotel
Apollo (893) Shaftesbury Avenue, W1.	working theatre
May Fair Hotel, Stratton Street, W1J.	working hotel

Demolished:

EALING, Walpole Cinema, Bond Street, W5.	(1981) office block
CHISWICK, Empire (2,154) Chiswick High Road, W4.	(1959) Empire House
SUTTON, Granada (2,000) Carshalton Road.	(1979) Sutton Park House
LEWISHAM, Hippodrome (3,492) 153 Rushey Green, CATFORD SE6.	(1960) Eros House

FINSBURY PARK, Empire (2,000) St. Thomass Road, N 4.	(1965) Vaudeville Court – flats
BRIXTON, Empress (1,900) Brighton Terrace, SW9.	(1992) housing

ESSEX

SOUTHEND, Odeon (2,750) Elmer Approach.	(dem. 2004) University of Essex
Palace Hotel, Pier Hill, SOUTHEND.	Park Inn Palace

THE BRITISH LOCATIONS

SOUTH COAST

MARGATE, Winter Gardens (1,533) Fort Crescent.	working theatre
St. Georges Hotel, CLIFTONVILLE.	(dem. 2006) awaiting development
Romney, Hythe & Dymchurch Railway, KENT.	fully operational
BRIGHTON, Hippodrome (1,850) Middle Street.	Grade II - closed
Grand Hotel, Kings Road, BRIGHTON.	refurbished hotel
Royal Crescent Hotel, BRIGHTON, King's Cliff	(converted) Royal Crescent Mansions
PORTSMOUTH, Royal (1,050) Guildhall Walk, PO1.	restored 2015
SOUTHSEA, Kings (1,780) Albert Road, PO5.	working theatre
Queens Hotel , Clarence Parade, SOUTHSEA.	working hotel
Royal Beach Hotel, St. Helens Parade, SOUTHSEA.	Western Royal Beach Hotel
SOUTHAMPTON, Gaumont (2,251) Commercial Road.	Mayflower Theatre
Polygon Hotel, Cumberland Place, SOUTHAMPTON.	(dem. 1999) flats
BOSCOMBE, Hippodrome (1,350) Christchurch Road.	Academy Nightclub
Chine Hotel, Boscombe Spa Road, BOURNEMOUTH.	working hotel
PLYMOUTH, Palace (1,200) Union Street.	derelict
Grand Hotel, Elliott Street, The Hoe, PLYMOUTH.	(converted) luxury duplexes

**PLYMOUTH
Palace**

(AJM: It was impracticable to list every theatre, public house, company, civic venue, hotel, etc. to which Laurel and Hardy paid a casual visit, but most are referred to in the text).

We hope you will use these Location pages as a guide to your own British Tours.

Note that they start with Stan Laurel's birthplace, and end at the theatre where Laurel & Hardy played their last ever performance. Can you beat that!!

Happy Hunting!

o-o-0-o-o

DATE SHEET – 1932

Jul 16	Saturday	Sail from NEW YORK on the *Aquitania*.
Jul 23	Saturday	Arrive SOUTHAMPTON, England. Train to Waterloo Station, LONDON. Afternoon: press reception, Savoy Hotel, LONDON.
Jul 24	Sunday	*Cheshire Cheese* and Embankment (Hardy). Watch the play *Cavalcade* at the Drury Lane Theatre, LONDON.
Jul 25	Monday	Empire Theatre, LEICESTER SQUARE. 9pm.
Jul 26	Tuesday 10:35pm	Watch the play *Party* at the Strand Theatre, LONDON. BBC Studios for radio broadcast, LONDON.
Jul 27	Wednesday	Coliseum Theatre – to watch *Casanova*. Dinner at 'Screen Artistes Federation' – LONDON. Overnight-train to Newcastle.
Jul 28	Thursday 3pm 9pm	Arrive NEWCASTLE Station. 5:49am. Car to Grand Hotel, TYNEMOUTH. Civic reception, Mayor's Parlour, NORTH SHIELDS. Luncheon – Albion Assembly Rooms, NORTH SHIELDS. Laurel visits Dockwray Square and Ayton House. Re-group Grand Hotel, TYNEMOUTH Plaza, TYNEMOUTH – for speeches and present-giving. Queen's Hall, NEWCASTLE. Stoll Picture House, NEWCASTLE.
Jul 29	Friday 1:35pm 7:30pm 9:30pm 10:47pm 12.00am	Central Station, NEWCASTLE. 11:10am. Arrive at Waverley Station, EDINBURGH. Staying at North British Station Hotel, EDINBURGH. Afternoon – visit to *Scottish National War Memorial* and Castle. Edinburgh Playhouse. Caledonian Station, EDINBURGH – train for Glasgow. Arrive Central Station, GLASGOW. Staying Central Hotel. Visit *Evening News* offices.
Jul 30	Saturday 4pm Evening:	Western Gailes Golf Course (Hardy). 9am. La Scala Cinema, Sauchiehall Street, GLASGOW. 'Mystery Tour.'
Jul 31	Sunday	Gleneagles Golf Course (Hardy).

DATE SHEET – 1932

ROUTES — 1932 Tour

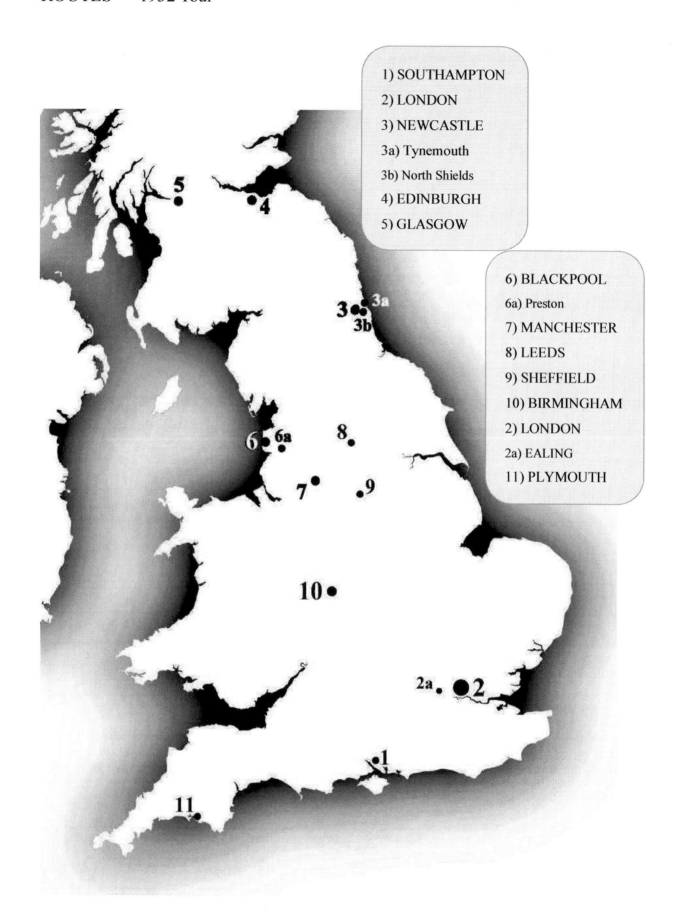

1) SOUTHAMPTON

2) LONDON

3) NEWCASTLE

3a) Tynemouth

3b) North Shields

4) EDINBURGH

5) GLASGOW

6) BLACKPOOL

6a) Preston

7) MANCHESTER

8) LEEDS

9) SHEFFIELD

10) BIRMINGHAM

2) LONDON

2a) EALING

11) PLYMOUTH

DATE SHEET – 1932

Aug 1	Monday	Central Station, GLASGOW. 10:05am
	2:20pm	Arrive PRESTON. Car to BLACKPOOL – Metropole Hotel.
	Evening	Winter Gardens, Palace Theatre, and Tower Ballroom.
	1:30am	Laurel goes walkabout.
Aug 2	Tuesday	Morning – Depart North Station, BLACKPOOL.
		Arrive Victoria Station, MANCHESTER. Staying at Midland Hotel.
	6:30pm	New Oxford Cinema, MANCHESTER.
		Visit to Bert Tracey's mother's house, Victoria Park.
		Manchester Opera House.
Aug 3	Wednesday	Arrive New Station, LEEDS. 1:07pm.
		Staying at Queen's Hotel, LEEDS.
	7:30pm	Majestic Cinema, LEEDS.
Aug 4	Thursday	Train leaves for Sheffield. 11am.
	12 pm	Arrive SHEFFIELD. Staying Grand Hotel.
	6:30pm	Cinema House, FARGATE.
Aug 5	Friday	Arrive New Street Station, BIRMINGHAM. 1:26pm.
		Staying Queen's Hotel, BIRMINGHAM.
	Afternoon	Council House, BIRMINGHAM.
	Evening	Gaumont Cinema, and West End Dance Hall.
Aug 6	Saturday	Leave Birmingham for London. 8:40am.
		Staying Savoy Hotel, LONDON.
Aug 8	Monday	Visit 49 Colebrook Avenue, EALING.
	8pm	Walpole Cinema, and Walpole Hall, EALING.
Aug 10	Wednesday	Morning – Victoria Station, LONDON – for boat train to France.
		Staying at Claridges Hotel, PARIS.
Aug 15	Monday	Return to LONDON, England.
Aug 16c		Palace Theatre, LONDON – to watch *The Cat and the Fiddle*.
Aug 18	Thursday	Columbia Recording Studios, LONDON.
Aug ??		Visit to Ealing Film Studios. (Laurel)
Aug ??		Laurel goes to watch Max Miller, at the Holborn Empire.
Aug 24	Wednesday	Sail on the *SS Paris* – PLYMOUTH to NEW YORK (arrive 30th)

o-o-0-o-o

1947

Feb 24 NEWCASTLE, Empire

The Three Redheads; Miss Louise & her Dogs; Slim Rhyder; Johnson Clark; Erikson; Mariora; Bob Lloyd & Betty; Keefe Bros & Annette.

Mar 3 BIRMINGHAM, Hippodrome

The Three Redheads; Miss Louise & her Dogs; Slim Rhyder; Erikson; Johnson Clark; Bob Lloyd & Betty; Keefe Brothers & Annette; Olga Varona.

Mar 10 (week 1) LONDON, Palladium

The Elwardos; Len & Bill Lowe; Louise & her Dogs; Tommy Fields; Billy Cotton Band; The Dolinoffs and Raya Sisters; Jack Train; Ronald Chesney; Richardo.

Mar 17 (week 2) LONDON, Palladium

The Elwardos; Len & Bill Lowe; Louise & her Dogs; Tommy Fields; Billy Cotton Band; The Hightowers; Jack Train; Ronald Chesney; Richardo.

Mar 24 (week 3) LONDON, Palladium

The Elwardos; Len & Bill Lowe; Louise & her Dogs; Tommy Fields; Charley Wood & Partner; Billy Russell; Darmora Ballet; The Two Beels; Jack Train; Ronald Chesney; Richardo.

Mar 31 LONDON, Wimbledon

The Four Bobrics; Len & Bill Lowe; Miss Louise & her Dogs; Mariora; Slim Rhyder; Johnson Clarke; Norman & Vonnie Munro.

Apr 7 LEWISHAM, Hippodrome

The Lai Founs; Len & Bill Lowe; Slim Rhyder; MacKenzie Reid & Dorothy; Jimmy Bruce; Palettes Dogs; Norman & Vonnie Munro.

Apr 14 (4 weeks) LONDON, Coliseum

Five Aussies; Tessa Deane; George Lacy; Rawicz & Landauer; Tommy Jover; Raf & Fe; Slim Rhyder; Elsie & Doris Waters; Darmora Ballet; Newman Twins.

Apr 27 (1 night) LONDON, Victoria Palace

Betty Blackler; George Doonan; Henry Lytton; Terry Wilson; Clarkson Rose; N'Gai; Bert Weston; Arthur Prince; Jack Martell; Binnie Hale; Noele Gordon; Neville Kennard; Vera Lynn; Will Fyffe; Norman Wisdom.

May 12 DUDLEY, Hippodrome

The Three Redheads; Len & Bill Lowe; Bob Lloyd & Betty; Olga Varona; Slim Rhyder; Mariora; Ann Yeaman's Sporting Dogs.

PROGRAMME BILLS – 1947

May 19   LIVERPOOL, Empire

The Three Redheads; Ivor E. Keys with Betty Ross; Slim Rhyder; Erikson;
The Newman Twins; Terri Carol; MacKenzie Reid & Dorothy;
Ann Yeaman's Sporting Dogs.

May 26   MORECAMBE, Winter Gardens (Victoria Pavilion)

The Three Redheads; Johnson Clark; Slim Rhyder; Connie Graham & Hal Scott;
The Newman Twins; MacKenzie Reid & Dorothy; Olga Varona.

Jun 2   BLACKPOOL, Palace

Vic Ray & Lucille; Velda & Vann; Olga Varona; Paul Rogers; Slim Rhyder;
Bobbie Kimber; Cynthia & Gladys; Levaine Bros.

Jun 9   (week 1)   GLASGOW, Empire

Newman Twins; Victor Barna & Alec Brook; Carl & Roger Yale;
Donald MacKay; Olga Varona; Slim Rhyder; Johnson Clark;
MacKenzie Reid & Dorothy; The Three Garcias.

Jun 16   (week 2)   GLASGOW, Empire

The Three Redheads; Ivor E. Keyes; Slim Rhyder; Joe King; Newman Twins;
Johnson Clark with 'Hodge'; MacKenzie Reid & Dorothy; Olga Varona.

Jun 23   SKEGNESS, Butlin Theatre

The Three Redheads; Jimmy Bruce; Ross Bayard Dancers; Len Clifford & Freda;
Slim Rhyder; Mariora; Olga Varona.

Jun 30   EDINBURGH, Empire

The Three Redheads; Bob Lloyd & Betty; Olga Varona; Claude Chandler;
Slim Rhyder; MacKenzie Reid & Dorothy; Baker & Verek.

Jul 7   HULL, New Theatre

The Three Redheads; Ivor E. Keyes; Olga Varona; Paul Rogers; Slim Rhyder;
MacKenzie Reid & Dorothy; The Perfectos.

Jul 14   BRISTOL, Hippodrome

The Three Redheads; Carl & Roger Yale; Jimmy Bruce; Palettes Dogs;
MacKenzie Reid & Dorothy; Mariora; Olga Varona.

Jul 21   (week 1)   MANCHESTER, Palace

Les Silvas; Olga Varona; the Raymonde Sisters & Allan; Johnson Clark;
Musical Derricks with Tony; Slim Rhyder; Rita Bernard & Lena Brown.

ROUTES — 1947 Tour – part 1

1) SOUTHAMPTON	5) Barkston
2) LONDON	2) LONDON
3) NEWCASTLE	2a) RH & DR
3a) Tynemouth	6) DUDLEY
3b) North Shields	7) LIVERPOOL
4) BIRMINGHAM	8) MORECAMBE
2) LONDON	8a) Ulverston
	8b) Whalley
	9) BLACKPOOL
	10) GLASGOW
	11) Grantham
	12) SKEGNESS
	13) EDINBURGH
	14) HULL
	15) BRISTOL
	15a) Weston
	16) MANCHESTER

PROGRAMME BILLS – 1947

Jul 28   (week 2)   MANCHESTER, Palace

Vickers Twins; Ivor E Keyes; Terri Carol; Bob Lloyd & Betty; Slim Rhyder;
Mills & Paulette; Young China Troupe; Yeaman's Dogs.

Aug 4   SOUTHSEA, Kings

Norman & Vonnie Munro; Ivor E Keyes; Terri Carol; Peter Raynor; Slim Rhyder;
MacKenzie Reid & Dorothy; Olga Varona; Palettes Dogs.

Aug 11   BOSCOMBE, Hippodrome

The Three Redheads; Ivor E. Keyes with Betty Ross; Mariora; Len Clifford &
Freda; Slim Rhyder; MacKenzie Reid & Dorothy; Olga Varona.

Aug 18   MARGATE, Winter Gardens

The Three Redheads; Peter Raynor; Frank Marx & Iris; Len Clifford & Freda;
Slim Rhyder; Musical Derricks & Tony; Palettes Dogs.

Aug 25   (2 weeks)   COVENTRY, Hippodrome

The Three Redheads; Bob Lloyd & Betty; Olga Varona; Carl & Roger Yale;
Slim Rhyder; Jack & Mary Kinson; MacKenzie Reid & Dorothy;
Cynthia & Gladys. [Week 2: Terri Carol replaced Jack & Mary Kinson.]

Sep 8   BOLTON, Lido

The Three Redheads; Lorraine & partner; Olga Varona; Len Clifford & Freda;
Slim Rhyder; MacKenzie Reid & Dorothy; Jackie & Partner.

Sep 15   SWINDON, Empire

Peter Raynor; The Three Redheads; Olga Varona; Two Pirates; Slim Rhyder;
Lorraine & partner; MacKenzie Reid & Dorothy; Yeaman's Sporting Dogs.

Sep 22   FINSBURY PARK, Empire

The Three Redheads; Johnson Clark; Olga Varona; Carl & Roger Yale; Ronalde;
Slim Rhyder; MacKenzie Reid & Dorothy; The Skating Merinos.

[doubling]   CHISWICK, Empire

Ray & Madge Lamar; Marie Wilson; Eddie Bayes; Jackie & Betty Lambert;
Johnnie Riscoe & Violet Terry; Dennis Lawes; Bex & Bex; Reg Redcliffe.

o-o-o-0-o-o-o

N.B.   HARRY MORENY played 'the cop' in Laurel & Hardy's sketch throughout the British
tour and accompanied them on the European tour which followed.

The stay at each venue is MON to SAT inclusive – unless otherwise stated.

The cast is not necessarily in order of appearance. Some acts appeared in both halves.

LAUREL & HARDY were the penultimate act on all their own shows.

o-o-0-o-o

ROUTES — 1947 Tour – part 2

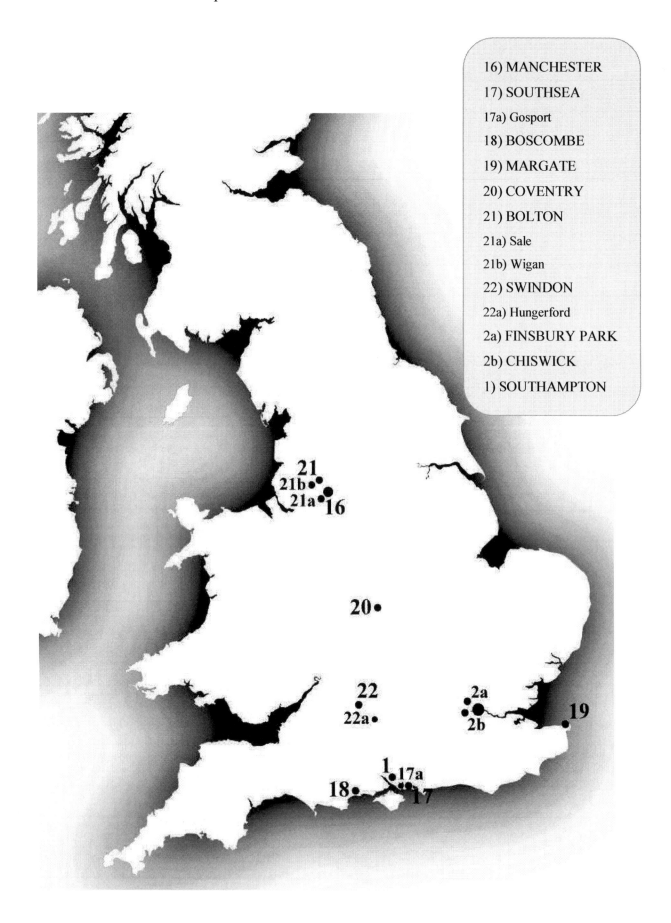

16) MANCHESTER

17) SOUTHSEA

17a) Gosport

18) BOSCOMBE

19) MARGATE

20) COVENTRY

21) BOLTON

21a) Sale

21b) Wigan

22) SWINDON

22a) Hungerford

2a) FINSBURY PARK

2b) CHISWICK

1) SOUTHAMPTON

Royal Variety Performance

LONDON PALLADIUM – 3rd November 1947

---0---

THE 'SKYROCKETS' ORCHESTRA – directed by Paul Fenoulhet

HY HAZELL with the ALEC THOMAS QUARTET – soubrette

MARILYN HIGHTOWER – dancer (*)

THREE SHADES – dancers

VALERIE TANDY – dancer/comedienne

BOBBIE TRANTER & TONY HULLEY – male dance duo

THE THREE ASTAIRES – variety dancing act

HORTOBAGYI TROUPE – springboard acrobats

BILLY RUSSELL – 'On Behalf of the Working Classes' – comedian (*)

WILSON, KEPPEL & BETTY – 'Sands of the Desert' – burlesque dancers

NORMAN EVANS – character comedian

BORRAH MINEVITCH'S HARMONICA RASCALS featuring JOHNNIE PULEO

MERVYN SAUNDERS – vocalist

MONA & OLIVIER – French dance act

WALLY BOAG – 'A lesson in Inflation' – comedy balloonist

THE 'CRAZY GANG' – Bud Flanagan; Nervo & Knox; Naughton & Gold

Assisted by: Frank Holloway; Willie Carlisle; Freddie Malcolm

JACK DURANT – impressions and acrobatic lunacy

ROBERT WILSON – Scottish singer

THE DAGENHAM GIRL PIPERS – all-girl bagpipe band

VIC & JOE CRASTONIAN – Scottish music on bagpipes and drum

JIMMIE CURRIE'S WATER SPECTACLE – water cascade

TERRI CAROL – paper-tearing (*)

CYNTHIA & GLADYS – jugglers (*)

THE THREE GARCIAS – female acrobatic dancers (*)

LEVANDA – foot equilibrist

MARIE LOUISE – aerial trapezist

MARIORA – The Amazing Girl Juggler (*)

OLGA VARONA – 'High on the Rope' – trapeze and rope artiste (*)

EVA MAY WONG – 'Charm from China'

BOBBIE KIMBER – ventriloquist (*)

DOLORES GRAY & BILL JOHNSON – American stars from 'Annie Get Your Gun'

STAN LAUREL & OLIVER HARDY – 'Hollywood's Comedy Couple'

– assisted by Harry Moreny.

LES ZORIS – speciality dance couple

TOMMY TRINDER – 'You Lucky People' – comedian

GRACIE FIELDS – 'The Lass from Lancashire' – singer

FINALE – There's No Business Like Showbusiness – the Entire Company

o-o-0-o-o

[(*) Indicates: also appeared on tour with Laurel & Hardy.]

Studio boss Hal Roach comes to wish Stan and Babe *Bon Voyage*, at the Santa Fe Depot,
Los Angeles — except that, "Yes, he never did." Puzzled? See below! [12 July 1932]

Roach Studio General Manager, Henry Ginsberg, comes to wish Stan and Babe *Bon Voyage*, at
the Santa Fe Depot, Los Angeles — and *he* really did. The top one is faked. Look for yourself!

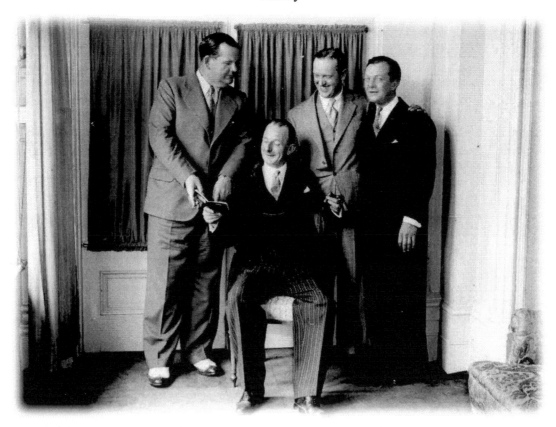

SAVOY HOTEL – 23 July 1932. Next to Laurel is comedian and newspaper columnist – Bobby Howes. Seated is Laurel's former boss, Frank O'Neil, who ran the Karno Company playing *Mumming Birds* at the Hulme Hippodrome, Manchester, which Stan joined in December 1909 [see page 12]

Meeting Peggy Wood, lead actress from *The Cat and the Fiddle*, who is sharing a dressing-room with Alice Delysia, at the Palace Theatre, Shaftesbury Avenue. (15 August 1932) [see page 53]

STARS IN GARTERS

Laurel pointing to two different gifts he has just received – a sprig of heather, and a pair of tartan garters – whilst praying that his American partner doesn't tell the press that they always wear suspenders under their trousers.

Scala Cinema, Glasgow — 30 July 1932 [see page 31]

No-one can accuse Oliver Hardy of being off his trolley, as the comedy duo await the boat train from Victoria Station, on the first leg of their trip to Paris. [10 August 1932].

The fun stopped when Babe, Stan, and Myrtle disembarked at St. Lazare Station, Paris, and they had to face the trials of the Customs Office. (10 August 1932) [see page 52]

ABOVE: Final farewell – 1932   BELOW: newly arrived – 1947

LIKE TWO PEAS IN A PORT
Considering the fifteen-year difference between the 1932 and 1947 arrivals at Southampton, the similarities are striking.

[see pages 10 and 67]

1947

The new look Mr. Laurel and Mr. Hardy   The new Mrs. Laurel and Mrs. Hardy

Red Lion Hotel GRANTHAM

Bill Healey (out of shot, left) and Olga, meeting up with Ida and the Boys at the Red Lion, before going on to the Plough Inn, to meet Stan's dad. (16 March 1947)   [see page 88]

Management and staff pose with McLaurel and McHardy, on the stage of the:
GLASGOW EMPIRE – 17 June 1947   [see page 123]

Hardy helping himself to golf clubs at the 'Enterprise Scotland Exhibition' — Royal Scottish Museum,
Edinburgh. But it's Laurel, the tee-caddie, who is having to carry the booty. (3 July 1947) [see page 130]

Brenda Bartlett, winner of this round of the 'Modern Venus Competition,' receives
a hearty handshake from Hardy, and a long lingering look from Laurel.
17 July 1947 Weston-super-Mare
[see page 134]

To show his affinity with all things Scottish, Hardy signs his autograph for members of the Dagenham Girl Pipers, in the bar at the London Palladium. [Royal Variety Performance. 3 November 1947] (B.S. Yes I know Dagenham is in Essex — so stop your droning.)

And this is how Laurel and Hardy's 1947 British tour ended — with the two legends being lauded by their peers, and applauded by Royalty.

[see *Royal Variety Performance* – pages 153-57]

o-o-o-0-o-o-o

LAUREL & HARDY – The British Tours

Part 2 – 'The Last Stage.' [The 1952 and 1953-4 Tours]

Second Edition – Extensively revised, reformatted and expanded

This engaging book is the story of the love which the British and Irish retained for these two comedy legends after the USA had turned its back on them, and how they adapted from film- to stage-work, and survived through the changing *modes* of comedy, and the changing *moods* of theatre audiences. Readers are given a full account of the theatres they played, the acts they worked with, their travel arrangements; the hotels at which they stayed; the people they met; and their many public appearances – all complemented by scores of rare photographs from these tours.

Second Edition. 208 pages. Lavishly illustrated — Softback — A4 [297mm x 210mm]

(ISBN 978-0-9521308-8-8) — Available via lulu.com

-----0-----

LAUREL and HARDY – The U.S. Tours

Second Edition – Extensively revised, reformatted. and expanded

After the two comedians meet at the Hal Roach Studios, the story takes an unexpected route. Instead of following them through the making of their films, we are led into a parallel world of public appearances, show business events, theatre tours, wartime fund raising tours, and troop shows. Revealed for the first time ever are details of three major U.S. city-to-city stage tours; numerous trips from the West to the East coast; three junkets to Mexico; and even a tour of Caribbean islands. On their travels, Laurel and Hardy meet a whole constellation of Hollywood stars; befriend a future President; and are invited to the White House. Stan and Babe emerge as warm and lovable, but vulnerable, men – and the reader will experience their every highlight and emotion throughout their long partnership.

Second Edition. 334 pages. Lavishly illustrated. Softback – A4 [297mm x 210mm]

(ISBN 978-0-9521308-6-4) — Available via lulu.com

-----0-----

LAUREL and HARDY – The European Tours

"The European Tours" details not only the 1947-48 stage tours Laurel and Hardy played around Denmark, Sweden, France, and Belgium, but the year the two Hollywood comedians spent in France, during the making of their 1950-51 film *Atoll K*. Included in this is a promotional visit to Italy; plus details of two earlier visits to France — one by Laurel in 1927, and one by both comedians in 1932.

Readers will get to see the real men behind the screen characters of "Stan and Ollie" — how they coped with being mobbed everywhere they went; the exhaustion of a life of touring; and how they both worked on through serious illness to complete their last film.

From it all, Stan Laurel and Oliver Hardy emerge as lovable, but vulnerable, men – and readers will experience their every emotion throughout these previously undocumented tours.

Second Print. 128 pages – 200 illustrations. Softback – A4 [297mm x 210mm]

(ISBN 978-0-9521308-4-0) — Available via lulu.com

-----0-----

LAUREL – Stage by Stage

"LAUREL - Stage by Stage" is the prequel to Marriots previous Laurel and Hardy's "Tours" books; and is a companion to "CHAPLIN – Stage by Stage."

It narrates for the first-time-ever all of Stan Laurel's stage shows, from his earliest appearances in British pantomime (as the teenage Stanley Jefferson), right up to his last-ever stage show before entering films.

Along the way he spends over three years touring with Charlie Chaplin, in the most-famous of all comedy troupes – the Fred Karno Company.

The next eight years are spent touring in U.S. vaudeville, playing in song-dance-and-comedy sketch acts with various partners.

Readers will experience every low and high as this comic genius tries to unshackle himself from the hardship and tedium of vaudeville, during a number of attempts to get into the world of film comedy. The amount of detail revealed about these "lost" tours is astounding.

272 pages – 200 illustrations. Softback – A4 [297mm x 210mm]

Second print (ISBN 978-1-78972-555-1) — Available via lulu.com

-----0-----

CHAPLIN – Stage by Stage

Contains every known stage appearance Chaplin made in the UK and, for the first time ever, the ones he made in Vaudeville, touring America with the Fred Karno Company of Comedians.

Along the way, many myths and mistakes from other works on Chaplin will be corrected, and many lies and legends exposed. But, in destroying the negative, a positive picture is built up of the very medium which created the man and the screen character "Chaplin."

Includes extracts from the scripts of the plays and sketches in which Chaplin appeared, complemented by reviews and plot descriptions, all of which help to complete the picture of the influences which affected Chaplin's later film work. Read and be Amazed!

[Although it is a companion to "LAUREL – Stage by Stage" it contains far more text relating to Chaplin, plus numerous different and previously unpublished photos of him.]

Chaplin Stage by Stage *provides a unique and indispensable record of Chaplin's career on the British stage and music hall and in American vaudeville in the formative fifteen years before he entered films. Marriot's phenomenal research gives us an exhaustive chronicle of Charlie's stage appearances – in addition to those of his father and his brother Sydney. —* [DAVID ROBINSON – Chaplin biographer.]

258 pages – 130 illustrations. Paperback – A4 [297mm x 210mm]

Second print (ISBN 978-1-78972-556-8) — Available via lulu.com

-----0-----

Have you bought your copies yet?

A sincere "Thank You" to those who have.

"A.J" Marriot

For information on the First Editions, and how to purchase, go to the author's website:

www.laurelandhardybooks.com

OR e-mail: ajmarriot@aol.com for any enquiries.

o-o-0-o-o

About the author:

"A.J" MARRIOT

In 1993, after twenty years as a stand-up comedian, including twelve seasons as a Holiday Camp entertainer, "A.J" Marriot turned his hand to writing. His first book, *LAUREL & HARDY – The British Tours*, has sold in over forty-five countries, and is still much sought after. His second, *CHAPLIN – Stage by Stage*, was acclaimed by biographers and critics alike as being the definitive account of Chaplin's pre-film days. Next came *The Lighter Side of LAUREL & HARDY,* which sold out seven print runs. In December 2011 readers were thrilled to receive the companion to "The British Tours" – namely: *LAUREL and HARDY – The U.S. Tours*, which again bears Marriot's hallmarks of unparalleled research, wit, and warmth towards his subjects.

Between 2001 and 2016 "A.J" was Editor and Features Writer of the *Laurel & Hardy Magazine*, which has the largest circulation of the many Laurel & Hardy fanzines, worldwide.

2014 brought us a second companion to "The British Tours" – *LAUREL and HARDY – The European Tours.* And then in 2017 he gave us the complete history of Stan Laurel's stage, music hall, and vaudeville appearances — before meeting up with screen and stage partner Oliver Hardy — in the book *"LAUREL – Stage by Stage."*

And so his quest to record every aspect of Laurel and Hardy's stage careers is complete, and readers can learn hundreds of previously unknown facts about their lives; and discover hundreds of previously unpublished photos. Best of all readers can do what Stan and Babe did, which is to get closer to the real Laurel and Hardy while they are engaged on these tours.

o-o-0-o-o

LAUREL & HARDY – The British Tours [1ˢᵗ Edition]

What they said:

This book is a must for theatregoers weaned on the music halls, as they will revel in the wealth of theatrical detail recorded. (WORDS & MUSIC)

The author's research is staggering, but from it Laurel and Hardy emerge as kind, sensitive men, always ready to spend time with their fans. (GRANTHAM JOURNAL)

Mr Marriot has produced an awesomely researched book which is absolutely unmissable for any Laurel and Hardy devotee. (MOVIE COLLECTOR)

I think you get more of a sense of them as people than from any other of the Laurel and Hardy books. (PEPPER BOOKS – California)

o-o-0-o-o

Printed in Great Britain
by Amazon

14587277R00120